Unity 2018 Shaders and Effects Cookbook

Third Edition

Transform your game into a visually stunning masterpiece
with over 70 recipes

John P. Doran

Alan Zucconi

BIRMINGHAM - MUMBAI

Unity 2018 Shaders and Effects Cookbook
Third Edition

Commissioning Editor: Kunal Chaudhari
Acquisition Editor: Larissa Pinto
Content Development Editor: Arun Nadar
Technical Editor: Surabhi Kulkarni
Copy Editor: Safis Editing
Project Coordinator: Sheejal Shah
Proofreader: Safis Editing
Indexer: Mariammal Chettiyar
Graphics: Jason Monteiro
Production Coordinator: Arvindkumar Gupta

First published: June 2013

Second edition: February 2016

Third edition: June 2018

Production reference: 1280618

Published by Packt Publishing Ltd.
Livery Place
35 Livery Street
Birmingham
B3 2PB, UK.

ISBN 978-1-78839-623-3

www.packtpub.com

`mapt.io`

Mapt is an online digital library that gives you full access to over 5,000 books and videos, as well as industry leading tools to help you plan your personal development and advance your career. For more information, please visit our website.

Why subscribe?

- Spend less time learning and more time coding with practical eBooks and Videos from over 4,000 industry professionals

- Improve your learning with Skill Plans built especially for you

- Get a free eBook or video every month

- Mapt is fully searchable

- Copy and paste, print, and bookmark content

PacktPub.com

Did you know that Packt offers eBook versions of every book published, with PDF and ePub files available? You can upgrade to the eBook version at `www.PacktPub.com` and as a print book customer, you are entitled to a discount on the eBook copy. Get in touch with us at `service@packtpub.com` for more details.

At `www.PacktPub.com`, you can also read a collection of free technical articles, sign up for a range of free newsletters, and receive exclusive discounts and offers on Packt books and eBooks.

Contributors

About the authors

John P. Doran is a passionate and seasoned technical game designer, software engineer, and author who is based in Redmond, Washington. For over a decade, John has built games in roles ranging from game designer to lead UI programmer. Additionally, John has taught game development in Singapore, South Korea, and the United States. To date, he has authored over 10 books pertaining to game development.

Thanks so much to my wife Hien and my family for all of their support while working on this book.

Alan Zucconi is a passionate developer, author, and lecturer, recognized as one of Develop's *30 under 30*. His expertise has been built over the past 10 years, working in the intersection between creativity and education. Starting in 2015, he published a series of educational tutorials for other developers and machine learning enthusiasts

About the reviewers

Andrew Hlynka is a software engineer and game developer from Windsor, Ontario, Canada. He earned his MSc degree in Computer Science in 2015 from the University of Windsor and has worked in the industry for over five years on software projects involving multimedia, interactive displays, games, mobile apps, and hybrid simulation systems. He continues his research in innovative animation techniques for games as an independent developer, publishing his projects under Dust Scratch Games.

I would like to thank my professors at the University of Windsor for their support and encouragement during my research as a student, and for introducing me to the Unity3D game engine nearly a decade ago, forever changing my workflow in the world of game development.

Michael Miles is a Manufacturing Engineer working in the aerospace industry by day and is a Unity game designer, C#, JavaScript, and Python developer at all other times. With these skills, and upon discovering Unity3D and Blender, Michael began creating interactive training and production-ready instruction tools for the assembly of the aircraft his company builds.

When not in front of the screen of a computer, he likes to play games with family and friends or immerse himself in books whose genres range from fantasy to theoretical physics.

Thanks to my parents for always being, there supporting every decision I made, however unwise you thought it was at the time.

Packt is searching for authors like you

If you're interested in becoming an author for Packt, please visit authors.packtpub.com and apply today. We have worked with thousands of developers and tech professionals, just like you, to help them share their insight with the global tech community. You can make a general application, apply for a specific hot topic that we are recruiting an author for, or submit your own idea.

Table of Contents

Preface

Unity 2018 Shaders and Effects Cookbook is your guide to becoming familiar with the creation of shaders and post-processing effects in Unity 2018. You will start your journey at the beginning, exploring the Post Processing Stack to see some of the possible ways you can use shaders to affect what you see without having to write scripts at all. Afterwards, we learn how to create shaders from scratch, starting by creating the most basic shaders and learning how the shader code is structured. This foundational knowledge will arm you with the means to progress further through each chapter, learning advanced techniques such as volumetric explosions and fur shading. We also explore the newly added Shader Graph editor to see how you can create shaders through a drag and drop interface as well! This edition of the book is written specifically for Unity 2018 and will help you to master physically-based rendering and global illumination to get as close to photorealism as possible.

By the end of each chapter, you will have gained new skills that will increase the quality of your shaders and even make your shader writing process more efficient. These chapters have been tailored so that you can jump into each section and learn a specific skill from beginner to expert. For those who are new to shader writing in Unity, you can progress through each chapter, one at a time, to build on your knowledge. Either way, you will learn the techniques that make modern games look the way they do.

Once you have completed this book, you will have a set of shaders that you can use in your Unity 3D games as well as the understanding to add to them, accomplish new effects, and address performance needs. So, let's get started!

Who this book is for

Unity Effects and Shader Cookbook is written for developers who want to create their first shaders in Unity 2018 or wish to take their game to a whole new level by adding professional post-processing effects. A solid understanding of Unity is required.

What this book covers

Chapter 1, *Post Processing Stack*, introduces readers to the Post Processing Stack, which will allow users to tweak their game's appearance without having to write any additional scripts.

Chapter 2, *Creating Your First Shader*, introduces you to the world of shader coding in Unity. You will build some basic shaders and learn how to introduce tweakable properties in your shaders to make them more interactive.

Chapter 3, *Surface Shaders and Texture Mapping*, covers the most common and useful techniques that you can implement with Surface Shaders, including how to use textures and normal maps for your models.

Chapter 4, *Understanding Lighting Models*, gives you an in-depth explanation of how shaders model the behavior of light. This chapter teaches you how to create custom lighting models used to simulate special effects, such as toon shading.

Chapter 5, *Physically-Based Rendering in Unity 5*, shows you that physically-based rendering is the standard technology used by Unity 5 to bring realism to your games. This chapter explains how to make the most out of it by mastering transparencies, reflective surfaces, and global illumination.

Chapter 6, *Vertex Functions*, teaches you how shaders can be used to alter the geometry of an object. This chapter introduces vertex modifiers and uses them to bring volumetric explosions, snow shaders, and other effects to life.

Chapter 7, *Fragment Shaders and Grab Passes*, explains how to use grab passes to make materials that emulate the deformations generated by semi-transparent materials.

Chapter 8, *Mobile Shader Adjustment*, helps you optimize your shaders to get the most out of any device.

Chapter 9, *Screen Effects with Unity Render Textures*, shows you how to create special effects and visuals that would otherwise be impossible to achieve.

Chapter 10, *Gameplay and Screen Effects*, tells you how post-processing effects can be used to complement your gameplay, simulating, for instance, a night-vision effect.

Chapter 11, *Advanced Shading Techniques*, introduces the most advanced techniques in this book, such as fur shading and heatmap rendering.

Chapter 12, *Shader Graph*, explains how to set up a project to use Unity's newly added Shader Graph editor. We cover how to create a simple shader graph, how to expose properties, and how to interact with the shader graph through code using a glow highlight system.

To get the most out of this book

Readers are expected to have experience of working with Unity and some scripting experience (C# or JavaScript is fine). The book is written with Unity 2018.1.0f2, but should work with future versions of the engine with some minor tweaks.

Download the example code files

You can download the example code files for this book from your account at www.packtpub.com. If you purchased this book elsewhere, you can visit www.packtpub.com/support and register to have the files emailed directly to you.

You can download the code files by following these steps:

1. Log in or register at www.packtpub.com.
2. Select the **SUPPORT** tab.
3. Click on **Code Downloads & Errata**.
4. Enter the name of the book in the **Search** box and follow the onscreen instructions.

Once the file is downloaded, please make sure that you unzip or extract the folder using the latest version of:

- WinRAR/7-Zip for Windows
- Zipeg/iZip/UnRarX for Mac
- 7-Zip/PeaZip for Linux

The code bundle for the book is also hosted on GitHub at https://github.com/PacktPublishing/Unity-2018-Shaders-and-Effects-Cookbook-Third-Edition. In case there's an update to the code, it will be updated on the existing GitHub repository.

We also have other code bundles from our rich catalog of books and videos available at https://github.com/PacktPublishing/. Check them out!

Download the color images

We also provide a PDF file that has color images of the screenshots/diagrams used in this book. You can download it here: https://www.packtpub.com/sites/default/files/downloads/Unity2018ShadersandEffectsCookbookThirdEdition_ColorImages.pdf.

Conventions used

There are a number of text conventions used throughout this book.

CodeInText: Indicates code words in text, database table names, folder names, filenames, file extensions, pathnames, dummy URLs, user input, and Twitter handles. Here is an example: "A Unity package is a single file that contains various Assets that can be used in Unity in a similar manner to a .zip file."

A block of code is set as follows:

```
Properties
{
   _MainTex("Texture", 2D) = "white"
}
```

When we wish to draw your attention to a particular part of a code block, the relevant lines or items are set in bold:

```
void surf (Input IN, inout SurfaceOutputStandard o) {
    // Use the tint provided as the base color for the material
    o.Albedo = _MainTint;

    // Get the normal data out of the normal map texture
    // using the UnpackNormal function
    float3 normalMap = UnpackNormal(tex2D(_NormalTex,
      IN.uv_NormalTex));

    normalMap.x *= _NormalMapIntensity;
    normalMap.y *= _NormalMapIntensity;

    // Apply the new normal to the lighting model
    o.Normal = normalize(normalMap.rgb);
}
```

Bold: Indicates a new term, an important word, or words that you see onscreen. For example, words in menus or dialog boxes appear in the text like this. Here is an example: "To finally bake the lights, open the **Lighting** window by going to **Window** | **Lighting** | **Settings**. Once there, select the **Global Maps** tab."

Warnings or important notes appear like this.

Tips and tricks appear like this.

Sections

In this book, you will find several headings that appear frequently (*Getting ready*, *How to do it...*, *How it works...*, *There's more...*, and *See also*).

To give clear instructions on how to complete a recipe, use these sections as follows:

Getting ready

This section tells you what to expect in the recipe and describes how to set up any software or any preliminary settings required for the recipe.

How to do it...

This section contains the steps required to follow the recipe.

How it works...

This section usually consists of a detailed explanation of what happened in the previous section.

There's more...

This section consists of additional information about the recipe in order to make you more knowledgeable about the recipe.

See also

This section provides helpful links to other useful information for the recipe.

Get in touch

Feedback from our readers is always welcome.

General feedback: Email `feedback@packtpub.com` and mention the book title in the subject of your message. If you have questions about any aspect of this book, please email us at `questions@packtpub.com`.

Errata: Although we have taken every care to ensure the accuracy of our content, mistakes do happen. If you have found a mistake in this book, we would be grateful if you would report this to us. Please visit `www.packtpub.com/submit-errata`, selecting your book, clicking on the Errata Submission Form link, and entering the details.

Piracy: If you come across any illegal copies of our works in any form on the internet, we would be grateful if you would provide us with the location address or website name. Please contact us at `copyright@packtpub.com` with a link to the material.

If you are interested in becoming an author: If there is a topic that you have expertise in and you are interested in either writing or contributing to a book, please visit `authors.packtpub.com`.

Reviews

Please leave a review. Once you have read and used this book, why not leave a review on the site that you purchased it from? Potential readers can then see and use your unbiased opinion to make purchase decisions, we at Packt can understand what you think about our products, and our authors can see your feedback on their book. Thank you!

For more information about Packt, please visit `packtpub.com`.

Post Processing Stack

1

In this chapter, you will learn about the following recipes:

- Installing the Post Processing Stack
- Getting a filmic look using grain, vignetting, and anti-aliasing
- Mimicking real life with bloom and anti-aliasing
- Setting the mood with color grading
- Creating a horror game look with fog

Introduction

It's great to write your own shaders and effects so that you can fine-tune your project to look just the way that you want, and this is what we will be spending the majority of the book looking into. However, it's also good to point out that Unity already comes with some prebuilt ways to get some of the more common effects that users like to have through the use of the Post Processing Stack.

For those who just want to get something up and running, the Post Processing Stack can be an excellent way for you to tweak the appearance of your game without having to write any additional code. Using the Post Processing Stack can also be useful in showing you just what shaders can do and how they can improve your game projects as, behind the scenes, the Post Processing Stack is itself a shader that is applied to the screen, aptly called a screen shader.

Installing the Post Processing Stack

Before we can use the Post Processing Stack, we must first get it from the newly introduced **Package Manager**. A Unity package is a single file that contains various assets that can be used in Unity in a similar manner to a `.zip` file. Previously, Unity used the **Asset Store** to share these files with users, but as time has gone on, the **Package Manager** has been added to give users an easy way to get free content from Unity. We will actually be using the **Package Manager** again in `Chapter 12`, *Shader Graph*, but right now we will be using it for the **Post-Processing** package that it contains.

Getting ready

To get started with this recipe, you will need to have Unity running and have created a new project. This chapter also requires you to have an environment to work from. The code files provided with this book will contain a basic scene and content to create the scene Unity's Standard Assets.

Open the `Chapter 1 | Starting Point` scene inside of the `Asset | Chapter 01 | Scenes` folder from the **Project** browser. If all goes well, you should see something like this from the **Game** tab:

This is a simple environment that will allow us to easily see how changes made in post-processing effects can modify how things are drawn on the screen.

 If you are interested in learning how to create the environment used, check out my previous book, *Unity 5.x Game Development Blueprints*, also available from Packt Publishing.

How to do it...

To begin:

1. Open up the **Package Manager** by going to **Window** | **Package Manager** (or by pressing *Ctrl + 9*):

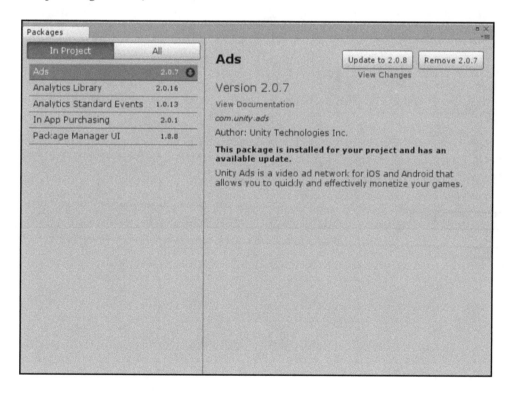

2. From the list view, click on the **All** button to display a list of all of the possible packages that are there. Once the list populates with all of the choices, select the **Post-processing** option:

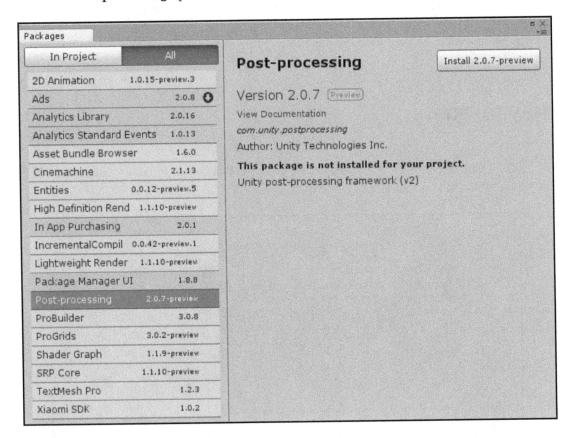

3. From there, at the top right of the menu, click on the **Install 2.0.7-preview** button. You may need to wait for a while for it to complete downloading the content. Once it's completed, you should be brought back to the **In Project** selection and now you'll see **Post-processing** added to the list:

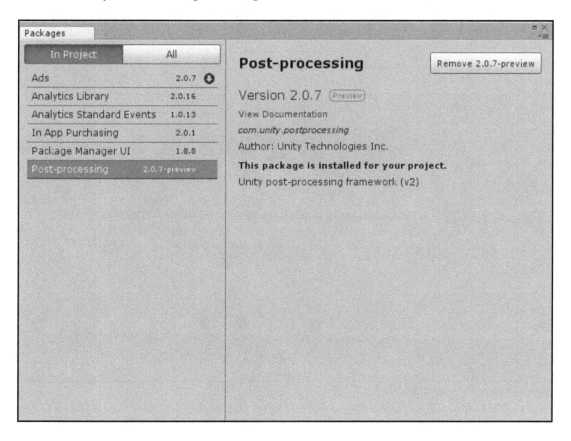

4. Close out of the **Packages** tab and go back to the **Scene** window to see the level. Then, from the **Hierarchy** window, we want to select the object that has our **Camera** component attached to it, as the Post Processing Stack needs to know which screen we want to modify. If you are using your own project, you may select the **MainCamera** object that comes with the default Unity scene, but the example project that is being used has the **Camera** located as a child of the FPSController object. To select it, click on the arrow next to the name to extend the object's children and then select the FirstPersonCharacter object:

This object has the **Camera** component on it, which is in charge of drawing what it sees to the **Game** tab when the game starts.

You can double-click on a game object in the **Hierarchy** tab to zoom the camera from the **Scene** tab to its location. This makes it very easy to find things, even in a large game level.

5. With the object selected and our **Camera** component attached to it, next we need to add the **Post-processing Behavior** component to the object by going into **Component | Rendering | Post-process Layer**:

6. Once added, from the **Inspector** tab, scroll down to the **Post Process Layer (Script)** component and, under **Layer**, change the dropdown to `PostProcessing`.

7. This tells the component which objects we want to draw on the screen. When setting this, an object must have its **Layer** property set to `PostProcessing` in order to be seen.

8. To create a **Post Process Volume**, go to the menu and select **GameObject | 3D Object | Post Process Volume**. From there, go to the **Inspector** tab and change the **Layer** property to `PostProcessing`. Finally, to make it easier to work with, change the **Position** to 0, 0, 0 and under the **Post Process Volume** component, check the **Is Global** property:

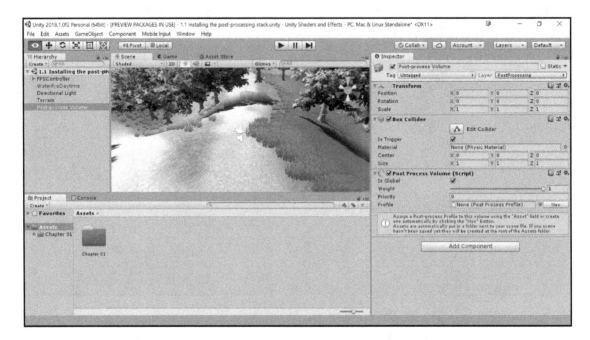

Notice that there is a **Profile** property to the volume. This property will contain information about how we wish to modify the screen. By checking **Is Global**, we are saying that this information should always be drawn on an object. By unchecking it, the effects will only be visible from a certain distance from where the volume is placed. Depending on the game, this could allow you to drastically modify how the game appears in certain areas, but we care only about getting the visual effect at this point.

Getting a filmic look using grain, vignetting, and depth of field

Now that we have the Post Processing Stack installed, we can create our first **Post-processing Volume**. The new Post Processing Stack relies on using volumes that describe how things should be drawn, either globally or within a certain area.

One of the most common appearances people like projects to have is that of a film. This is used quite frequently in titles such as the *Uncharted* series and *Grand Theft Auto V*. It's also used quite effectively in the *Left 4 Dead* series, as its creator are trying to emulate the B-movie zombie films that the games are based on.

Getting ready

Make sure you have completed the *Installing the Post Processing Stack* recipe before starting this one.

How to do it...

1. We first create a new **Post Processing Profile** by right-clicking within the Assets | Chapter 1 folder in the **Project** window and then selecting **Create | Post Processing Profile**. Once selected, it will allow us to rename the item. Go ahead and set the name to FilmicProfile:

If you happen to not enter the name correctly, you can rename an item from the **Project** tab by clicking on the name and then clicking again.

2. Once created, you should notice that, when selected, the **Inspector** window will now contain a button that says **Add effect...** (as you can see in the preceding image), which will allow us to augment what is normally drawn on the screen.
3. From the **Hierarchy** tab, select the **Post-process Volume** object again and from the **Inspector** tab go to the **Post Process Volume** component and assign the **Profile** property to the FilmicProflie we just created:

Notice that, once the **Profile** has been set, the **Add effect...** button shows up here as well. We can use this at either place and the changes will be saved in the file.

4. To get started, click on the **Add effect...** button and select the **Unity |
   Grain** option. By default, you'll only see the **Grain** option with a check, so click
   on the arrow to expand its contents:

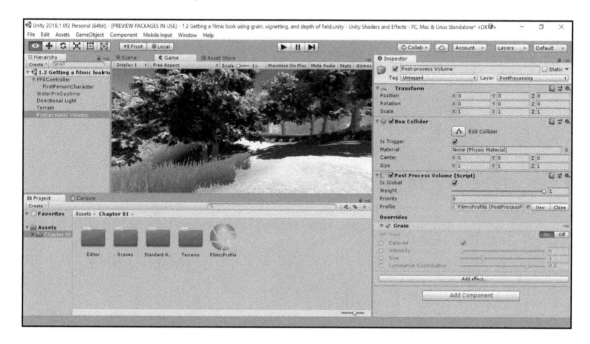

By default, you'll see that everything is greyed out. In order to have it affect
anything, you have to click on the checkbox on the left-hand side. You can quickly
turn them all on or off by pressing the **All** or **None** buttons on the screen.

5. In our case, check the **Intensity** option and set it to 0.2. Then, check the **Size** property and set it to 0.3. Afterward, switch to the **Game** tab to see a representation of what our tweaks have done:

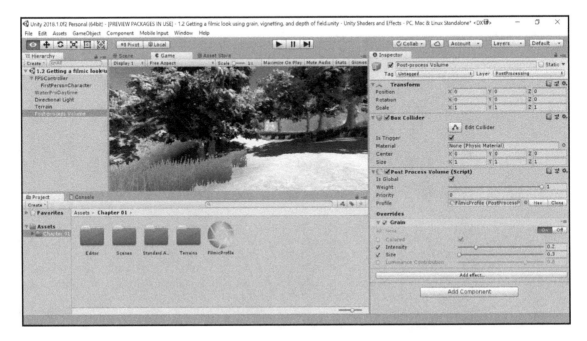

6. You will notice that the screen has become much fuzzier than before. Decrease the **Intensity** to 0.2, the **Size** to 0.3, and uncheck the **Colored** option.

Unlike how users typically work in Unity, due to Post Processing Profiles being filed, you can modify them while playing your game and, upon stopping the game, the values are still saved. This can be useful for tweaking values to achieve the exact look that you're after.

7. The next property we want to tweak is the **Vignette** property. Note the blackened edges around the screen. Click on **Add effect...** and select **Unity | Vignette**. Open up the properties and change the **Intensity** to 0.5 and the **Smoothness** to 0.35:

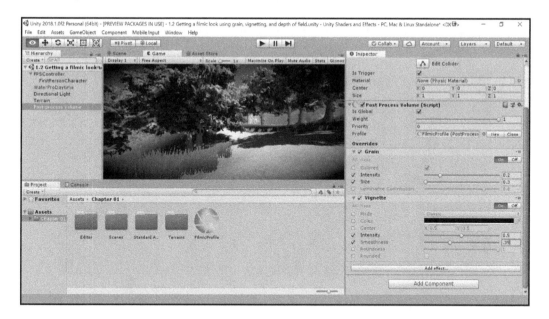

8. Next, select **Add effect...** again and, this time, select **Unity | Depth of Field**. Check the **Depth of Field** option. It may be difficult to see a change right off the bat, but change the **Focus Distance** to 6 and **Focal Length** to 80 and you should notice the grass in front of the background and the mountain in the distance are now blurred:

9. Now, if we go into the game itself, you should see our filmic look in action:

The final result of the filmic look

And with that, we now have a scene that looks much more like a film than what we had to begin with!

How it works...

Each time we add an effect to a **Post-processing Volume**, we are overriding what would normally be put onto the screen.

If you've been to a movie theater that still uses film, you may have noticed how there were little specks in the filmstock while the film was playing. The **grain** effect simulates this film grain, causing the effect to become more pronounced the more the movie is played. This is often used in horror games to obscure the player's vision.

For more information on the grain effect, check out: https://github.com/ Unity-Technologies/PostProcessing/wiki/Grain.

In the film world, **vignetting** can be an unintended effect of using the wrong type of lens for the type of shot you are trying to achieve or the aspect ratio that you are shooting for. In game development, we typically use vignetting for dramatic effect or to have players focus on the center of the screen by darkening and/or desaturating the edges of the screen compared to the center.

For more information on the vignette effect, check out: `https://github.com/Unity-Technologies/PostProcessing/wiki/Vignette`.

The **depth of field** setting basically determines what is blurry and what isn't. The idea is to have items of importance in focus while items in the background are not.

 For more information on the depth of field effect, check out: `https://github.com/Unity-Technologies/PostProcessing/wiki/Depth-of-Field`.

Mimicking real life with bloom and anti-aliasing

The **bloom** optical effect aims to mimic the imaging effects of real-world cameras, where things in areas with lights will glow along the edges, thus overwhelming the camera. The bloom effect is very distinctive and you've likely seen it employed in areas in a game that are magical or heaven-like.

Getting ready

Make sure you have completed the *Installing the Post Processing Stack* recipe before starting this one.

How to do it...

1. We first create a new **Post Processing Profile** by right-clicking within the `Assets` folder in the **Project** window and then selecting **Create | Post Processing Profile**. Once selected, it will allow us to rename the item. Go ahead and set the name to `BloomProfile`.
2. Select the `Post-process volume` object and, from the **Inspector** window, go to the **Post Processing Volume** component and assign the **Profile** property to the `BloomProflie` we just created.

3. Afterward, select the **Game** tab, if it hasn't been selected already to see the results of the changes we are about to make in the following steps.

4. Select the **Add effect...** button and select **Unity | Bloom**. Once the effect has been added to the **Overrides** section of the **Post Processing Volume** component, select the arrow to open its properties. Check the **Intensity** property and set it to 3. Afterward, check and set the **Threshold** to 0.75, the **Soft Knee** to 0.1, and the **Radius** to 3:

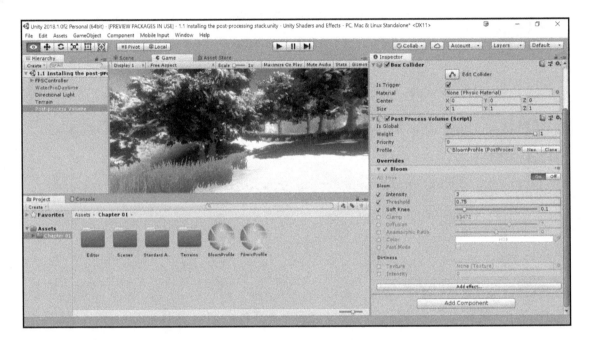

5. Next, select the object with the **Post Process Layer** component attached to it (in the example, it is the FPSController | FirstPersonCharacter object) and, from the **Inspector** tab, scroll down to the **Post Process Layer** script. From there, change the **Anti-aliasing** property dropdown to Fast Approximate Anti-aliasing:

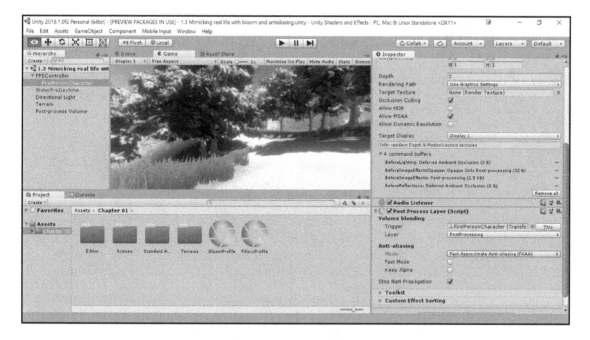

6. Afterward, save your scene and hit the Play button to check out your project:

The final result of using bloom and anti-aliasing

How it works...

As mentioned before, bloom will make bright things even brighter while adding a glow to lighter areas. In this recipe, you may notice that the path is much lighter than it was previously. This can be used in order to ensure that players will follow the path to get to the next section of gameplay.

> For more information on bloom, check out: `https://github.com/Unity-Technologies/PostProcessing/wiki/Bloom`.

Anti-aliasing attempts to reduce the appearance of aliasing, which is the effect of lines appearing jagged on the screen. This is typically due to the fact that the display the player is using to play the game doesn't have a high enough resolution to be displayed properly. Anti-aliasing will combine colors with nearby lines in order to remove their prominence, at the cost of the game appearing blurry.

> For more information on anti-aliasing and what each mode means, check out: `https://github.com/Unity-Technologies/PostProcessing/wiki/Anti-aliasing`.

Setting mood with color grading

One of the best ways to easily change the mood of a scene is by changing the colors a scene uses. One of the best examples of this is in the *Matrix* series of films, where the real world is always blue-tinted, while the computer-generated world of the Matrix is always tinted green. We can emulate this in our games through the use of color grading.

Getting ready

Make sure you have completed the *Installing the Post Processing Stack* recipe before starting this one.

How to do it...

1. We first create a new **Post Processing Profile** by right-clicking within the `Assets` folder in the **Project** window and then selecting **Create | Post Processing Profile**. Once selected, it will allow us to rename the item. Go ahead and set it to `ColorProfile`.

2. Select the `Post-process volume` object and, from the **Inspector** window, go to the **Post Processing Volume** component and assign the **Profile** property to the `ColorProflie` we just created.

3. Afterward, select the **Game** tab, if it hasn't been selected already, to see the results of the changes to be made.

4. Select the **Add effect...** button and select **Unity | Color Grading**.

5. Check the **Mode** property and set it to **Low Definition Range** (LDR). From there, you'll see a number of properties that can be used to adjust the colors on the screen in a similar manner to how Photoshop's hue/saturation menu works. Check the **Temperature** property and set it to 30. Afterward, set the **Hue Shift** property to –20 and the **Saturation** to 15:

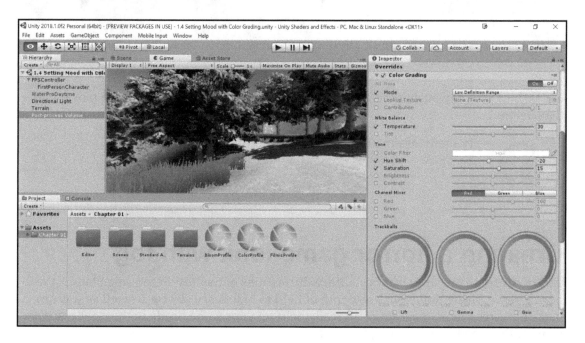

6. After making the changes, dive into the game to see what it looks like when playing:

The final result of using color grading

Notice how the previously very green environment is now much warmer and more yellow than before.

For more information on the color grading effect, check out: `https://github.com/Unity-Technologies/PostProcessing/wiki/Color-Grading`.

Creating a horror game look with fog

One of the types of games that best utilize the features of the Post Processing Stack is the horror genre. Using things such as depth of field to hide scary objects, as well as static to make the screen more menacing, can really help set your game firmly in the right place and provide the mood you are going for.

Getting ready

Make sure you have completed the *Installing the Post Processing Stack* recipe before starting this one.

How to do it...

1. We first create a new Post Processing Profile by right-clicking within the Assets folder in the **Project** window and then selecting **Create | Post Processing Profile**. Once selected, it will allow us to rename the item. Go ahead and set the name to HorrorProfile.

2. Select the Post-process volume object and, from the **Inspector** window, go to the **Post Processing Volume** component and assign the **Profile** property to the HorrorProflie we just created.

3. Unlike previous settings, though, the fog settings are located in the **Lighting** window, which can be accessed by going into **Window | Lighting**.

4. From there, scroll all the way to the bottom until you reach the **Other Settings** option. Once there, check **Fog** and set the color to a value that is close to the skybox. I used the following settings:

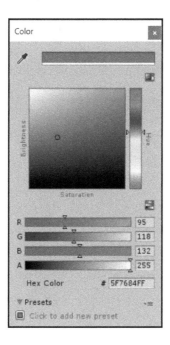

If you know the hex values of the color from your graphic editing software you can just type it in the **Hex Color** property of the **Color** window.

5. Next, change the **Mode** to `Exponential` and the **Density** to `0.03`:

As you can see, it's already much more spooky that it was previously, but there are still more options that we can change.

6. Open up the **HorrorProfile** again and go to the **Inspector** tab. Press the **Add effect...** button and select **Unity | Ambient Occlusion**. Check the **Mode** option and select Scalable Ambient Obscurance. Afterward, change the **Intensity** to 2 and the **Radius** to 20:

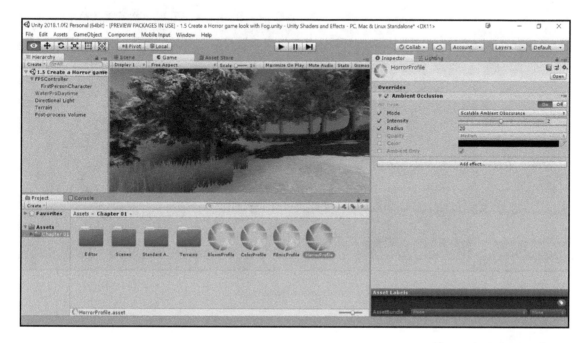

7. Lastly, lighting often has a big effect on the theme of a scene as well. If you're using the example map, select the Directional Light object in the **Hierarchy** tab and, from the **Inspector** tab under the **Light** component, change the **Intensity** to 0.5 and then adjust the **Color** to something darker. (I used the same color as in *step 4* with a **HEX** of 5F7684FF.)

8. Save your game and then start it to see the effect of all of the changes:

The final result of our horror look

How it works...

The **Ambient Occlusion** option will calculate areas that should have additional shadows. Since our scene is filled with trees, this will make the undersides much darker than they were previously.

 For more information on the Ambient Occlusion effect, check out: `https:/ /github.com/Unity-Technologies/PostProcessing/wiki/Ambient- Occlusion`. If you are interested in looking into the other options that the Post Processing stack has, check out: `https://github.com/Unity- Technologies/PostProcessing/wiki`.

Creating Your First Shader

2

In this chapter, you will learn about the following recipes:

- Creating a basic Standard Shader
- Adding properties to a shader
- Using properties in a Surface Shader

Introduction

This chapter will cover some of the more common diffuse techniques found in today's game development shading pipelines. Let's imagine a cube that has been painted white uniformly in a 3D environment with a directional light. Even if the color used is the same on each face, they will all have different shades of white on them depending on the direction that the light is coming from and the angle that we are looking at it from. This extra level of realism is achieved in 3D graphics through the use of shaders, special programs that are mostly used to simulate how light works. A wooden cube and a metal one may share the same 3D model, but what makes them look different is the shader that they use.

This first chapter will introduce you to shader coding in Unity. If you have little to no previous experience with shaders, this chapter is what you need in order to understand what shaders are, how they work, and how to customize them. By the end of this chapter, you will have learned how to build basic shaders that perform basic operations. Armed with this knowledge, you will be able to create just about any Surface Shader.

Creating a basic Standard Shader

In Unity, when we create a game object, we then attach additional functionality through the use of **components**. In fact, every game object is required to have a Transform component; there are a number of components included in Unity already, and we create components of our own when we write scripts that extend from `MonoBehaviour`.

All the objects that are part of a game contain a number of components that affect their look and behavior. While scripts determine how objects should behave, renderers decide how they should appear on the screen. Unity comes with several renderers, depending on the type of object that we are trying to visualize; every 3D model typically has a `MeshRenderer` component attached to it. An object should have only one renderer, but the renderer itself can contain several materials. Each material is a wrapper for a single shader, the final ring in the food chain of 3D graphics. The relationships between these components can be seen in the following diagram:

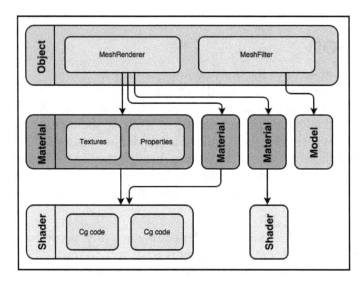

Understanding the difference between these components is essential for understanding how shaders work.

Getting ready

To get started with this recipe, you will need to have Unity running and must have a project opened. As mentioned before, there will also be a Unity project included with this cookbook, so you can use that one as well and simply add your own custom shaders to it as you step through each recipe. With this completed, you are now ready to step into the wonderful world of real-time shading!

Before getting into our first shader, let's create a small scene for us to work with:

1. Let's create a scene by navigating to **File** | **New Scene.**
2. Once you create the scene, create a plane to act as the ground by going to **GameObject** | **3D Objects** | **Plane** in the Unity editor. Next, select the object in the **Hierarchy** tab and then go into the **Inspector** tab. From there, right-click on the **Transform** component and select the **Reset Position** option:

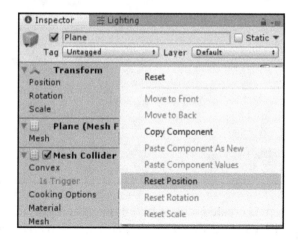

This will reset the position property of the object to be at 0, 0, 0:

3. To make it easier to see what our shaders will look like when applied, let's add some shapes to visualize what each of our shaders will do. Create a sphere by going to **GameObject** | **3D Objects** | **Sphere**. Once created, select it and go to the **Inspector** tab. Next, change the **Position** to 0, 1, 0 so it is above the origin of the world (which is at 0, 0, 0) and our previously created plane:

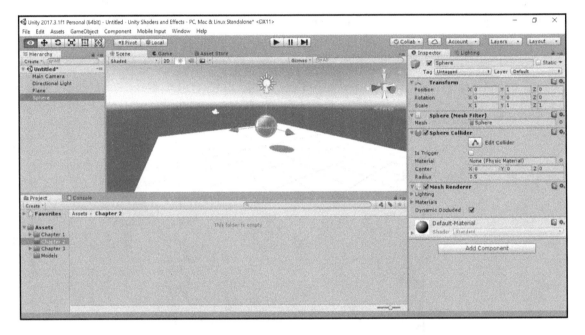

4. Once this sphere is created, create two more spheres, placing them to the left and right of the spheres at positions –2, 1, 0 and 2, 1, 0 respectively:

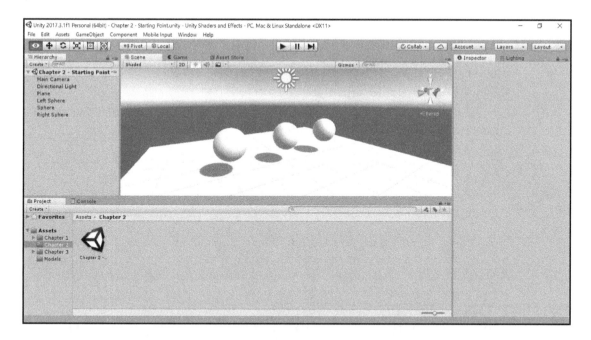

5. Lastly, confirm that you have a directional light (it should be seen in the Hierarchy tab). If not, you can add one by selecting **GameObject | Light | Directional Light** to make it easier to see the effect of your changes and how your shaders react to light.

 If you are using the Unity project that came with the cookbook, you can open up the Chapter 2 | Starting Point scene instead as it has been set up already.

How to do it...

With our scene generated, we can move on to the shader writing steps:

1. In the **Project** tab in your Unity editor, right-click on the Chapter 2 folder and select **Create | Folder**.
2. Rename the folder that you created as Shaders by right-clicking on it and selecting **Rename** from the drop-down list, or by selecting the folder and hitting *F2* on the keyboard.

3. Create another folder and rename it as `Materials`.

4. Right-click on the `Shaders` folder and select **Create** | **Shader** | **Standard Surface Shader**. Then, right-click on the `Materials` folder and select **Create** | **Material**.

5. Rename both the shader and material as `StandardDiffuse`.

6. Launch the `StandardDiffuse` shader by double-clicking on the file. This will automatically launch a scripting editor for you and display the shader's code.

 You will see that Unity has already populated our shader with some basic code. This, by default, will get you a basic shader that accepts one texture in the Albedo (RGB) property. We will be modifying this base code so that you can learn how to quickly start developing your own custom shaders.

7. Now let's give our shader a custom folder from which it's selected. The very first line of code in the shader is the custom description that we have to give the shader so that Unity can make it available in the shader drop-down list when assigning to materials. We have renamed our path as `Shader "CookbookShaders/StandardDiffuse"`, but you can name it whatever you want and rename it at any time so don't worry about any dependencies at this point. Save the shader in your script editor and return to the Unity editor. Unity will automatically compile the shader when it recognizes that the file has been updated. This is what your shader should look like at this point:

```
Shader "CookbookShaders/StandardDiffuse" {
  Properties {
    _Color ("Color", Color) = (1,1,1,1)
    _MainTex ("Albedo (RGB)", 2D) = "white" {}
    _Glossiness ("Smoothness", Range(0,1)) = 0.5
    _Metallic ("Metallic", Range(0,1)) = 0.0
  }
  SubShader {
    Tags { "RenderType"="Opaque" }
    LOD 200

    CGPROGRAM
    // Physically based Standard lighting model, and enable shadows
on all light types
    #pragma surface surf Standard fullforwardshadows

    // Use shader model 3.0 target, to get nicer looking lighting
    #pragma target 3.0

    sampler2D _MainTex;

    struct Input {
```

```
      float2 uv_MainTex;
    };

    half _Glossiness;
    half _Metallic;
    fixed4 _Color;

    // Add instancing support for this shader. You need to check
'Enable Instancing' on materials that use the shader.
    // See https://docs.unity3d.com/Manual/GPUInstancing.html for
more information about instancing.
    // #pragma instancing_options assumeuniformscaling
    UNITY_INSTANCING_BUFFER_START(Props)
      // put more per-instance properties here
    UNITY_INSTANCING_BUFFER_END(Props)

    void surf (Input IN, inout SurfaceOutputStandard o) {
      // Albedo comes from a texture tinted by color
      fixed4 c = tex2D (_MainTex, IN.uv_MainTex) * _Color;
      o.Albedo = c.rgb;
      // Metallic and smoothness come from slider variables
      o.Metallic = _Metallic;
      o.Smoothness = _Glossiness;
      o.Alpha = c.a;
    }
    ENDCG
  }
  FallBack "Diffuse"
}
```

8. Technically speaking, this is a Surface Shader based on **physically-based rendering (PBR)**. As the name suggests, this type of shader achieves realism by simulating how light physically behaves when hitting objects.

9. After your shader is created, we need to connect it to a material. Select the material called `StandardDiffuse` that we created in *step 4* and look at the **Inspector** tab. From the **Shader** drop-down list, select **CookbookShaders | StandardDiffuse**. (Your shader path might be different if you chose to use a different path name.) This will assign your shader to your material and make it ready for you to assign to an object.

 To assign material to an object, you can simply click and drag your material from the **Project** tab to the object in your scene. You can also drag material to the **Inspector** tab of an object in the Unity editor in order to assign it.

The screenshot of an example is as follows:

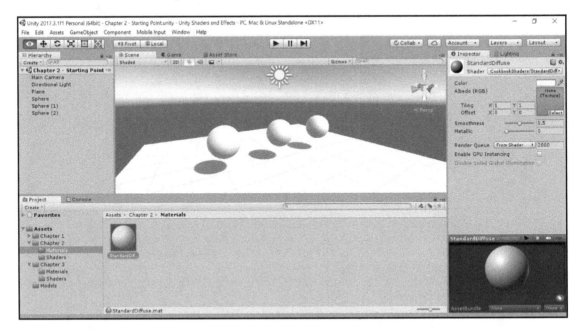

Not much to look at at this point, but our shader development environment is set up and we can now start to modify the shader to suit our needs.

How it works...

Unity has made the task of getting your shader environment up and running very easy for you. It is simply a matter of a few clicks and you are good to go. There are a lot of elements working in the background with regard to the Surface Shader itself. Unity has taken the Cg shader language and made it more efficient to write by doing a lot of the heavy Cg code lifting for you. The Surface Shader language is a more component-based way of writing shaders. Tasks such as processing your own texture coordinates and transformation matrices have already been done for you, so you don't have to start from scratch any more. In the past, we would have to start a new shader and rewrite a lot of code over and over again. As you gain more experience with Surface Shaders, you will naturally want to explore more of the underlying functions of the Cg language and how Unity is processing all of the low-level **graphics processing unit** (**GPU**) tasks for you.

All the files in a Unity project are referenced independently from the folder that they are in. We can move shaders and materials from within the editor without the risk of breaking any connection. Files, however, should never be moved from outside the editor as Unity will not be able to update their references.

So, by simply changing the shader's path name to a name of our choice, we have got our basic diffuse shader working in the Unity environment, with lights and shadows and all that, just by changing one line of code!

There's more...

The source code of the built-in shaders is typically hidden in Unity. You cannot open this from the editor as you do with your own shaders. For more information on where to find a large portion of the built-in Cg functions for Unity, go to your Unity install directory and navigate to the `Editor` | `Data` | `CGIncludes` folder:

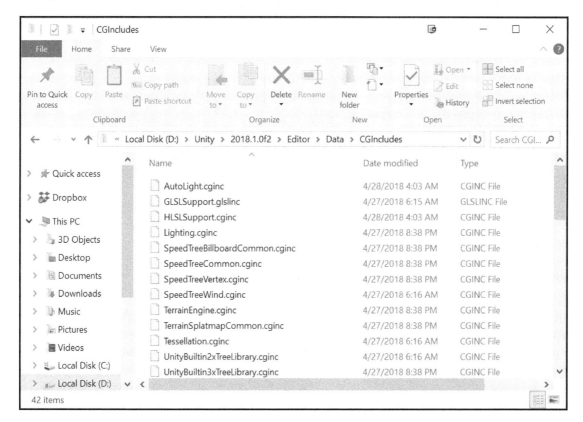

In this folder, you can find the source code of the shaders shipped with Unity. Over time, they have changed a lot; you can visit the **Unity download archive** (`https://unity3d.com/get-unity/download/archive`) if you need to access the source codes of a shader used in a different version of Unity. After choosing the right version, select **Built in shaders** from the drop-down list, as shown in the following screenshot:

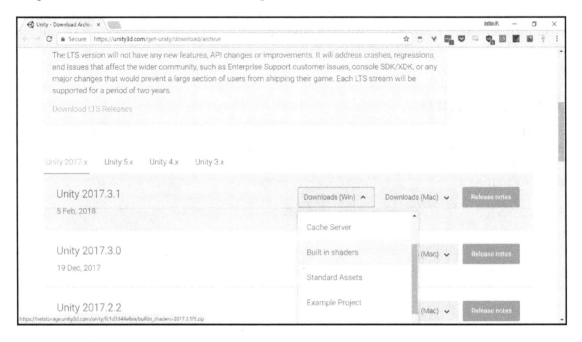

There are three files that are of note at this point: `UnityCG.cginc`, `Lighting.cginc`, and `UnityShaderVariables.cginc`. Our current shader is making use of all these files at the moment. In `Chapter 11`, *Advanced Shading Techniques*, we will explore in depth how to use CGInclude for a modular approach to shader coding.

Adding properties to a shader

Properties of a shader are very important for the shader pipeline as they are the method that you use to let the artist or user of the shader assign textures and tweak your shader values. Properties allow you to expose GUI elements in a material's **Inspector** tab without you having to use a separate editor, which provides visual ways to tweak a shader. With your shader opened in your IDE of choice, look at the block of lines two through seven. This is called the `Properties` block of the script. Currently, it will have one texture property in it called `_MainTex`.

If you look at your material that has this shader applied to it, you will notice that there is one **texture** GUI element in the **Inspector** tab. These lines of code in our shader are creating this GUI element for us. Again, Unity has made this process very efficient in terms of coding and the amount of time it takes to iterate through changing your properties.

Getting ready

Let's see how this works in our current shader called `StandardDiffuse` by creating our own properties and learning more about the syntax involved. For this example, we will refit the shader previously created. Instead of using a texture, it will only use its color and some other properties that we will be able to change directly from the **Inspector** tab. Start by duplicating the `StandardDiffuse` shader. You can do this by selecting it in the **Inspector** tab and pressing *Ctrl + D*. This will create a copy called `StandardDiffuse 1`. Go ahead and rename it as `StandardColor`.

You can give a friendlier name to your shader in its first line. For instance, `Shader "CookbookShaders/StandardDiffuse"` tells Unity to call this shader `StandardDiffuse` and move it to a group called `CookbookShaders`. If you duplicate a shader using *Ctrl + D*, your new file will share the same name. To avoid confusion, make sure to change the first line of each new shader so that it uses a unique alias in this and future recipes.

How to do it...

Once the `StandardColor` shader is ready, we can start changing its properties:

1. In the first line of the script, update the name to the following:

   ```
   Shader "CookbookShaders/Chapter 02/StandardColor" {
   ```

   Downloading the example code

2. In the `Properties` block of our shader, remove the current property by deleting the following code from our current shader:

```
_MainTex ("Albedo (RGB)", 2D) = "white" {}
```

3. As we have removed an essential property, this shader will not compile until the other references to _MainTex are removed. Let's remove this other line inside of the `SubShader` section:

```
sampler2D _MainTex;
```

4. The original shader used _MainTex to color the model. Let's change this by replacing the first line of code of the `surf()` function with this:

```
fixed4 c = _Color;
```

Just as you may be used to the `float` type being used for floating point values when writing code in C# and other programming languages, `fixed` is used for fixed-point values and is the type used when writing shaders. You may also see the `half` type used as well, which is like the `float` type but takes up half the space. This is useful for saving memory but is less precise in how it is presented. We will be discussing this in much greater detail in the *Techniques to make shaders more efficient* recipe in `Chapter 8`, *Mobile Shader Adjustment*.

 For more information on fixed-point values, check out `https://en.wikipedia.org/wiki/Fixed-point_arithmetic`.

The `4` in `fixed4` stands for the fact that the color is a single variable that contains four `fixed` values: red, green, blue, and alpha. You will learn more about how this works and how to modify these values in more detail in the next chapter, `Chapter 3`, *Surface Shaders and Texture Mapping*.

5. When you save and return to Unity, the shader will compile, and you will see that now our material's **Inspector** tab doesn't have a texture swatch any more. To complete the refit of this shader, let's add one more property to the `Properties` block and see what happens. Enter the following code:

```
_AmbientColor ("Ambient Color", Color) = (1,1,1,1)
```

6. We have added another color swatch to the material's **Inspector** tab. Now let's add one more in order to get a feel for other kinds of properties that we can create. Add the following code to the `Properties` block:

```
_MySliderValue ("This is a Slider", Range(0,10)) = 2.5
```

7. We have now created another GUI element that allows us to visually interact with our shader. This time, we created a slider with the name **This is a Slider**, as shown in the following screenshot:

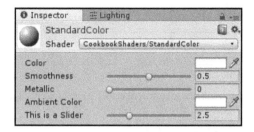

8. Properties allow you to create a visual way to tweak shaders without having to change values in the shader code itself. The next recipe will show you how these properties can actually be used to create a more interesting shader.

 While properties belong to shaders, the values associated with them are stored in materials. The same shader can be safely shared between many different materials. On the other hand, changing the property of a material will affect the look of all the objects that are currently using it.

How it works...

Every Unity shader has a built-in structure that it is looking for in its code. The **Properties** block is one of those functions that are expected by Unity. The reason behind this is to give you, the shader programmer, a means of quickly creating GUI elements that tie directly into your shader code. These properties (variables) that you declare in the **Properties** block can then be used in your shader code to change values, colors, and textures. The syntax to define a property is as follows:

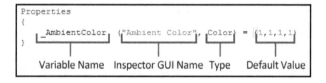

Let's take a look at what is going on under the hood here. When you first start writing a new property, you will need to give it a **Variable Name**. The **Variable Name** is going to be the name that your shader code is going to use in order to get the value from the GUI element. This saves us a lot of time because we don't have to set up this system ourselves. The next elements of a property are the **Inspector GUI Name** and **Type** of the property, which is contained within parentheses. The **Inspector GUI Name** is the name that is going to appear in the material's **Inspector** tab when the user is interacting with and tweaking the shader. The **Type** is the type of data that this property is going to control. There are many types that we can define for properties inside of Unity shaders. The following table describes the types of variables that we can have in our shaders:

Surface Shader property types	Description
Range (min, max)	This creates a `float` property as a slider from the minimum value to the maximum value
Color	This creates a color swatch in the **Inspector** tab that opens up a `color picker = (float, float, float, float)`
2D	This creates a texture swatch that allows a user to drag a texture into the shader
Rect	This creates a non-power of two texture swatch and functions the same as the 2D GUI element
Cube	This creates a cube map swatch in the **Inspector** tab and allows a user to drag and drop a cube map into the shader
float	This creates a float value in the **Inspector** tab but without a slider
Vector	This creates a four-float property that allows you to create directions or colors

Finally, there is the **Default Value**. This simply sets the value of this property to the value that you place in the code. So, in the previous example diagram, the default value for the property named `_AmbientColor`, which is of the `Color` type, is set to a value of `1, 1, 1, 1`. As this is a `Color` property expecting a color that is RGBA or `float4` or `r, g, b, a = x, y, z, w`, this `Color` property, when first created, is set to white.

See also

The properties are documented in the Unity manual at `http://docs.unity3d.com/Documentation/Components/SL-Properties.html`.

Using properties in a Surface Shader

Now that we have created some properties, let's actually hook them up to the shader so that we can use them as tweaks to our shader and make the material process much more interactive. We can use the **Properties** values from the material's **Inspector** tab because we have attached a variable name to the property itself, but in the shader code, you have to set up a couple of things before you can start calling the value by its variable name.

How to do it...

The following steps show you how to use the properties in a Surface Shader:

1. Continuing from the previous example, let's create another shader with the name `ParameterExample`. Just like before, remove the `_MainTex` property in the same manner as was done in the *Adding properties to a shader* recipe of this chapter:

```
// Inside the Properties block
_MainTex ("Albedo (RGB)", 2D) = "white" {}

// Below the CGPROGRAM line
sampler2D _MainTex;

// Inside of the surf function
fixed4 c = tex2D (_MainTex, IN.uv_MainTex) * _Color;
```

2. Afterward, update the `Properties` section to the following code:

```
Properties {
  _Color ("Color", Color) = (1,1,1,1)
  _AmbientColor ("Ambient Color", Color) = (1,1,1,1)
  _MySliderValue ("This is a Slider", Range(0,10)) = 2.5

  _Glossiness ("Smoothness", Range(0,1)) = 0.5
  _Metallic ("Metallic", Range(0,1)) = 0.0
}
```

3. Next, add the following lines of code to the shader, below the `CGPROGRAM` line:

```
float4 _AmbientColor;
float _MySliderValue;
```

4. With *step 3* complete, we can now use the values from the properties in our shader. Let's do this by adding the value from the _Color property to the _AmbientColor property and giving the result of this to the o.Albedo line of code. So, let's add the following code to the shader in the surf() function:

```
void surf (Input IN, inout SurfaceOutputStandard o) {
        // We can then use the properties values in our shader
        fixed4 c = pow((_Color + _AmbientColor), _MySliderValue);

        // Albedo comes from property values given from slider and
colors
        o.Albedo = c.rgb;

        // Metallic and smoothness come from slider variables
        o.Metallic = _Metallic;
        o.Smoothness = _Glossiness;
        o.Alpha = c.a;
    }
    ENDCG
```

5. Finally, your shader should look like the following shader code. If you save your shader and re-enter Unity, your shader will compile. If there were no errors, you will now have the ability to change the ambient and emissive colors of the material as well as increase the saturation of the final color using the slider value. Pretty neat:

```
Shader "CookbookShaders/Chapter02/ParameterExample" {
    // We define Properties in the properties block
    Properties {
      _Color ("Color", Color) = (1,1,1,1)
      _Glossiness ("Smoothness", Range(0,1)) = 0.5
      _Metallic ("Metallic", Range(0,1)) = 0.0
    }
    SubShader {
      Tags { "RenderType"="Opaque" }
      LOD 200

        // We need to declare the properties variable type inside of
the
        // CGPROGRAM so we can access its value from the properties
block.

        CGPROGRAM
        // Physically based Standard lighting model, and enable shadows
on all light types
        #pragma surface surf Standard fullforwardshadows
```

```
    // Use shader model 3.0 target, to get nicer looking lighting
    #pragma target 3.0

    float4 _AmbientColor;
    float _MySliderValue;

    struct Input {
      float2 uv_MainTex;
    };

    half _Glossiness;
    half _Metallic;
    fixed4 _Color;

    // Add instancing support for this shader. You need to check
'Enable Instancing' on materials that use the shader.
    // See https://docs.unity3d.com/Manual/GPUInstancing.html for
more information about instancing.
    // #pragma instancing_options assumeuniformscaling
    UNITY_INSTANCING_BUFFER_START(Props)
      // put more per-instance properties here
    UNITY_INSTANCING_BUFFER_END(Props)

    void surf (Input IN, inout SurfaceOutputStandard o) {
      // We can then use the properties values in our shader
      fixed4 c = pow((_Color + _AmbientColor), _MySliderValue);

      // Albedo comes from property values given from slider and
colors
      o.Albedo = c.rgb;

      // Metallic and smoothness come from slider variables
      o.Metallic = _Metallic;
      o.Smoothness = _Glossiness;
      o.Alpha = c.a;
    }
    ENDCG
  }
  FallBack "Diffuse"
}
```

The pow(arg1, arg2) function is a built-in function that will perform the equivalent math function of power. So, argument 1 is the value that we want to raise to a power and argument 2 is the power that we want to raise it to.

To find out more about the pow() function, look at the Cg tutorial. It is a great free resource that you can use to learn more about shading and there is a glossary of all the functions available to you in the Cg shading language at http://http.developer.nvidia.com/CgTutorial/cg_tutorial_appendix_e.html.

The following screenshot demonstrates the result obtained using our properties to control our material's colors and saturation from within the material's **Inspector** tab:

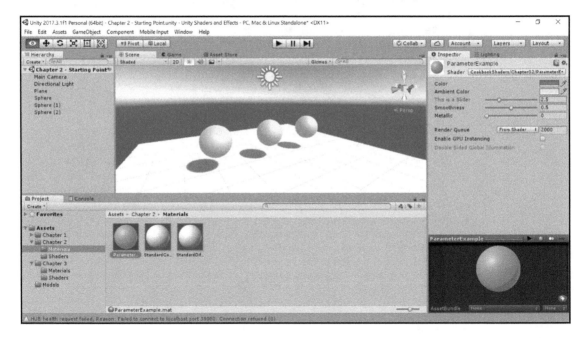

How it works...

When you declare a new property in the Properties block, you are providing a way for the shader to retrieve the tweaked value from the material's **Inspector** tab. This value is stored in the variable name portion of the property. In this case, _AmbientColor, _Color, and _MySliderValue are the variables in which we are storing the tweaked values.

In order for you to be able to use the value in the `SubShader` block, you need to create three new variables with the same names as the property's variable name. This automatically sets up a link between these two so that they know they have to work with the same data. Additionally, it declares the type of data that we want to store in our `SubShader` variables, which will come in handy when we look at optimizing shaders in a later chapter. Once you have created the `SubShader` variables, you can then use the values in the `surf()` function. In this case, we want to add the `_Color` and `_AmbientColor` variables together and take it to a power of whatever the `_MySliderValue` variable is equal to in the material's **Inspector** tab. The vast majority of shaders start out as Standard Shaders and get modified until they match the desired look. We have now created the foundation for any Surface Shader you will create that requires a diffuse component.

 Materials are assets. This means that any change made to them while your game is running in the editor are permanent. If you have changed the value of a property by mistake, you can undo it using *Ctrl + Z*.

There's more...

Like any other programming language, Cg does not allow mistakes. As such, your shader will not work if you have a typo in your code. When this happens, your materials are rendered in unshaded magenta:

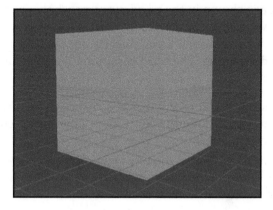

When a script does not compile, Unity prevents your game from being exported or even executed. Conversely, errors in shaders do not stop your game from being executed. If one of your shaders appears as magenta, it is time to investigate where the problem is. If you select the incriminated shader, you will see a list of errors displayed in its **Inspector** tab:

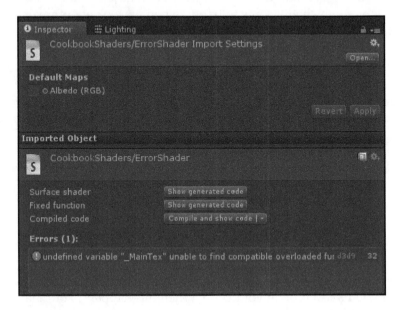

Despite showing the line that raised the error, it rarely means that this is the line that has to be fixed. The error message shown in the previous screenshot is generated by deleting the `sampler2D _MainTex` variable from the `SubShader{}` block. However, the error is raised by the first line that tries to access such a variable. Finding and fixing what's wrong with code is a process called **debugging**. The most common mistakes that you should check for are as follows:

- A missing bracket. If you forgot to add a curly bracket to close a section, the compiler is likely to raise errors at the end of the document, at the beginning, or in a new section.
- A missing semicolon. One of the most common mistakes, but luckily one of the easiest to spot and fix. When looking at the Error definition, first check if the line above it has a semicolon or not.
- A property that has been defined in the `Properties` section but has not been coupled with a variable in the `SubShader{}` block.
- Compared to what you might be used to in C# scripts, the floating point values in Cg do not need to be followed by an `f`. It's `1.0`, not `1.0f`.

The error messages raised by shaders can be very misleading, especially due to their strict syntactic constraints. If you are in doubt about their meaning, it's best to search the internet. The Unity forums are filled with other developers who are likely to have encountered (and fixed) your problem before.

See also

- More information on how to master Surface Shaders and their properties can be found in Chapter 3, *Surface Shaders and Texture Mapping*.
- If you are curious to see what shaders can actually do when used at their full potential, have a look at Chapter 11, *Advanced Shading Techniques*, for some of the most advanced techniques covered in this book.

Surface Shaders and Texture Mapping

3

In this chapter, we will explore the topic of Surface Shaders in greater detail than in the previous chapter. We will start from building a very simple matte material and end with holographic projections and the advanced blending of terrains. We will also see how you can use textures to animate, blend, and drive any other property that they like.

In this chapter, you will learn about the following methods:

- Diffuse shading
- Accessing and modifying packed arrays
- Adding a texture to a shader
- Scrolling textures by modifying UV values
- Creating a shader with normal mapping
- Creating a transparent material
- Creating a Holographic Shader
- Packing and blending textures
- Creating a circle around your terrain

Introduction

Surface Shaders were introduced in Chapter 2, *Creating Your First Shader*, as the main type of shader that's used in Unity. This chapter will show you in detail what these actually are and how they work. Generally speaking, there are two essential steps in every Surface Shader. First, you have to specify certain physical properties of the material that you want to describe, such as its diffuse color, smoothness, and transparency. These properties are initialized in a function called the **surface function** and are stored in a structure called the SurfaceOutput. Secondly, the SurfaceOutput is passed to a lighting model. This is a special function that will also take information about the nearby lights in the scene. Both of these parameters are then used to calculate the final color for each pixel of your model. The lighting function is where the real calculations of a shader take place as it's the piece of code that determines how light should behave when it touches a material.

The following diagram loosely summarizes how a Surface Shader works. Custom lighting models will be explored in Chapter 4, *Understanding Lighting Models*, while Chapter 6, *Vertex Functions*, will focus on vertex modifiers:

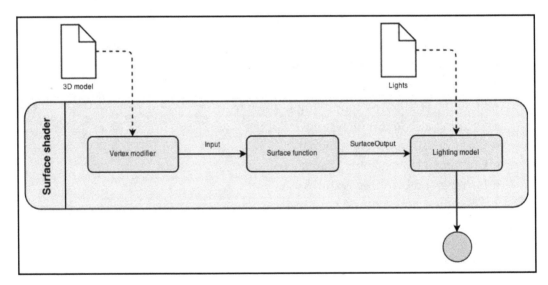

Diffuse shading

Before starting our journey into texture mapping, it is important to understand how diffuse materials work. Certain objects might have a uniform color and smooth surface, but are not smooth enough to shine in reflected light. These matte materials are best represented with a Diffuse Shader. While, in the real world pure diffuse materials do not exist, Diffuse Shaders are relatively cheap to implement and are largely applied in games with low-poly aesthetics, so they're worth learning about.

There are several ways in which you can create your own Diffuse Shader. A quick way is to start with Unity's Standard Surface Shader and edit it to remove any additional texture information.

Getting ready

Before starting this recipe, you should have created a Standard Surface Shader with the name `SimpleDiffuse`. For instructions on creating a Standard Surface Shader, look at the *Creating a basic Standard Surface Shader* recipe located in `Chapter 2`, *Creating Your First Shader*, if you haven't done so already.

How to do it...

Open up the `SimpleDiffuse` shader you've created and make the following changes:

1. In the `Properties` section, remove all of the variables except for `_Color`:

   ```
   Properties
   {
     _Color ("Color", Color) = (1,1,1,1)
   }
   ```

2. From the `SubShader{}` section, remove the `_MainTex`, `_Glossiness`, and `_Metallic` variables. You should not remove the reference to `uv_MainTex` as Cg does not allow the `Input` struct to be empty. The value will simply be ignored.

3. Also, remove the `UNITY_INSTANCING_BUFFER_START/END` macros and the comments used with them.

4. Remove the content of the `surf()` function and replace it with the following:

```
void surf (Input IN, inout SurfaceOutputStandard o)
{
  o.Albedo = _Color.rgb;
}
```

5. Your shader should look as follows:

```
Shader "CookbookShaders/Chapter03/SimpleDiffuse" {
  Properties
  {
    _Color ("Color", Color) = (1,1,1,1)
  }
  SubShader
  {
    Tags { "RenderType"="Opaque" }
    LOD 200

    CGPROGRAM
    // Physically based Standard lighting model, and enable shadows
on all light types
    #pragma surface surf Standard fullforwardshadows

    // Use shader model 3.0 target, to get nicer looking lighting
    #pragma target 3.0


    struct Input
    {
      float2 uv_MainTex;
    };

    fixed4 _Color;

    void surf (Input IN, inout SurfaceOutputStandard o)
    {
      o.Albedo = _Color.rgb;
    }

    ENDCG
  }
  FallBack "Diffuse"
}
```

The two lines below CGPROGRAM is actually one line and is cut off due to the size of the book.

6. As this shader has been refitted with a Standard Shader, it will use physically-based rendering to simulate how light behaves on your models.

If you are trying to achieve a non-photorealistic look, you can change the first #pragma directive so that it uses Lambert rather than Standard. If you do so, you should also replace the SurfaceOutputStandard parameter of the surf function with SurfaceOutput. For more information on this and the other lighting models that Unity supports, Jordan Stevens put together a very nice article about it, which you can see here: http://www.jordanstevenstechart.com/lighting-models

7. Save the shader and dive back into Unity. Using the same instructions as in the *Creating a basic Standard Surface Shader* recipe located in Chapter 2, *Creating Your First Shader*, create a new material called SimpleDiffuseMat and apply our newly created shader to it. Change the color to something different, such as red, by clicking on the window next to the **Color** property in the **Inspector** window while selected.

8. Then, go into the Models folder of this book's example code and bring the bunny object into our scene by dragging and dropping it from the **Project** window into the **Hierarchy** window. From there, assign the SimpleDiffuseMat material to the object:

9. You can double-click on an object in the **Hierarchy** tab in order to center the camera on the object that's been selected.

How it works...

The way shaders allow you to communicate the rendering properties of your material to their lighting model is via their `SurfaceOutput`. It is basically a wrapper around all the parameters that the current lighting model needs. It should not surprise you that different lighting models have different `SurfaceOutput` structs. The following table shows the three main output structs used in Unity and how they can be used:

Type of shaders	Standard	Physically-Based Lighting Models
Diffuse	Any Surface Shader `SurfaceOutput`	**Standard** `SurfaceOutputStandard`
Specular	Any Surface Shader `SurfaceOutput`	**Standard (Specular setup)** `SurfaceOutputStandardSpecular`

The `SurfaceOutput` struct has the following properties:

- `fixed3 Albedo;`: This is the diffuse color of the material
- `fixed3 Normal;`: This is the tangent space, normal, if written
- `fixed3 Emission;`: This is the color of the light emitted by the material (this property is declared as `half3` in the Standard Shaders)
- `fixed Alpha;`: This is the transparency of the material
- `half Specular;`: This is the specular power from 0 to 1
- `fixed Gloss;`: This is the specular intensity

The `SurfaceOutputStandard` struct has the following properties:

- `fixed3 Albedo;`: This is the base color of the material (whether it's diffuse or specular)
- `fixed3 Normal;`
- `half3 Emission;`: This property is declared as `half3`, while it was defined as `fixed3` in `SurfaceOutput`
- `fixed Alpha;`
- `half Occlusion;`: This is the occlusion (default 1)
- `half Smoothness;`: This is the smoothness (0 = rough, 1 = smooth)
- `half Metallic;`: 0 = non-metal, 1= metal

The `SurfaceOutputStandardSpecular` struct has the following properties:

- `fixed3 Albedo;`
- `fixed3 Normal;`
- `half3 Emission;`
- `fixed Alpha;`
- `half Occlusion;`
- `half Smoothness;`
- `fixed3 Specular;`: This is the specular color. This is very different from the `Specular` property in `SurfaceOutput` as it allows you to specify a color rather than a single value.

Using a Surface Shader correctly is a matter of initializing the `SurfaceOutput` with the correct values.

 For more information on creating Surface Shaders, check out the following link: `https://docs.unity3d.com/Manual/SL-SurfaceShaders.html`

Accessing and modifying packed arrays

Loosely speaking, the code inside a shader has to be executed for at least every pixel in your screen. This is the reason why GPUs are highly optimized for parallel computing; they can execute multiple processes at the same time. This philosophy is also evident in the standard type of variables and operators available in Cg. Understanding them is essential, not just so that you can use the shaders correctly, but also to write highly optimized ones.

How to do it...

There are two types of variables in Cg: single values and packed arrays. The latter can be identified because their type ends with a number such as `float3` or `int4`. As their names suggest, these types of variables are similar to structs, which means that they each contain several single values. Cg calls them packed arrays, though they are not exactly *arrays* in the traditional sense.

The elements of a packed array can be accessed as a normal struct. They are typically called x, y, z, and w. However, Cg also provides you with another alias for them, that is, r, g, b, and a. Despite there being no difference between using x or r, it can make a huge difference for the readers. Shader coding, in fact, often involves calculation with positions and colors. You might have seen this in the Standard Shaders:

```
o.Alpha = _Color.a;
```

Here, o was a struct and _Color was a packed array. This is also why Cg prohibits the mixed usage of these two syntaxes: you cannot use _Color.xgz.

There is also another important feature of packed arrays that has no equivalent in C#: **swizzling**. Cg allows addressing and reordering elements within packed arrays in just a single line. Once again, this appears in the Standard Shader:

```
o.Albedo = _Color.rgb;
```

Albedo is fixed3, which means that it contains three values of the fixed type. However, _Color is defined as a fixed4 type. A direct assignment would result in a compiler error as _Color is bigger than Albedo. The C# way of doing this would be as follows:

```
o.Albedo.r = _Color.r;
o.Albedo.g = _Color.g;
o.Albedo.b = _Color.b;
```

However, it can be compressed in Cg:

```
o.Albedo = _Color.rgb;
```

Cg also allows reordering elements, for instance, using _Color.bgr to swap the red and blue channels.

Lastly, when a single value is assigned to a packed array, it is copied to all of its fields:

```
o.Albedo = 0; // Black =(0,0,0)
o.Albedo = 1; // White =(1,1,1)
```

This is referred to as **smearing**.

Swizzling can also be used on the left-hand side of an expression, allowing only certain components of a packed array to be overwritten:

```
o.Albedo.rg = _Color.rg;
```

In this case, it is called **masking**.

There's more...

Where swizzling really shows its full potential is when it's applied to packed matrices. Cg allows types such as float4x4, which represents a matrix of floats with four rows and four columns. You can access a single element of the matrix using the _mRC notation, where *R* is the row and *C* is the column:

```
float4x4 matrix;
// ...
float first = matrix._m00;
float last = matrix._m33;
```

The _mRC notation can also be chained:

```
float4 diagonal = matrix._m00_m11_m22_m33;
```

An entire row can be selected using squared brackets:

```
float4 firstRow = matrix[0];
// Equivalent to
float4 firstRow = matrix._m00_m01_m02_m03;
```

See also

- In addition to being easier to write, swizzling, smearing, and masking properties have performance benefits as well
- However, inappropriate use of swizzling can also make your code harder to understand at first glance, and may make it harder for the compiler to automatically optimize your code
- Packed arrays are one of the nicest features of Cg. You can discover more about them here: http://http.developer.nvidia.com/CgTutorial/cg_tutorial_chapter02.html

Adding a texture to a shader

Textures can bring our shaders to life very quickly in terms of achieving very realistic effects. In order to effectively use textures, we need to understand how a 2D image is mapped to a 3D model. This process is called texture mapping, and it requires some work to be done on the shader and 3D model that we want to use. Models, in fact, are made out of triangles, which are often referred to as polygons; each vertex on the model can store data that shaders can access and use to determine what to draw.

One of the most important pieces of information that are stored in vertices is the **UV data**. It consists of two coordinates, *U* and *V*, ranging from 0 to 1. They represent the *XY* position of the pixel in the 2D image that will be mapped to the vertices. UV data is present only for vertices; when the inner points of a triangle have to be texture-mapped, the GPU interpolates the closest UV values to find the right pixel in the texture to be used. The following diagram shows you how a **2D Texture** is mapped to a triangle from a 3D model:

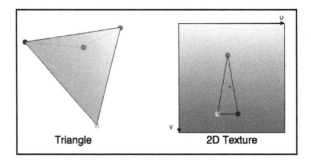

The UV data is stored in the 3D model and requires modeling software to be edited. Some models lack the UV component, hence they cannot support texture mapping. The Stanford bunny, for example, was not originally provided with one.

Getting ready

For this recipe, you'll need a 3D model with UV data and its texture. They both need to be imported to Unity before starting. You can do this simply by dragging them to the editor. As the Standard Shader supports texture mapping by default, we'll use this and then explain how it works in detail.

How to do it...

Adding a texture to your model using the Standard Shader is incredibly simple, as follows:

1. In the Sample Code for this chapter that's provided with this book, you can find the `basicCharacter` model which, by default, has UV information embedded into it, making it so that when we attach a material, it will draw the texture using that information.

2. Create a new Standard Surface Shader called `TexturedShader` by going to the **Project** tab and then selecting **Create** | **Shaders** | **Standard Surface Shader**. Once created, you can type in a new name for the shader and then press *Enter*.

3. For organization's sake, open the shader and change the first line to the following:

```
Shader "CookbookShaders/Chapter03/TexturedShader" {
```

4. This will allow us to find the shader inside of the organization we have been using so far for this book.

5. Create a new material called `TexturedMaterial` by going to the **Project** tab and then selecting **Create** | **Material**. Once created, you can type in a new name for the material and then press *Enter* to confirm the change.

6. Assign the shader to the material by going to the **Inspector** tab and then clicking on the **Shader** dropdown before selecting `CookbookShaders/Chapter 03/TexturedShader`:

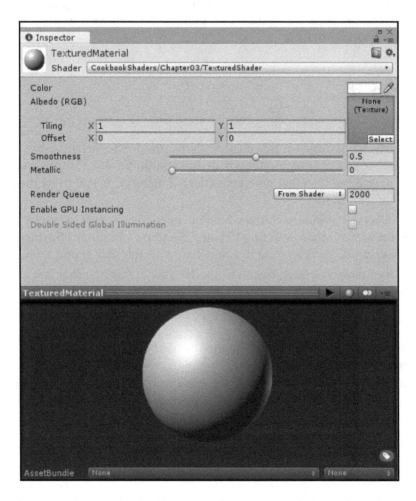

You may also do this by first selecting the material and then dragging the shader file over it in the **Project** tab.

7. After selecting the material, drag your texture to the empty rectangle called **Albedo (RGB)**. If you are missing some, there are textures located in this chapter's example code that can be used. If you have followed all of these steps correctly, your material **Inspector** tab should look like this:

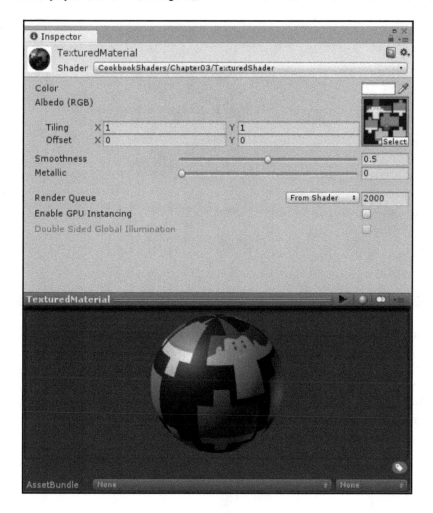

 The Standard Shader knows how to map a 2D image to a 3D model using its UV models and textures used in this example were created by Kenney Vleugels and Casper Jorissen. You can find these and many other public domain game assets at Kenney.nl.

8. To see the UV data in action, in the example code's `Models` folder, drag and drop the model into the **Hierarchy** tab. Once there, double-click on the newly created object to zoom in so that you can see the object:

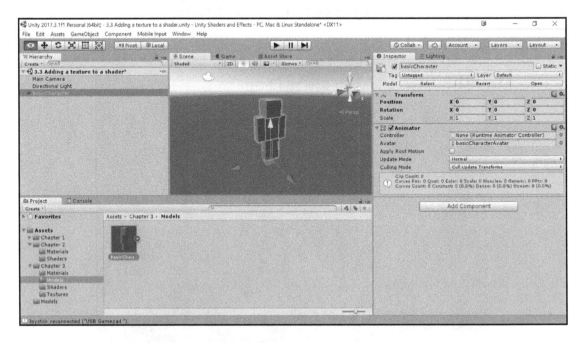

9. Once there, you may go to the **Project** tab and open up the `Chapter 3 | Materials` folder and drag and drop our `Textured Material` onto the character. Note that the model consists of different objects, each of which provides direction to draw in a particular place. This means that you will need to drop the material on each part of the model (`ArmLeft1`, `ArmRight1`, `Body1`, and so on); trying to apply this to the top level of the hierarchy only (`basicCharacter`) will not work:

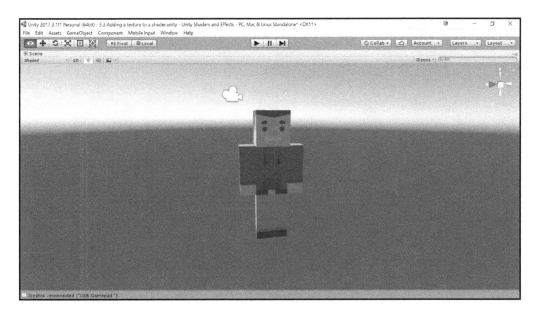

9. It is also possible to change what the object looks like by changing the texture that's being used. For instance, if we use the other texture provided (`skin_womanAlternative`), we have a very different looking character:

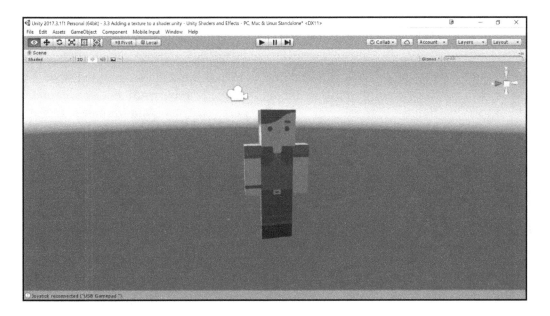

This is often used in games to provide different kinds of characters with minimal cost.

How it works...

When the Standard Shader is used from the **Inspector** of a material, the process behind texture mapping is completely transparent to developers. If we want to understand how it works, it's necessary to take a closer look at `TexturedShader`. From the `Properties` section, we can see that the `Albedo (RGB)` texture is actually referred to in the code as `_MainTex`:

```
_MainTex ("Albedo (RGB)", 2D) = "white" {}
```

In the `CGPROGRAM` section, this texture is defined as `sampler2D`, the standard type for 2D textures:

```
sampler2D _MainTex;
```

The following line shows a `struct` called `Input`. This is the input parameter for the surface function and contains a packed array called `uv_MainTex`:

```
struct Input {
  float2 uv_MainTex;
};
```

Every time the `surf()` function is called, the `Input` structure will contain the UV of `_MainTex` for the specific point of the 3D model that needs to be rendered. The Standard Shader recognizes that the name `uv_MainTex` refers to `_MainTex` and initializes it automatically. If you are interested in understanding how the UV is actually mapped from a 3D space to a 2D texture, you can check out `Chapter 5`, *Understanding Lighting Models*.

Finally, the UV data is used to sample the texture in the first line of the surface function:

```
fixed4 c = tex2D (_MainTex, IN.uv_MainTex) * _Color;
```

This is done using the `tex2D()` function of Cg; it takes a texture and UV and returns the color of the pixel at that position.

The *U* and *V* coordinates go from *0* to *1*, where (0,0) and (1,1) correspond to two opposite corners. Different implementations associate UV with different corners; if your texture happens to appear reversed, try inverting the V component.

There's more...

When you import a texture to Unity, you are setting up some of the properties that `sampler2D` will use. The most important is the **Filter** mode, which determines how colors are interpolated when the texture is sampled. It is very unlikely that the UV data will point exactly to the center of a pixel; in all other cases, you might want to interpolate between the closest pixels to get a more uniform color. The following is a screenshot of the **Inspector** tab of an example texture:

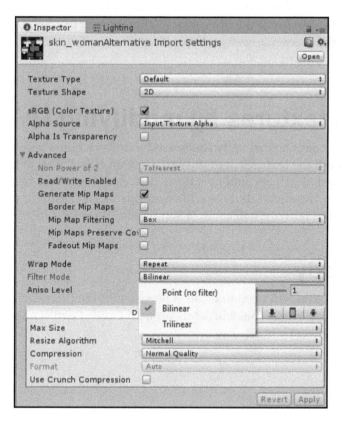

For most applications, **Bilinear** provides an inexpensive, yet effective, way to smooth the texture. If you are creating a 2D game, however, **Bilinear** might produce blurred tiles. In this case, you can use **Point** to remove any interpolation from the texture sampling.

When a texture is seen from a steep angle, texture sampling is likely to produce visually unpleasant artifacts. You can reduce them by setting the **Aniso Level** to a higher value. This is particularly useful for floor and ceiling textures, where glitches can break the illusion of continuity.

See also

- If you would like to know more about the inner workings of how textures are mapped to a 3D surface, you can read the information available at http:// developer.nvidia.com/CgTutorial/cg_tutorial_chapter03.html.
- For a complete list of the options available when importing a 2D texture, you can refer to the following website: http://docs.unity3d.com/Manual/class-TextureImporter.html

Scrolling textures by modifying UV values

One of the most common texture techniques used in today's game industry is the process of allowing you to scroll the textures over the surface of an object. This allows you to create effects such as waterfalls, rivers, and lava flows. It's also a technique that is the basis of creating animated sprite effects, but we will cover this in a subsequent recipe of this chapter. First, let's see how we will create a simple scrolling effect in a Surface Shader.

Getting ready

To begin this recipe, you will need to create a new shader file (ScrollingUVs) and material (ScrollingUVMat). This will set us up with a nice clean shader that we can use to study the scrolling effect by itself.

How to do it...

To begin with, we will launch our new shader file that we just created and enter the code mentioned in the following steps:

1. The shader will need two new properties that will allow us to control the speed of the texture scrolling. So, let's add a speed property for the *X* direction and a speed property for the *Y* direction, as shown in the following code:

```
Properties {
    _Color ("Color", Color) = (1,1,1,1)
    _MainTex ("Albedo (RGB)", 2D) = "white" {}
    _ScrollXSpeed ("X Scroll Speed", Range(0,10)) = 2
    _ScrollYSpeed ("Y Scroll Speed", Range(0,10)) = 2
}
```

2. When working in ShaderLab, `Properties` has a syntax that looks like the following:

```
Properties
{
    _propertyName("Name in Inspector", Type) = value
}
```

Each property contained in the `Properties` block first has a name that is used in code to refer to the object, here specified as _propertyName. The underscore isn't required but is a common standard in place. Inside the parenthesis, you'll see two parameters. The first is a string that defines what text will be displayed in the **Inspector** for what this property is. The second parameter is the type of data we wish to store.

In our case, for the *X* and *Y* Scroll Speed, we are creating a number with a possible Range from 0 to 10. Lastly, we can initialize the property with a default value which is done on the end. As we've seen before, these properties will show up in the **Inspector** if you select a material that is using this shader.

 For more information on Properties and how to create them, check out https://docs.unity3d.com/Manual/SL-Properties.html.

For this example, we don't need the `Smoothness` or `Metallic` properties, so we can remove them as well.

3. Modify the Cg properties in the CGPROGRAM section above the definition of _MainTex and create new variables so that we can access the values from our properties:

```
fixed _ScrollXSpeed;
fixed _ScrollYSpeed;
sampler2D _MainTex;
```

4. We also need to remove the _Glossiness and _Metallic definitions as we are not using them anymore.

5. Modify the surface function to change the UVs given to the tex2D() function. Then, use the built-in _Time variable to animate the UVs over time when the **Play** button is pressed in the editor:

```
void surf (Input IN, inout SurfaceOutputStandard o) {
    // Create a separate variable to store our UVs
    // before we pass them to the tex2D() function
    fixed2 scrolledUV = IN.uv_MainTex;
    // Create variables that store the individual x and y
    // components for the UV's scaled by time
    fixed xScrollValue = _ScrollXSpeed * _Time;
    fixed yScrollValue = _ScrollYSpeed * _Time;
    // Apply the final UV offset
    scrolledUV += fixed2(xScrollValue, yScrollValue);
    // Apply textures and tint
    half4 c = tex2D(_MainTex, scrolledUV);
    o.Albedo = c.rgb * _Color;
    o.Alpha = c.a;
}
```

6. Once the script is finished, save it and then go back to the Unity editor. Go to the Materials folder and assign ScrollingUVsMat to use our ScrollingUVs shader. Once that is done, under the **Albedo (RGB)** property, drag and drop the water texture from the example code provided with this book to assign the property:

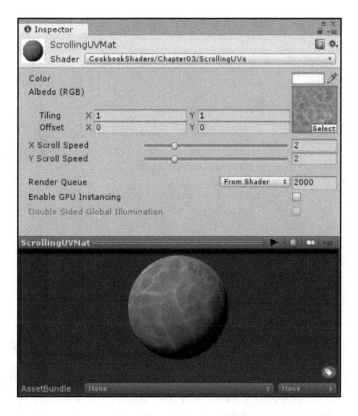

7. After this is created, we need to create an object that can use the shader. From a new scene, go ahead and select **GameObject** | **3D Object** | **Plane** and drag and drop the ScrollingUVMat material onto it.

8. Once applied, go ahead and play the game to see the shader in action:

While it's not visible in this still image, you will notice that in the Unity editor, the object will now move in both the *X* and *Y* axes! Feel free to drag the **X Scroll Speed** and **Y Scroll Speed** properties in the **Inspector** tab to see how the changes affect how the object moves. Also, feel free to move the camera to make it easier to see if you would like.

If you modify a variable on a **Material** during gameplay, the value will stay changed, unlike how Unity typically works.

Pretty cool! With this knowledge, we can take this concept much further to create interesting visual effects. The following screenshot demonstrates the result of utilizing the scrolling UV system with multiple materials in order to create a simple river motion for your environments:

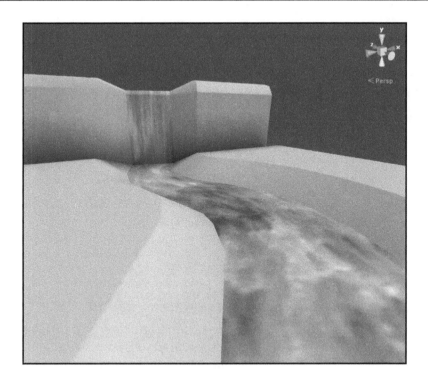

How it works...

The scrolling system starts with the declaration of a couple of properties, which will allow the user of this shader to increase or decrease the speed of the scrolling effect itself. At their core, they are float values being passed from the material's **Inspector** tab to the surface function of the shader. For more information on shader properties, see `Chapter 2`, *Creating Your First Shader*.

Once we have these float values from the material's **Inspector** tab, we can use them to offset our UV values in the shader.

To begin this process, we first store the UVs in a separate variable called `scrolledUV`. This variable has to be `float2/fixed2` because the UV values are being passed to us from the `Input` structure:

```
struct Input
{
    float2 uv_MainTex;
}
```

Once we have access to the mesh's UVs, we can offset them using our scroll speed variables and built-in _Time variable. This built-in variable returns a variable of the float4 type, meaning that each component of this variable contains different values of time as it pertains to game time.

A complete description of these individual time values is described at the following link: http://docs.unity3d.com/Manual/SL-UnityShaderVariables.html

This _Time variable will give us an incremented float value based on Unity's game time clock. So, we can use this value to move our UVs in a UV direction and scale that time with our scroll speed variables:

```
// Create variables that store the individual x and y
// components for the uv's scaled by time
fixed xScrollValue = _ScrollXSpeed * _Time;
fixed yScrollValue = _ScrollYSpeed * _Time;
```

With the correct offset being calculated by time, we can add the new offset value back to the original UV position. This is why we are using the += operator in the next line. We want to take the original UV position, add the new offset value, and then pass this to the tex2D() function as the texture's new UVs. This creates the effect of the texture moving on the surface. What we are really doing is manipulating the UVs, so we are faking the effect of the texture moving:

```
scrolledUV += fixed2(xScrollValue, yScrollValue);
half4 c = tex2D (_MainTex, scrolledUV);
```

Creating a shader with normal mapping

Every triangle of a 3D model has a *facing direction*, which is the direction that it is pointing toward. It is often represented with an arrow placed in the center of the triangle and is orthogonal to the surface. The facing direction plays an important role in the way light reflects on a surface. If two adjacent triangles face different directions, they will reflect lights at different angles, hence they'll be shaded differently. For curved objects, this is a problem: it is obvious that the geometry is made out of flat triangles.

To avoid this problem, the way the light reflects on a triangle doesn't take into account its facing direction, but its *normal direction* instead. As stated in the *Adding a texture to a shader* recipe, vertices can store data; the normal direction is the most used information after the UV data. This is a vector of unit length (which means it has a length of 1) that indicates the direction faced by the vertex.

Regardless of the facing direction, every point within a triangle has its own normal direction that is a linear interpolation of the ones stored in its vertices. This gives us the ability to fake the effect of high-resolution geometry on a low-resolution model.

The following screenshot shows the same geometric shape rendered with different per-vertex normals. In the image, on the left, normals are orthogonal to the face represented by its vertices; this indicates that there is a clear separation between each face. On the right, normals are interpolated along the surface, indicating that even if the surface is rough, a light should reflect as if it's smooth. It's easy to see that even if the three objects in the following screenshot share the same geometry, they reflect light differently. Despite being made out of flat triangles, the object on the right reflects light as if its surface was actually curved:

Smooth objects with rough edges are a clear indication that per-vertex normals have been interpolated. This can be seen if we draw the direction of the normal stored in every vertex, as shown in the following screenshot. You should note that every triangle has only three normals, but as multiple triangles can share the same vertex, more than one line can come out of it:

Calculating the normals from the 3D model is a technique that has rapidly declined in favor of a more advanced one-normal mapping. Similar to what happens with texture mapping, the normal directions can be provided using an additional texture, usually called a normal map or bump map.

Normal maps are usually images where the red, green, and blue channels of the image are used to indicate the *X*, *Y*, and *Z* components of the normal direction. There are many ways to create normal maps these days. Some applications, such as CrazyBump (`http://www.crazybump.com/`) and NDO Painter (`http://quixel.se/ndo/`), will take in 2D data and convert it to normal data for you. Other applications such as Zbrush 4R7 (`http://www.pixologic.com/`) and AUTODESK (`http://usa.autodesk.com`) will take 3D-sculpted data and create normal maps for you. The actual process of creating normal maps is out of the scope of this book, but the links in the previous text should help you get started.

Unity makes the process of adding normals to your shaders quite an easy process in the Surface Shader realm using the `UnpackNormals()` function. Let's see how this is done.

Getting ready

To begin this recipe, first create a new scene by selecting **File** | **New Scene**. Then, create a sphere game object by going to **GameObject** | **3D Objects** | **Sphere**. Double-click on the object in the **Hierarchy** tab to bring the object into focus in the **Scene** tab. You will also need to create a new standard Surface Shader file (`NormalShader`) and material (`NormalShaderMat`). Once created, set the material to a sphere in the **Scene** view. This will give us a clean workspace in which we can look at just the normal mapping technique:

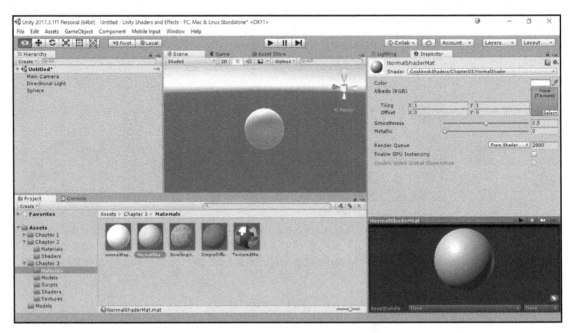

You will need a normal map for this recipe, but there is also one in the Unity project included with this book.

An example normal map included with this book's content is shown here:

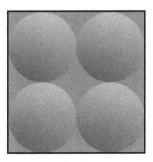

You can see it for yourself in the Assets | Chapter 03 | Textures folder under normalMapExample.

How to do it...

The following are the steps to create a normal map shader:

1. Let's get the Properties block set up in order to have a color Tint and texture:

```
Properties
{
  _MainTint ("Diffuse Tint", Color) = (0,1,0,1)
  _NormalTex ("Normal Map", 2D) = "bump" {}
}
```

In this case, I have 1 in the green and alpha channels and 0 for red and blue, so the default color will be green. For the _NormalTex property, we are using a 2D type, which means we can use a 2D image to dictate what each pixel will use. By initializing the texture as bump, we are telling Unity that _NormalTex will contain a normal map (sometimes referred to as bump maps as well, hence the bump name). If the texture is not set, it will be replaced by a grey texture. The color used (0.5, 0.5, 0.5, 1) indicates no bump at all.

2. In the `SubShader{}` block, scroll below the `CGPROGRAM` statement and remove the original `_MainText`, `_Glossiness`, `_Metallic`, and `_Color` definitions. Afterward, add in our `_NormalTex` and `_MainTint`:

```
CGPROGRAM
// Physically based Standard lighting model, and enable shadows
// on all light types
#pragma surface surf Standard fullforwardshadows

// Use shader model 3.0 target, to get nicer looking lighting
#pragma target 3.0

// Link the property to the CG program
sampler2D _NormalTex;
float4 _MainTint;
```

3. We need to make sure that we update the `Input` struct with the proper variable name so that we can use the model's UVs for the normal map texture:

```
// Make sure you get the UVs for the texture in the struct
struct Input
{
    float2 uv_NormalTex;
}
```

4. Finally, we extract the normal information from the normal map texture using the built-in `UnpackNormal()` function. Then, you only have to apply these new normals to the output of the Surface Shader:

```
void surf (Input IN, inout SurfaceOutputStandard o) {
    // Use the tint provided as the base color for the material
    o.Albedo = _MainTint;

    // Get the normal data out of the normal map texture
    // using the UnpackNormal function
    float3 normalMap = UnpackNormal(tex2D(_NormalTex,
        IN.uv_NormalTex));

    // Apply the new normal to the lighting model
    o.Normal = normalMap.rgb;
}
```

5. Save your script and return to the Unity editor. You should notice that the sphere has now become green by default if added. More importantly though, notice the **Normal Map** property that has been added. Drag and drop the normal map texture into the slot.

6. You may notice some changes, but it may be hard to visually see what is going on. In the **Normal Map** property, change the **Tiling** to (10, 10). This way, you can see the normal map duplicated 10 times over the course of the sphere in the *X* and *Y* axes instead of only once:

7. The following screenshot demonstrates the result of our normal map shader:

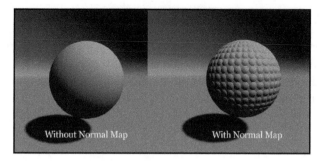

Shaders can have both a texture map and a normal map. It is not uncommon to use the same UV data to address both. However, it is possible to provide a secondary set of UVs in the vertex data (UV2), which are specifically used for the normal map.

How it works...

The actual math to perform the normal mapping effect is definitely beyond the scope of this chapter, but Unity has done it all for us already. It has created the functions for us so that we don't have to keep doing it over and over again. This is another reason why Surface Shaders are a really efficient way to write shaders.

If you look in the `UnityCG.cginc` file found in the `Editor | Data| CGIncludes` folder in your Unity installation directory, you will find the definitions for the `UnpackNormal()` function. When you declare this function in your Surface Shader, Unity takes the normal map provided and processes it for you, giving you the correct type of data so that you can use it in your per-pixel lighting function. It's a huge time-saver! When sampling a texture, you get RGB values from 0 to 1; however, the directions of a normal vector range from -1 to 1. `UnpackNormal()` brings these components into the right range.

Once you have processed the normal map with the `UnpackNormal()` function, you send it back to your `SurfaceOutput` struct so that it can be used in the lighting function. This is done by using `o.Normal = normalMap.rgb;`. We will see how the normal is actually used to calculate the final color of each pixel in `Chapter 4`, *Understanding Lighting Models*.

There's more...

You can also add some controls to your normal map shader that lets a user adjust the intensity of the normal map. This is easily done by modifying the x and y components of the normal map variable and then adding it all back together. Add another property to the `Properties` block and name it `_NormalMapIntensity`:

```
_NormalMapIntensity("Normal intensity", Range(0,3)) = 1
```

In this case, we are giving the property the ability to be between 0 and 3 with a default value of 1. Once created, you'll need to add the variable inside the SubShader:

```
// Link the property to the CG program
sampler2D _NormalTex;
float4 _MainTint;
float _NormalMapIntensity;
```

After the property is added, we can make use of it. Multiply the x and y components of the unpacked normal map and reapply this value to the normal map variable with the bolded changes:

```
void surf (Input IN, inout SurfaceOutputStandard o) {
    // Use the tint provided as the base color for the material
    o.Albedo = _MainTint;

    // Get the normal data out of the normal map texture
    // using the UnpackNormal function
    float3 normalMap = UnpackNormal(tex2D(_NormalTex,
      IN.uv_NormalTex));

    normalMap.x *= _NormalMapIntensity;
    normalMap.y *= _NormalMapIntensity;

    // Apply the new normal to the lighting model
    o.Normal = normalize(normalMap.rgb);
}
```

Normal vectors are supposed to have lengths equal to one. Multiplying them for _NormalMapIntensity changes their length, making normalization necessary. The normalize function will take the vector and adjust it so that it is pointing in the correct direction but with a length of one, which is what we are looking for.

Now, you can let a user adjust the intensity of the normal map in the material's **Inspector** tab, as follows:

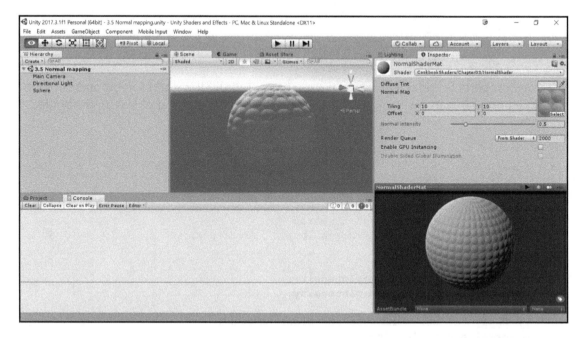

The following screenshot shows the result of modifying the normal map with our scalar values:

Creating a transparent material

All the shaders we have seen so far have something in common; they are used for solid materials. If you want to improve the look of your game, transparent materials are often a good way to start. They can be used for anything from a fire effect to a glass window. Working with them, unfortunately, is slightly more complicated. Before rendering solid models, Unity orders them according to the distance from the camera (*Z ordering*) and skips all the triangles that are facing away from the camera (**culling**). When rendering transparent geometries, there are instances in which these two aspects can cause problems. This recipe will show you how to solve some of these issues when it comes to creating a transparent Surface Shader. This topic will be heavily revisited in `Chapter 7`, *Fragment Shaders and Grab Passes*, where realistic glass and water shaders will be provided.

Getting ready

This recipe requires a new shader, which we'll be calling `Transparent`, and a new material (`TransparentMat`) so that it can be attached to an object. As this is going to be a transparent glass window, a quad or plane is perfect (**GameObject | 3D Objects | Quad**). We will also need several other non-transparent objects to test the effect:

In this example, we will use a PNG image file for the glass texture since it has support for an alpha channel that will be used to determine the transparency of the glass. The process of creating such an image depends on the software that you are using. However, these are the main steps that you will need to follow:

1. Find the image of the glass you want for your windows.
2. Open it with a photo editing software, such as *GIMP* or *Photoshop*.
3. Select the parts of the image that you want to be semi-transparent.
4. Create a white (full opacity) layer mask on your image.
5. Use the selection previously made to fill the layer mask with a darker color. White is treated as fully visible, black will be treated as invisible, and grey will be somewhere in the middle.
6. Save the image and import it into Unity.

The toy image used in this recipe is a picture of stained glass from the *Meaux Cathedral* in *France* (`https://en.wikipedia.org/wiki/Stained_glass`). If you have followed all of these steps, your image should look like this (**RGB** channels on the left, and **A** channel on the right):

You can also make use of the image file in provided the example code for this book in `Chapter 3 | Textures` **folder** (`Meaux_Vitrail.psd`).

Attaching this image to the material will cause the image to show up, but we cannot see it behind the glass:

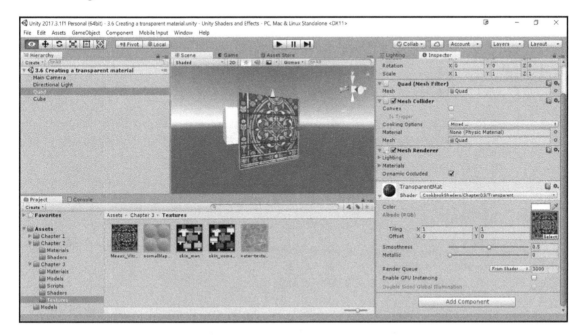

As we would like to see behind this, we can make adjustments to the shader to do exactly that.

How to do it...

As mentioned previously, there are a few aspects that we need to take care of while using a Transparent Shader:

1. Remove the `_Glossiness` and `_Metallic` variables from the `Properties` and `SubShader` sections of the code as they aren't needed for this example.

2. In the `SubShader{}` section of the shader, modify the `Tags` section to the following so that we can signal that the shader is transparent:

```
Tags
{
    "Queue" = "Transparent"
    "IgnoreProjector" = "True"
    "RenderType" = "Transparent"
}
```

Tags are used by the SubShader to know how and when items should be rendered. Similar to the dictionary type, tags are key-value pairs where the left-hand side is the tag name and the right-hand side is the value you wish for it to be set to.

 For more information on tags in ShaderLab, check out: https://docs. unity3d.com/Manual/SL-SubShaderTags.html

3. As this shader is designed for 2D materials, make sure that the back geometry of your model is not drawn by adding the following below the LOD 200 line:

```
LOD 200

// Do not show back
Cull Back

CGPROGRAM
// Physically based Standard lighting model, and enable shadows
on all light types
#pragma surface surf Standard alpha:fade
```

4. Tell the shader that this material is transparent and needs to be blended with what was drawn on the screen before:

```
#pragma surface surf Standard alpha:fade
```

5. Use this Surface Shader to determine the final color and transparency of the glass:

```
void surf(Input IN, inout SurfaceOutputStandard o)
{
  float4 c = tex2D(_MainTex, IN.uv_MainTex) * _Color;
  o.Albedo = c.rgb;
  o.Alpha = c.a;
}
```

6. Afterward, save your script and dive back to the Unity editor:

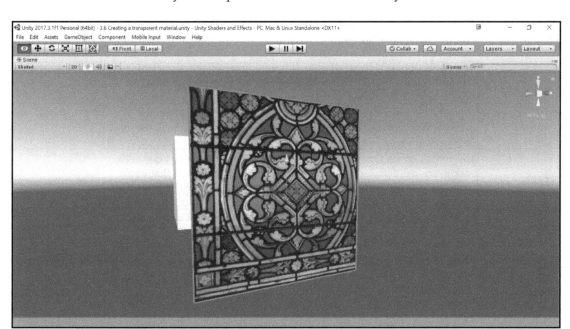

Notice that you can now see the cube behind the glass. Perfect!

How it works...

This shader introduces several new concepts. First of all, `Tags` are used to add information about how the object is going to be rendered. The really interesting one here is `Queue`. Unity, by default, will sort your objects for you based on the distance from the camera. So, as an object gets nearer to the camera, it is going to be drawn over all the objects that are further away from the camera. For most cases, this works out just fine for games, but you will find yourself in certain situations where you will want to have more control over the sorting of your objects in your scene. Unity has provided us with some default render queues, each with a unique value that directs Unity when to draw the object to the screen. These built-in render queues are called `Background`, `Geometry`, `AlphaTest`, `Transparent`, and `Overlay`. These queues weren't just created arbitrarily; they actually serve a purpose to make our lives easier when writing shaders and interacting with the real-time renderer.

Refer to the following table for descriptions on the usage of each of these individual render queues:

Render queue	Render queue description	Render queue value
Background	This render queue is rendered first. It is used for skyboxes and so on.	1000
Geometry	This is the default render queue. This is used for most objects. Opaque geometry uses this queue.	2000
AlphaTest	Alpha-tested geometry uses this queue. It's different from the Geometry queue as it's more efficient to render alpha-tested objects after all the solid objects are drawn.	2450
Transparent	This render queue is rendered after Geometry and AlphaTest queues in back-to-front order. Anything alpha-blended (that is, shaders that don't write to the depth buffer) should go here, for example, glass and particle effects.	3000
Overlay	This render queue is meant for overlay effects. Anything rendered last should go here, for example, lens flares.	4000

So, once you know which render queue your object belongs to, you can assign its built-in render queue tag. Our shader used the Transparent queue, so we wrote Tags{"Queue"="Transparent"}.

The fact that the Transparent queue is rendered after Geometry does *not* mean that our glass will appear on top of all the other solid objects. Unity will draw the glass last, but it will not render pixels that belong to pieces of geometry hidden behind something else. This control is done using a technique called **ZBuffering**. More information on how models are rendered can be found at the following link: http://docs.unity3d.com/Manual/SL-CullAndDepth.html.

The IgnoreProjector tag makes this object unaffected by Unity's projectors. Lastly, RenderType plays a role in **shader replacement**, a topic that will be covered briefly in Chapter 10, *Gameplay and Screen Effects*.

The last concept introduced is alpha:fade. This indicates that all the pixels from this material have to be blended with what was on the screen before according to their alpha values. Without this directive, the pixels will be drawn in the correct order, but they won't have any transparency.

Creating a Holographic Shader

More and more space-themed games are being released every year. An important part of a good sci-fi game is the way futuristic technology is presented and integrated into gameplay. There's nothing that screams futuristic more than holograms. Despite being present in many flavors, holograms are often represented as semi-transparent, thin projections of an object. This recipe shows you how to create a shader that simulates such effects. Take this as a starting point: you can add noise, animated scan lines, and vibrations to create a truly outstanding holographic effect. The following screenshot shows an example of a Holographic effect:

Getting ready

Create a shader called `Holographic`. Attach it to a material (`HolographicMat`) and assign it to a 3D model in your scene:

How to do it...

The following changes will change our existing shader into a holographic one:

1. Remove the following properties as they will not be used:
   - `_Glossiness`
   - `_Metallic`

2. Add the following property to the shader:

   ```
   _DotProduct("Rim effect", Range(-1,1)) = 0.25
   ```

3. Add its respective variable to the CGPROGRAM section:

   ```
   float _DotProduct;
   ```

4. As this material is transparent, add the following tags:

   ```
   Tags
   {
     "Queue" = "Transparent"
     "IgnoreProjector" = "True"
     "RenderType" = "Transparent"
   }
   ```

 According to the type of object that you will use, you might want its backside to appear. If this is the case, add `Cull Off` so that the back of the model won't be removed (*culled*).

5. This shader is not trying to simulate a realistic material, so there is no need to use the PBR lighting model. **Lambertian reflectance**, which is very cheap, is used instead. Additionally, we should disable any lighting with `nolighting` and signal to Cg that this is a Transparent Shader using `alpha:fade`:

   ```
   #pragma surface surf Lambert alpha:fade nolighting
   ```

6. Change the `Input` structure so that Unity will fill it with the current view direction and the world normal direction:

   ```
   struct Input
   {
     float2 uv_MainTex;
     float3 worldNormal;
     float3 viewDir;
   };
   ```

7. Use the following surface function. Remember that since this shader is using Lambertian reflectance as its lighting function, the name of the `SurfaceOutput` structure should be changed accordingly to `SurfaceOutput` instead of `SurfaceOutputStandard`:

```
void surf(Input IN, inout SurfaceOutput o)
{
    float4 c = tex2D(_MainTex, IN.uv_MainTex) * _Color;
    o.Albedo = c.rgb;

    float border = 1 - (abs(dot(IN.viewDir,
        IN.worldNormal)));
    float alpha = (border * (1 - _DotProduct) + _DotProduct);
    o.Alpha = c.a * alpha;
}
```

8. Save your script and dive into Unity. From there, change the **Color** property in the **HolographicMat** and see your hologram come to life:

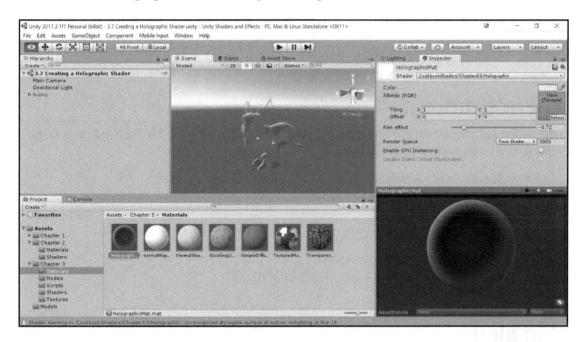

You can now use the **Rim effect** slider to choose the strength of the holographic effect.

How it works...

As mentioned previously, this shader works by showing only the silhouette of an object. If we look at the object from another angle, its outline will change. Geometrically speaking, the edges of a model are all those triangles whose *normal direction* is orthogonal (90 degrees) to the current *view direction*. The `Input` structure declares these parameters, `worldNormal` and `viewDir`, respectively.

The problem of understanding when two vectors are orthogonal can be solved using `_DotProduct`. This is an operator that takes two vectors and returns zero if they are orthogonal. We use `_DotProduct` to determine how close to zero the `_DotProduct` has to be for the triangle to fade completely.

The second aspect that is used in this shader is the gentle fading between the edge of the model (fully visible) and the angle determined by `_DotProduct` (invisible). This linear interpolation is effected as follows:

```
float alpha = (border * (1 - _DotProduct) + _DotProduct);
```

Finally, the original `alpha` from the texture is multiplied with the newly calculated coefficient to achieve the final look.

There's more...

This technique is very simple and relatively inexpensive, and yet it can be used for a large variety of effects, such as the following:

- The slightly colored atmosphere of a planet in sci-fi games
- The edge of an object that has been selected or is currently under the mouse
- A ghost or specter
- Smoke coming out of an engine
- The shockwave of an explosion
- The bubble shield of a spaceship under attack

See also

The `_DotProduct` plays an important role in the way reflections are calculated. Chapter 4, *Understanding Lighting Models*, will explain in detail how it works and why it is widely used in so many shaders.

Packing and blending textures

Textures are useful for storing not only loads of data, not just pixel colors as we generally tend to think of them, but also for multiple sets of pixels in both the x and y directions and RGBA channels. We can actually pack multiple images into a single RGBA texture and use each of the R, G, B, and A components as individual textures themselves by extracting each of these components from the shader code.

The result of packing individual grayscale images into a single RGBA texture can be seen in the following screenshot:

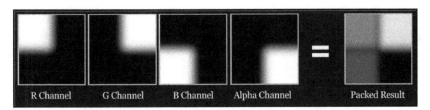

Why is this helpful? Well, in terms of the amount of actual memory that your application takes up, textures are a large portion of your application's size. We can, of course, reduce the size of the image, but then we would lose details in how it can be represented. So, to begin reducing the size of your application, we can look at all of the images that we are using in our shader and see if we can merge these textures into a single texture. Using a single texture with multiple images in them requires fewer draw calls and less overhead than separate files. We can also use this concept to combine irregularly shaped textures (that being, those that are not squares) into a single one to take up less space than giving them their own full texture.

Any texture that is grayscale can be packed into one of the RGBA channels of another texture. This might sound a bit odd at first, but this recipe is going to demonstrate one of the uses of packing a texture and using these packed textures in a shader.

One example of using these packed textures is when you want to blend a set of textures together onto a single surface. You see this most often in terrain type shaders, where you need to blend into another texture nicely using some sort of control texture or the packed texture, in this case. This recipe covers this technique and shows you how to construct the beginnings of a nice four-texture blended terrain shader.

Getting ready

Let's create a new shader file in your `Shaders` folder (`TextureBlending`) and then create a new material for this shader (`TextureBlendingMat`). The naming convention is entirely up to you for your shader and material files, so try your best to keep them organized, and easy to reference later on.

Once you have your shader and material ready, create a new scene in which we can test our shader. Inside to the scene, place the `Terrain_001` object from the `Chapter 3 | Models` folder and assign the `TextureBlendingMat` material to it:

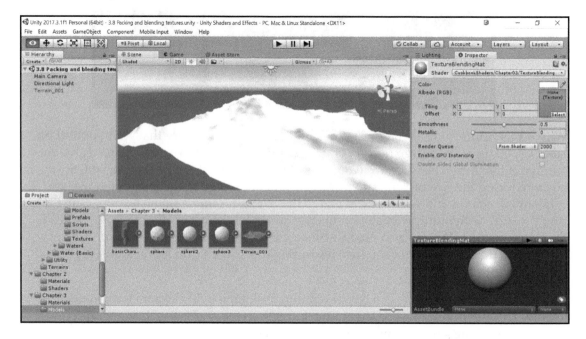

You will also need to gather up four textures that you would want to blend together. These can be anything, but for a nice terrain shader, you will want grass, dirt, rocky dirt, and rock textures. You can find these assets in `Chapter 1 | Standard Assets | Environment | TerrainAssets | SurfaceTextures` folder in the example code for this book.

Finally, we will also need a blending texture that is packed with grayscale images. This will give us the four blending textures that we can use to direct how the color textures will be placed on the object surface.

We can use very intricate blending textures to create a very realistic distribution of terrain textures over a terrain mesh, as shown in the following screenshot:

| R Channel | G Channel | B Channel | Alpha Channel | Packed Result |

How to do it...

Let's learn how to use packed textures by entering the code shown in the following steps:

1. We need to add a few properties to our `Properties` block. We will need five `sampler2D` objects, or textures, and two `Color` properties:

```
Properties
{
 _MainTint ("Diffuse Tint", Color) = (1,1,1,1)
//Add the properties below so we can input all of our
   textures
 _ColorA ("Terrain Color A", Color) = (1,1,1,1)
 _ColorB ("Terrain Color B", Color) = (1,1,1,1)
 _RTexture ("Red Channel Texture", 2D) = ""{}
 _GTexture ("Green Channel Texture", 2D) = ""{}
 _BTexture ("Blue Channel Texture", 2D) = ""{}
 _ATexture ("Alpha Channel Texture", 2D) = ""{}
 _BlendTex ("Blend Texture", 2D) = ""{}
}
```

As always, remove the properties we are not using from the base shader from our code.

2. We then need to create the `SubShader{}` section variables that will be our link to the data in the `Properties` block:

```
CGPROGRAM
#pragma surface surf Lambert

// Use shader model 3.5 target, to support enough textures
#pragma target 3.5
float4 _MainTint;
float4 _ColorA;
float4 _ColorB;
sampler2D _RTexture;
sampler2D _GTexture;
sampler2D _BTexture;
sampler2D _BlendTex;
sampler2D _ATexture;
```

3. Due to the number of items inside of our shader, we will need to update the target level version of our shader model to `3.5`:

For more information on Shader Compilation Target Levels, check out: `https://docs.unity3d.com/Manual/SL-ShaderCompileTargets.html`.

4. So, now we have our texture properties and we are passing them to our `SubShader{}` function. In order to allow the user to change the tiling rates on a per-texture basis, we will need to modify our `Input` struct. This will allow us to use the tiling and offset parameters on each texture:

```
struct Input
{
    float2 uv_RTexture;
    float2 uv_GTexture;
    float2 uv_BTexture;
    float2 uv_ATexture;
    float2 uv_BlendTex;
};
```

5. In the `surf()` function, get the texture information and store it in its own variables so that we can work with the data in a clean, easy-to-understand way:

```
void surf (Input IN, inout SurfaceOutput o) {
  //Get the pixel data from the blend texture
  //we need a float 4 here because the texture
  //will return R,G,B,and A or X,Y,Z, and W
  float4 blendData = tex2D(_BlendTex, IN.uv_BlendTex);
  //Get the data from the textures we want to blend
  float4 rTexData = tex2D(_RTexture, IN.uv_RTexture);
  float4 gTexData = tex2D(_GTexture, IN.uv_GTexture);
  float4 bTexData = tex2D(_BTexture, IN.uv_BTexture);
  float4 aTexData = tex2D(_ATexture, IN.uv_ATexture);
```

Remember that due to us using Lambert, we will be using `SurfaceOutput` instead of `SurfaceOutputStandard` for the `surf` function.

6. Let's blend each of our textures together using the `lerp()` function. It takes three arguments, `lerp(value : a, value : b,` and `blend: c)`. The `lerp()` function takes in two textures and blends them with the float value given in the last argument:

```
//No we need to construct a new RGBA value and add all
//the different blended texture back together
float4 finalColor;
finalColor = lerp(rTexData, gTexData, blendData.g);
finalColor = lerp(finalColor, bTexData, blendData.b);
finalColor = lerp(finalColor, aTexData, blendData.a);
finalColor.a = 1.0;
```

7. Finally, we multiply our blended texture by the color tint values and use the red channel to determine where the two different terrain tint colors go:

```
//Add on our terrain tinting colors
float4 terrainLayers = lerp(_ColorA, _ColorB, blendData.r);
finalColor *= terrainLayers;
finalColor = saturate(finalColor);
o.Albedo = finalColor.rgb * _MainTint.rgb;
o.Alpha = finalColor.a;
}
```

8. Save your script and go back into Unity. Once there, you can assign the `TerrainBlend` texture to the **Blend Texture** property. Once you've done that, place different textures in the different channels in order to see our script in action:

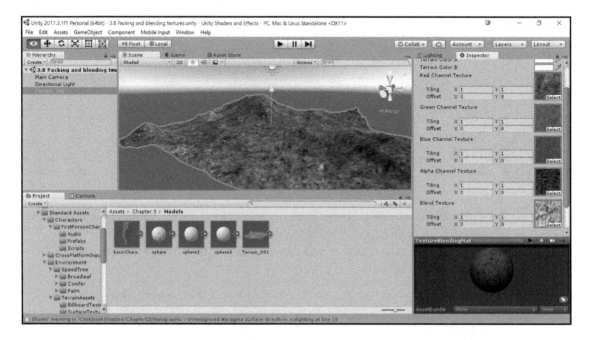

9. This effect can be taken even further by using different textures and terrain tinting to create some great looking terrains with minimal effort. The result of blending together four terrain textures and creating a terrain tinting technique can be seen in the following screenshot:

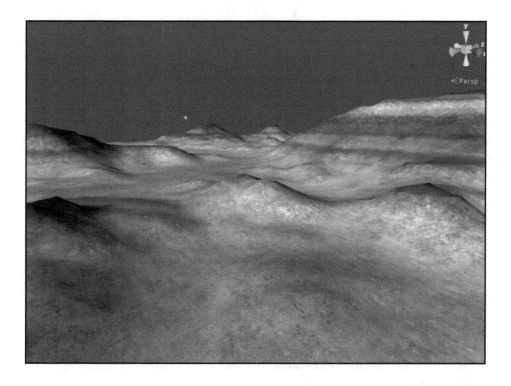

How it works...

This might seem like quite a few lines of code, but the concept behind blending is actually quite simple. For the technique to work, we have to employ the built-in `lerp()` function from the CgFX standard library. This function allows us to pick a value between argument one and argument two using argument three as the blend amount:

Function	Description
`lerp(a, b, f )`	This involves linear interpolation: $(1 - f)* a + b * f$ Here, a and b are matching vector or scalar types. The f parameter can be either a scalar or vector of the same type as a and b.

So, for example, if we wanted to find the mid-value between 1 and 2, we could feed the value 0.5 as the third argument to the lerp() function and it would return the value 1.5. This works perfectly for our blending needs as the values of an individual channel in an RGBA texture are single float values, usually in the range of 0 to 1.

In the shader, we simply take one of the channels from our **Blend Texture** and use it to drive the color that is picked in a lerp() function for each pixel. For instance, we take our grass texture and dirt texture, use the red channel from our blending texture, and feed this to a lerp() function. This will give us the correct blended color result for each pixel on the surface.

A more visual representation of what is happening when using the lerp() function is shown in the following diagram:

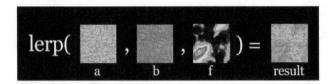

The shader code simply uses the four channels of the **Blend Texture** and all the color textures to create a final **Blended Texture**. This final texture then becomes the color that we can multiply with our diffuse lighting.

Creating a circle around your terrain

Many RTS games display distances (range attack, moving distance, sight, and so on) by drawing a circle around the selected unit. If the terrain is flat, this can be done simply by stretching a quad with the texture of a circle. If that's not the case, the quad will most likely be clipped behind a hill or another piece of geometry. This recipe will show you how to create a shader that allows you to draw circles around an object of arbitrary complexity. If you want to be able to move or animate your circle, we will need both a shader and C# script.

The following screenshot shows an example of drawing a circle in a hilly region using a shader:

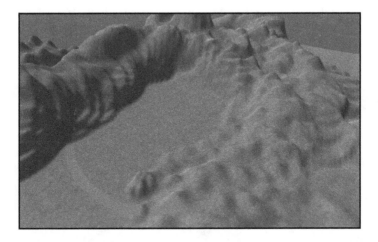

Getting ready

Despite working with every piece of geometry, this technique is oriented to terrains. Hence, the first step is setting up a terrain in Unity, but instead of using a model, we will create one within the Unity editor:

1. Let's start by creating a new shader called `RadiusShader` and the respective material, `RadiusMat`.
2. Have the character for your object ready; we will draw a circle around it.
3. From the menu, navigate to **GameObject** | **3D Object** | **Terrain** to create a new terrain.
4. Create the geometry for your terrain. You can either import an existing one or draw your own using the tools available (**Raise/Lower Terrain**, **Paint Height**, **Smooth Height**).

5. The terrains are special objects in Unity, and the way texture mapping works on them is different from traditional 3D models. You cannot provide `_MainTex` from a shader as it needs to be provided directly from the terrain itself. To do this, select **Paint Texture** and then click on **Add Texture...**:

The creation of a terrain isn't covered in this book, but if you would like to learn more about it, check out the following link: `https://docs.unity3d.com/Manual/terrain-UsingTerrains.html`

6. Now that the texture is set, you have to change the material of the terrain so that a custom shader can be provided. From **Terrain Settings**, change the **Material** property to `Custom`, and then drag the **Radius** material to the `Custom Material` box:

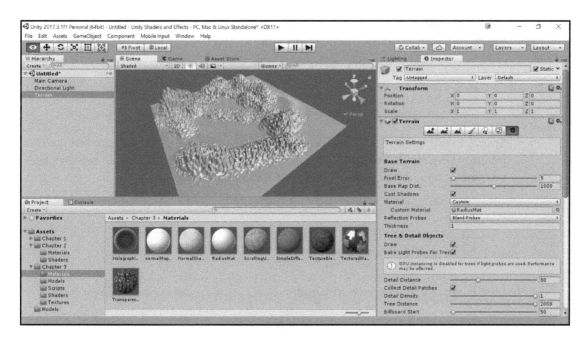

You are now ready to create your shader.

How to do it...

Let's start by editing the `RadiusShader` file:

1. In the new shader, remove the `_Glossiness` and `_Metallic` properties and add these four properties:

    ```
    _Center("Center", Vector) = (200,0,200,0)
    _Radius("Radius", Float) = 100
    _RadiusColor("Radius Color", Color) = (1,0,0,1)
    _RadiusWidth("Radius Width", Float) = 10
    ```

2. Add their respective variables to the CGPROGRAM section, remembering to remove the declaration of _Glossiness and _Metallic:

```
float3 _Center;
float _Radius;
fixed4 _RadiusColor;
float _RadiusWidth;
```

3. Input to our surface function requires not only the UV of the texture but also the position (in world coordinates) of every point of the terrain. We can retrieve this parameter by changing the struct Input as follows:

```
struct Input
{
    float2 uv_MainTex; // The UV of the terrain texture
    float3 worldPos;   // The in-world position
};
```

4. Lastly, we use this surface function:

```
void surf(Input IN, inout SurfaceOutputStandard o)
{
    // Get the distance between the center of the
    // place we wish to draw from and the input's
    // world position
    float d = distance(_Center, IN.worldPos);

    // If the distance is larger than the radius and
    // it is less than our radius + width change the color
    if ((d > _Radius) && (d < (_Radius + _RadiusWidth)))
    {
        o.Albedo = _RadiusColor;
    }
    // Otherwise, use the normal color
    else
    {
        o.Albedo = tex2D(_MainTex, IN.uv_MainTex).rgb;
    }
}
```

These steps are all it takes to draw a circle on your terrain. You can use the material's Inspector tab to change the position, radius, and color of the circle:

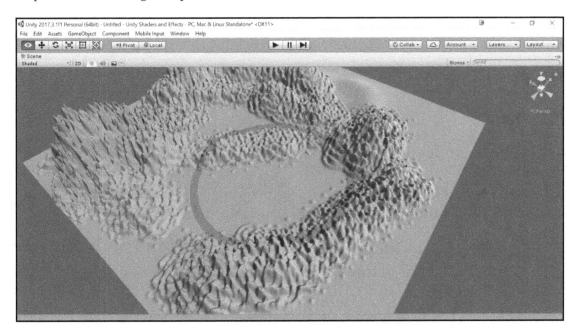

Moving the circle

This is great, but you'll likely also want to change where the circle is at run-time, which we can do via code. If you want the circle to follow your character, other steps are necessary:

1. Create a new C# script called `SetRadiusProperties`.
2. Since you may wish to see this change both in the game and outside, we can add a tag to the top of the class saying to execute this code while in the editor, in addition to when the game is being played, by adding the following tag:

   ```
   [ExecuteInEditMode]
   public class SetRadiusProperties : MonoBehaviour
   ```

3. Add these properties to the script:

```
public Material radiusMaterial;
public float radius = 1;
public Color color = Color.white;
```

4. In the `Update()` method, add these lines of code:

```
if(radiusMaterial != null)
{
    radiusMaterial.SetVector("_Center", transform.position);
    radiusMaterial.SetFloat("_Radius", radius);
    radiusMaterial.SetColor("_RadiusColor", color);
}
```

5. Attach the script to the object you wish to have the circle drawn around.

6. Finally, drag the `RadiusMat` material to the **Radius Material** slot of the script:

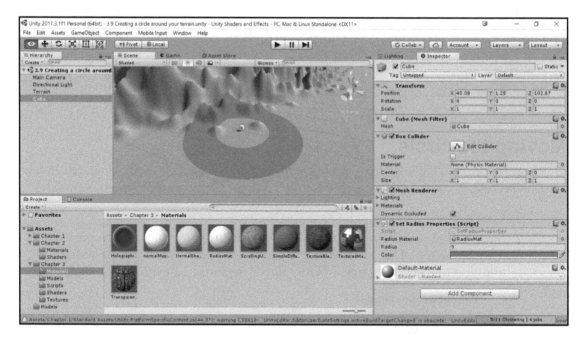

You can now move your character around and this will create a nice circle around it. Changing the properties of the `Radius` script will change the radius as well.

How it works...

The relevant parameters to draw a circle are its center, radius, and color. They are all available in the shader with the names _Center, _Radius, and _RadiusColor. By adding the worldPos variable to the Input structure, we are asking Unity to provide us with the position of the pixel that we are drawing expressed in world coordinates. This is the actual position of an object in the editor.

The surf() function is where the circle is actually drawn. It calculates the distance from the point being drawn and the center of the radius, and then it checks whether it is between _Radius and _Radius + _RadiusWidth; if this is the case, it uses the chosen color. In the other case, it just samples the texture map like all the other shaders we have seen so far.

Understanding Lighting Models

4

In the previous chapters, we introduced Surface Shaders and explained how we can change physical properties (such as Albedo and Specular) to simulate different materials. How does this really work? At the heart of every Surface Shader, there is its **lighting model**. It's the function that takes these properties and calculates the final shade of each pixel. Unity usually hides this from the developers because in order to write a lighting model, you have to understand how light reflects and refracts onto surfaces. This chapter will finally show you how lighting models work and give you the basics to create your own.

In this chapter, you will learn the following recipes:

- Creating a custom diffuse lighting model
- Creating a toon shader
- Creating a Phong Specular type
- Creating a BlinnPhong Specular type
- Creating an Anisotropic Specular type

Introduction

Simulating the way light works is a very challenging and resource-consuming task. For many years, video games have used very simple lighting models which, despite lacking realism, were very believable. Even if most 3D engines are now using physically-based renderers, it is worth exploring some simpler techniques. The ones presented in this chapter are reasonably realistic and widely adopted on devices with low resources such as mobile phones. Understanding these simple lighting models is also essential if you want to create your own.

Creating a custom diffuse lighting model

If you are familiar with Unity 4, you may know that the default shader it provided was based on a lighting model called **Lambertian reflectance**. This recipe will show you how it is possible to create a shader with a custom lighting model and explains the mathematics involved and implementation. The following diagram shows the same geometry rendered with a Standard Shader (right) and a diffuse Lambert one (left):

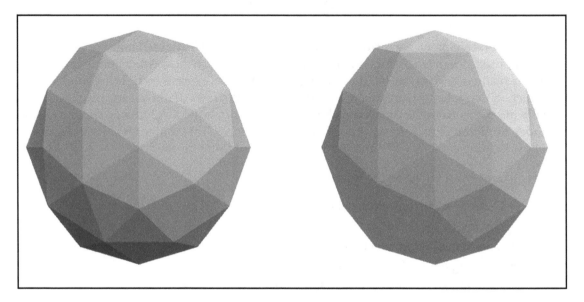

Shaders based on Lambertian reflectance are classified as non-photorealistic; no object in the real world really looks like this. However, Lambert Shaders are still often used in low-poly games as they produce a neat contrast between the faces of complex geometries. The lighting model used to calculate the Lambertian reflectance is also very efficient, making it perfect for mobile games.

Unity has already provided us with a lighting function that we can use for our shaders. It is called the Lambertian lighting model. It is one of the more basic and efficient forms of reflectance, which you can find in a lot of games even today. As it is already built in the Unity Surface Shader language, we thought it best to start with this first and build on it. You can also find an example in the Unity reference manual, but we will go into more depth and explain where the data is coming from and why it is working the way it is. This will help you get a nice grounding in setting up custom lighting models so that we can build on this knowledge in the future recipes in this chapter.

Getting ready

Let's start by carrying out the following steps:

1. Create a new shader and give it a name (`SimpleLambert`).
2. Create a new material, give it a name (`SimpleLambertMat`), and assign the new shader to its `shader` property.
3. Then, create a sphere object and place it roughly in the center of the scene and attach the new material to it.
4. Finally, let's create a directional light to cast some light on our object if one isn't created already.
5. When your assets have been set up in Unity, you should have a scene that resembles the following screenshot:

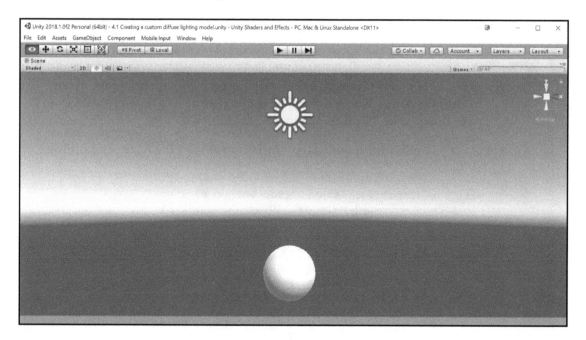

How to do it...

The Lambertian reflectance can be achieved with the following changes to the shader:

1. Begin by replacing the shader's `Properties` block with the following :

```
Properties
{
    _MainTex("Texture", 2D) = "white"
}
```

2. Since we are removing all of the other properties, remove the `_Glossiness`, `_Metallic`, and `_Color` declarations inside of the `SubShader` section.

3. Change the `#pragma` directive of the shader so that, instead of `Standard`, it uses our custom lighting model:

```
#pragma surface surf SimpleLambert
```

 If you try to run the script now, it will complain that it doesn't know what the `SimpleLambert` lighting model is. We will need to create a function called `Lighting` + the name that we gave here with instructions on how to light the object, which we will be writing later on in this recipe. In this case, it would be `LightingSimpleLambert`.

4. Use a very simple surface function, which just samples the texture according to its UV data:

```
void surf(Input IN, inout SurfaceOutput o) {
    o.Albedo = tex2D(_MainTex, IN.uv_MainTex).rgb;
}
```

5. Add a function called `LightingSimpleLambert()` that will contain the following code for the Lambertian reflectance:

```
// Allows us to use the SimpleLambert lighting mode
half4 LightingSimpleLambert (SurfaceOutput s, half3 lightDir,
                             half atten)
{
    // First calculate the dot product of the light direction and the
    // surface's normal
    half NdotL = dot(s.Normal, lightDir);

    // Next, set what color should be returned
    half4 color;
```

```
color.rgb = s.Albedo * _LightColor0.rgb * (NdotL * atten);
color.a = s.Alpha;

// Return the calculated color
return color;
}
```

6. Save your script and return to the Unity editor. You should notice that it looks somewhat different than what was there before:

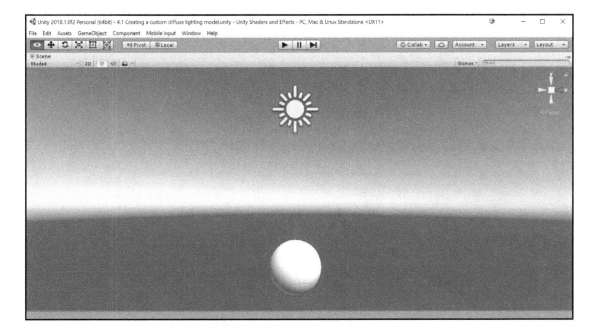

7. The effect is even easier to see if we use the cylinders we used in the previous chapter, Chapter 3, *Surface Shaders and Texture Mapping*:

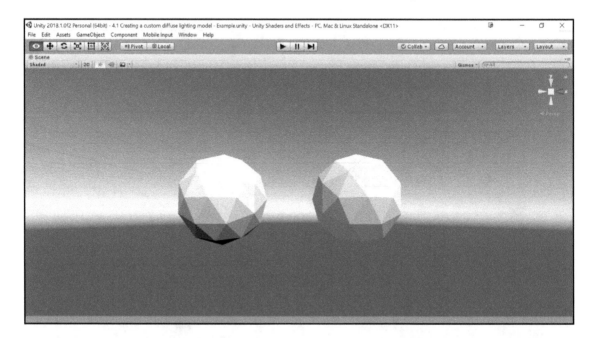

How it works...

As previously seen in Chapter 2, *Creating Your First Shader*, the #pragma directive is used to specify which surface function to use. Choosing a different lighting model works in a similar fashion: SimpleLambert forces Cg to look for a function called LightingSimpleLambert(). Note the Lighting at the beginning, which is omitted in the directive.

The Lighting function takes three parameters: the *surface output* (which contains the physical properties such as the albedo and transparency), the *direction* the light is coming from, and its *attenuation*.

According to Lambertian reflectance, the amount of light a surface reflects depends on the angle between the incident light and surface normal. If you have played pool billiards, you are surely familiar with this concept; the direction of a ball depends on its incident angle against the wall. If you hit a wall at a 90 degree angle, the ball will come back at you; if you hit it with a very low angle, its direction will be mostly unchanged. The Lambertian model makes the same assumption; if the light hits a triangle at a 90 degree angle, all the light gets reflected back. The lower the angle, the less light is reflected back to you. This concept is shown in the following diagram:

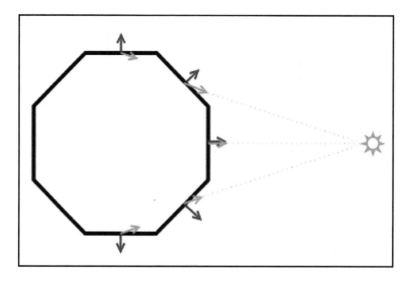

This simple concept has to be translated into a mathematical form. In vector algebra, the angle between two unit vectors can be calculated via an operator called **dot product**. When the dot product is equal to zero, two vectors are orthogonal, which means that they make a 90-degree angle. When it is equal to one (or minus one), they are parallel to each other. Cg has a function called dot(), which implements the dot product extremely efficiently.

The following diagram shows a light source (sun) shining on a complex surface. **L** indicates the light direction (called `lightDir` in the shader) and **N** is the normal to the surface. The light is reflected with the same angle that it hits the surface with:

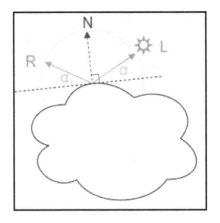

 For more information on normals and what they mean mathematically check out: `https://en.wikipedia.org/wiki/Normal_(geometry)`

Lambertian reflectance simply uses the `NdotL` dot product as a multiplicative coefficient for the intensity of light:

$$I = N \cdot L$$

When N and L are parallel, all the light is reflected back to the source, causing the geometry to appear brighter. The `_LightColor0` variable contains the color of the light that is calculated.

 Prior to Unity 5, the intensity of the lights was different. If you are using an old diffuse shader based on the Lambertian model, you may notice that `NdotL` is multiplied by two: `(NdotL * atten * 2)`, rather than `(NdotL * atten)`. If you are importing a custom shader from Unity 4, you will need to correct this manually. Legacy Shaders, however, have already been designed taking this aspect into account.

When the dot product is negative, the light is coming from the opposite side of the triangle. This is not a problem for opaque geometries as triangles that are not facing the camera frontally are culled (discarded) and not rendered.

This basic Lambert is a great starting point when you are prototyping your shaders as you can get a lot accomplished in terms of writing the core functionality of the shader while not having to worry about the basic `Lighting` functions.

Unity has provided us with a lighting model that has already taken the task of creating a Lambert lighting for you. If you look at the `UnityCG.cginc` file found in your Unity's installation directory under the `Data` folder, you will notice that you have Lambert and BlinnPhong lighting models available for you to use. The moment you compile your shader with `#pragma surface surf Lambert`, you are telling the shader to utilize Unity's implementation of the Lambert `Lighting` function in the `UnityCG.cginc` file so that you don't have to write that code over and over again. We will explore how the BlinnPhong model works later in this chapter.

Creating a toon shader

One of the most used effects in games is **toon shading**, which is also known as **celluloid** (**CEL**) shading. It is a non-photorealistic rendering technique that makes 3D models appear flat. Many games use it to give the illusion that the graphics are being hand-drawn rather than being 3D modeled. You can see, in the following diagram, a sphere rendered with a toon Shader (left) and a Standard Shader (right):

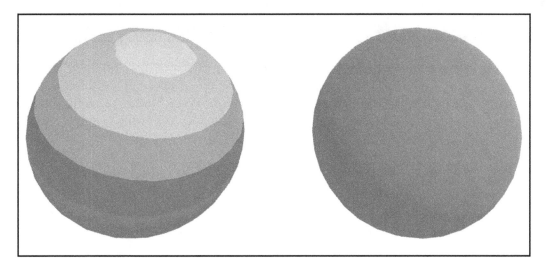

Achieving this effect using just surface functions is not impossible, but it would be extremely expensive and time consuming. The surface function, in fact, only works on the properties of the material, not its actual lighting condition. As toon shading requires us to change the way light reflects, we need to create our custom lighting model instead.

Getting ready

Let's start this recipe by creating a shader and its material and importing a special texture, as follows:

1. Start by creating a new shader; in this example, we will duplicate the one made in the previous recipe by selecting it in the **Project** tab and then hit *Ctrl + D*. We will change the name of this new `shader` to `ToonShader`.

> You can rename an object in the **Project** window by single-clicking on the name.

2. Create a new material for the shader (`ToonShaderMat`) and attach it to a 3D model. Toon shading works best on curved surfaces.
3. This recipe requires an additional texture called a **ramp map**, which will be used to dictate when we want to use certain colors depending on the shade received:

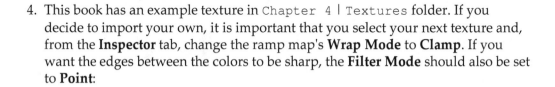

4. This book has an example texture in `Chapter 4 | Textures` folder. If you decide to import your own, it is important that you select your next texture and, from the **Inspector** tab, change the ramp map's **Wrap Mode** to **Clamp**. If you want the edges between the colors to be sharp, the **Filter Mode** should also be set to **Point**:

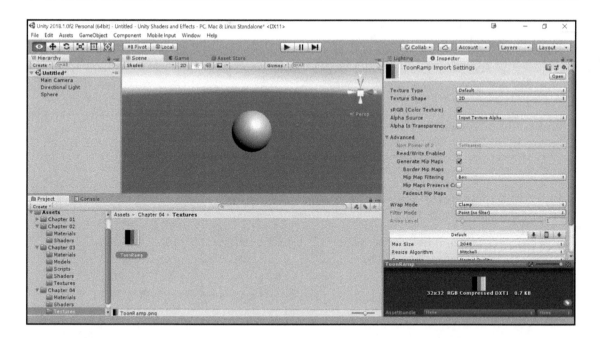

 The example project included with this book already has this step completed in the `Assets` | `Chapter 4` | `Texture` | `ToonRamp` file, but it is a good idea to verify that this is the case before moving forward.

How to do it...

The toon aesthetic can be achieved with the following changes to the shader:

1. Add a new property for a texture called `_RampTex`:

   ```
   _RampTex ("Ramp", 2D) = "white" {}
   ```

2. Add its relative variable in the `CGPROGRAM` section:

   ```
   sampler2D _RampTex;
   ```

3. Change the `#pragma` directive so that it points to a function called `LightingToon()`:

   ```
   #pragma surface surf Toon
   ```

4. Replace the `LightingSimpleLambert` function with the following function instead:

```
fixed4 LightingToon (SurfaceOutput s, fixed3 lightDir,
                fixed atten)
{
    // First calculate the dot product of the light direction and the
    // surface's normal
    half NdotL = dot(s.Normal, lightDir);
    // Remap NdotL to the value on the ramp map
    NdotL = tex2D(_RampTex, fixed2(NdotL, 0.5));

    // Next, set what color should be returned
    half4 color;

    color.rgb = s.Albedo * _LightColor0.rgb * (NdotL * atten );
    color.a = s.Alpha;

    // Return the calculated color
    return color;
}
```

5. Save the script, open up the `ToonShaderMat`, and assign the `Ramp` property to your ramp map. If all goes well, you should see something like the following in your scene:

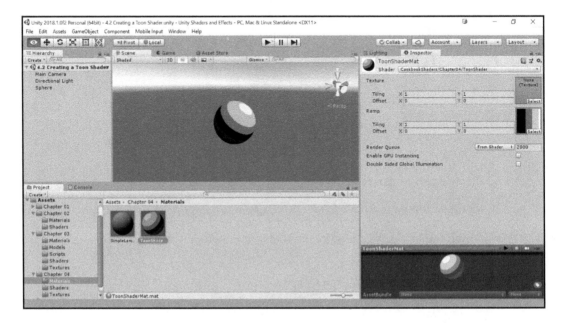

This effect may be modified by the lighting in the scene. You can change the illumination of the scene by going to **Window** | **Lighting** | **Settings** and changing the **Environment** | **Environment Lighting** | **Intensity Multiplier** property to 0.

How it works...

The main characteristic of toon shading is the way the light is rendered; surfaces are not shaded uniformly. To achieve this effect, we need a ramp map. Its purpose is to remap the Lambertian light intensity `NdotL` to another value. Using a ramp map without a gradient, we can force the lighting to be rendered in steps. The following diagram shows how the ramp map is used to correct the light intensity:

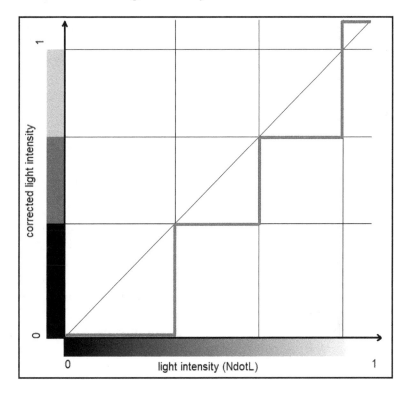

There's more...

There are many different ways whereby you can achieve a toon shading effect. Using different ramps can produce dramatic changes in the way your models look, so you should experiment in order to find the best one.

An alternative to ramp textures is to **snap** the light intensity NdotL so that it can only assume a certain number of values equidistantly sampled from 0 to 1:

```
half4 LightingCustomLambert (SurfaceOutput s, half3 lightDir,
              half3 viewDir, half atten)
{
  half NdotL = dot (s.Normal, lightDir);

  // Snap instead
  half cel = floor(NdotL * _CelShadingLevels) /
          (_CelShadingLevels - 0.5);

  // Next, set what color should be returned
  half4 color;

  color.rgb = s.Albedo * _LightColor0.rgb * (cel * atten );
  color.a = s.Alpha;

  // Return the calculated color
  return color;
}
```

To snap a number we first multiply NdotL by the _CelShadingLevels variable, round the result to an integer through the floor function, and then divides it back. This rounding is done by the floor function which will effectively remove the decimal point from a number. By doing this, the cel quantity is forced to assume one of the _CelShadingLevels equidistant values from 0 to 1. This removes the need for a ramp texture and makes all the color steps of the same size. If you are going for this implementation, remember to add a property called _CelShadingLevels to your shader. You can find an example of this in the example code for this chapter. Try dragging the **Levels** property to see how it affects how the screenshot is shown:

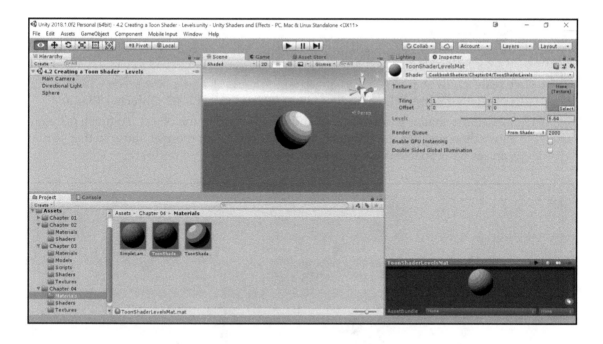

Creating a Phong Specular type

The specularity of an object surface simply describes how shiny it is. These types of effects are often referred to as view-dependent effects in the shader world. This is because, in order to achieve a realistic Specular effect in your shaders, you need to include the direction of the camera or the user facing the object's surface. The most basic and performance-friendly Specular type is the Phong Specular effect. It is the calculation of the light direction reflecting off of the surface compared to the user's view direction. It is a very common Specular model used in many applications, from games to movies. While it isn't the most realistic in terms of accurately modeling the reflected Specular, it gives a great approximation of what is expected of shininess that performs well in most situations. Additionally, if your object is further away from the camera and there is no need for a very accurate Specular, this is a great way to provide a Specular effect to your shaders.

In this recipe, we will be covering how to implement the per-vertex version of the shader and also the per-pixel version using some new parameters in the Surface Shader's `Input` struct. We will see the difference and discuss when and why to use these two different implementations for different situations.

Getting ready

To start with this recipe, perform the following steps:

1. Create a new shader (`Phong`), material(`PhongMat`), and a new scene with a sphere in it with a **Plane** underneath it (**GameObject** | **3D Objects** | **Plane**).

2. Attach the shader to the material and the material to the object. To finish off your new scene, create a new directional light if one is not there already, so that you can see your Specular effect as you code it:

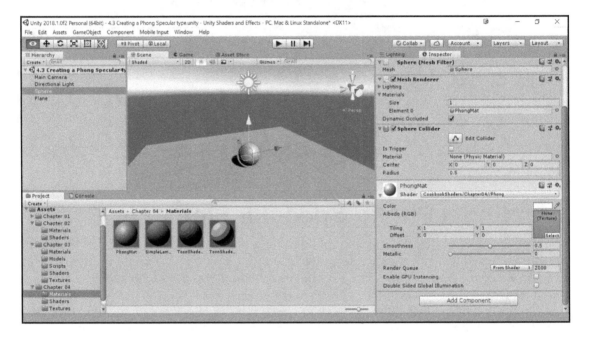

How to do it...

Follow these steps to create a Phong lighting model:

1. You might be seeing a pattern at this point, but we always like to start out with our most basic part of the shader writing process: the creation of properties. So, let's remove all of the current properties with their definitions in the `SubShader` block and then add the following properties to the shader:

   ```
   Properties
   {
   ```

```
_MainTint ("Diffuse Tint", Color) = (1,1,1,1)
_MainTex ("Base (RGB)", 2D) = "white" {}
_SpecularColor ("Specular Color", Color) = (1,1,1,1)
_SpecPower ("Specular Power", Range(0,30)) = 1
}
```

2. We then have to make sure to add the corresponding variables to our CGPROGRAM block in our SubShader{} block:

```
float4 _SpecularColor;
sampler2D _MainTex;
float4 _MainTint;
float _SpecPower;
```

3. Now, we have to add our custom lighting model so that we can compute our own Phong Specular. Don't worry if it doesn't make sense at this point; we will cover each line of code in the *How it works...* section of this recipe. Add the following code to the shader's SubShader{} function:

```
fixed4 LightingPhong (SurfaceOutput s, fixed3 lightDir,
                      half3 viewDir, fixed atten)
{
  // Reflection
  float NdotL = dot(s.Normal, lightDir);
  float3 reflectionVector = normalize(2.0 * s.Normal *
    NdotL - lightDir);

  // Specular
  float spec = pow(max(0, dot(reflectionVector, viewDir)),
    _SpecPower);
  float3 finalSpec = _SpecularColor.rgb * spec;

  // Final effect
  fixed4 c;
  c.rgb = (s.Albedo * _LightColor0.rgb * max(0,NdotL) *
    atten) + (_LightColor0.rgb * finalSpec);
  c.a = s.Alpha;
  return c;
}
```

4. Next, we have to tell the CGPROGRAM block that it needs to use our custom Lighting function instead of one of the built-in ones. We do this by changing the #pragma statement to the following:

```
CGPROGRAM
#pragma surface surf Phong
```

5. Finally, let's update the `surf` function to the following:

```
void surf (Input IN, inout SurfaceOutput o)
{
 half4 c = tex2D (_MainTex, IN.uv_MainTex) * _MainTint;
 o.Albedo = c.rgb;
 o.Alpha = c.a;
}
```

6. The following screenshot demonstrates the result of our custom Phong lighting model using our own custom reflection vector:

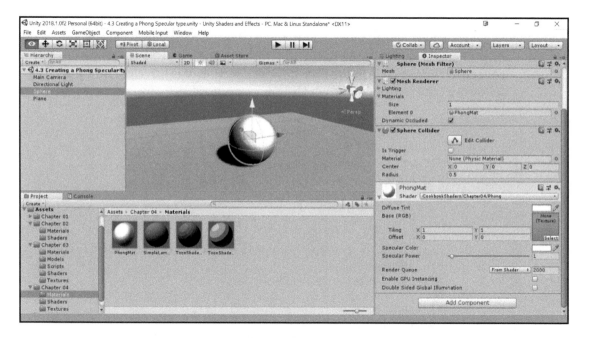

Try changing the **Specular Power** property and notice the effect that you see.

How it works...

Let's break down the Lighting function by itself, as the rest of the shader should be pretty familiar to you at this point.

In the previous recipes, we have used a Lighting function that provided only the light direction, lightDir.

Unity comes with a set of Lighting functions that you can use, including one that provides the view direction, viewDir.

To figure out how to write your own custom lighting mode refer to the following table replacing NameYouChoose with the lighting function name you gave in the #pragma statement or go to http://docs.unity3d.com/Documentation/Components/SL-SurfaceShaderLighting.html for more details:

Not view-dependent	half4 LightingNameYouChoose (SurfaceOutput s, half3 lightDir, half atten);
View-dependent	half4 LightingNameYouChoose (SurfaceOutput s, half3 lightDir, half3 viewDir, half atten);

In our case, we are using a Specular shader, so we need to have the view-dependent Lighting function structure. We have to write the following:

```
CPROGRAM
#pragma surface surf Phong
fixed4 LightingPhong (SurfaceOutput s, fixed3 lightDir, half3 viewDir,
fixed atten)
{
  // ...
}
```

This will tell the shader that we want to create our own view-dependent shader. Always make sure that your Lighting function name is the same in your Lighting function declaration and the #pragma statement, or Unity will not be able to find your lighting model.

The components that play a role in the `Phong` model are described in the following image. We have the light direction **L** (coupled with its perfect reflection **R**) and normal direction **N**. They have all been encountered before in the Lambertian model, with the exception of **V**, which is the **view direction**:

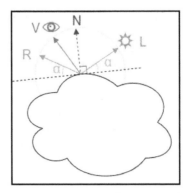

The `Phong` model assumes that the final light intensity of a reflective surface is given by two components, its diffuse color, and Specular value, as follows:

$$I = D + S$$

The diffuse component D remains unchanged from the Lambertian model:

$$D = N \cdot L$$

The Specular component S is defined as follows:

$$S = (R \cdot V)^p$$

Here, p is the Specular power defined as `_SpecPower` in the shader. The only unknown parameter is R, which is the reflection of L according to N. In vector algebra, this can be calculated as follows:

$$R = 2N \cdot (N \cdot L) - L$$

This is exactly what is calculated in the following:

```
float3 reflectionVector = normalize(2.0 * s.Normal * NdotL -
                                    lightDir);
```

This has the effect of bending the normal towards the light; as a vertex, normal is pointing away from the light, it is forced to look at the light. Refer to the following diagram for a more visual representation. The script that produces this debug effect is included in this book's support page at `https://www.packtpub.com/books/content/support`:

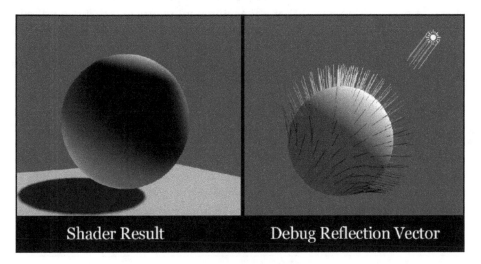

The following diagram displays the final result of our Phong Specular calculation isolated in the shader:

Creating a BlinnPhong Specular type

Blinn is another more efficient way of calculating and estimating specularity. It is done by getting the half vector from the view direction and light direction. It was brought into the world of Cg by Jim Blinn. He found that it was much more efficient to just get the half vector instead of calculating our own reflection vectors. It cut down on the code and processing time. If you actually look at the built-in BlinnPhong lighting model included in the `UnityCG.cginc` file, you will notice that it is using the half vector as well, hence it is named BlinnPhong. It is just a simpler version of the full Phong calculation.

Getting ready

To start with this recipe, perform the following steps:

1. This time, instead of creating a whole new scene, let's just use the objects and scene that we have by using **File** | **Save Scene As...**, and create a new shader (BlinnPhong) and material (`BlinnPhongMat`):

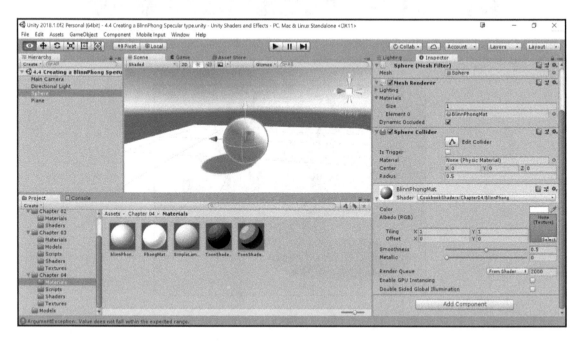

2. Once you have a new shader, double-click on it to launch your IDE of choice so that you can start editing your shader.

How to do it...

Perform the following steps to create a BlinnPhong lighting model:

1. First, let's remove all of the current properties with their definitions in the
   `SubShader` block. Then we need to add our own properties to the `Properties`
   block so that we can control the look of the Specular highlight:

```
Properties
{
  _MainTint ("Diffuse Tint", Color) = (1,1,1,1)
  _MainTex ("Base (RGB)", 2D) = "white" {}
  _SpecularColor ("Specular Color", Color) = (1,1,1,1)
  _SpecPower ("Specular Power", Range(0.1,60)) = 3
}
```

2. Then we need to make sure that we have created the corresponding variables in
   our `CGPROGRAM` block so that we can access the data from our `Properties` block,
   in our subshader:

```
sampler2D _MainTex;
float4 _MainTint;
float4 _SpecularColor;
float _SpecPower;
```

3. Now it's time to create our custom lighting model that will process our Diffuse
   and Specular calculations. The code is as follows:

```
fixed4 LightingCustomBlinnPhong (SurfaceOutput s,
                    fixed3 lightDir,
                    half3 viewDir,
                    fixed atten)
{
  float NdotL = max(0,dot(s.Normal, lightDir));

  float3 halfVector = normalize(lightDir + viewDir);
  float NdotH = max(0, dot(s.Normal, halfVector));
  float spec = pow(NdotH, _SpecPower) * _SpecularColor;

  float4 color;
  color.rgb = (s.Albedo * _LightColor0.rgb * NdotL) +
        (_LightColor0.rgb * _SpecularColor.rgb * spec) * atten;
  color.a = s.Alpha;
  return color;
}
```

4. Then update the `surf` function to the following:

```
void surf (Input IN, inout SurfaceOutput o)
{
 half4 c = tex2D (_MainTex, IN.uv_MainTex) * _MainTint;
 o.Albedo = c.rgb;
 o.Alpha = c.a;
}
```

5. To complete our shader, we will need to tell our CGPROGRAM block to use our custom lighting model rather than a built-in one by modifying the `#pragma` statement with the following code:

```
CPROGRAM
#pragma surface surf CustomBlinnPhong
```

6. The following screenshot demonstrates the results of our BlinnPhong lighting model:

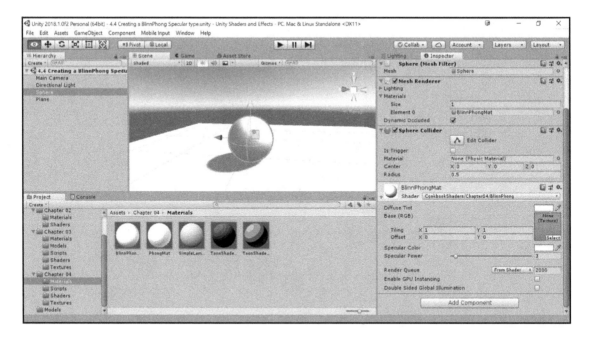

How it works...

The BlinnPhong Specular is almost exactly like the Phong Specular, except that it is more efficient because it uses less code to achieve almost the same effect. Before the introduction of physically-based rendering, this approach was the default choice for Specular reflection in Unity 4.

Calculating the reflection vector **R** is generally expensive. The BlinnPhong Specular replaces it with the half vector **H** between the view direction **V** and light direction **L**:

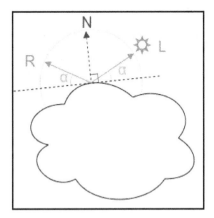

Instead of calculating our own reflection vector, we are simply going to get the vector halfway between the view direction and light direction, basically simulating the reflection vector. It has actually been found that this approach is more physically accurate than the last approach, but we thought it necessary to show you all the possibilities:

$$S_{Phong} = (R \cdot V)^p, \quad S_{BlinnPhong} = (N \cdot H)^p$$

According to vector algebra, the half vector can be calculated as follows:

$$H = \frac{V + L}{|V + L|}$$

Here |V+L| is the length of the vector V+L. In Cg, we simply need to add the view direction and light direction together and then normalize the result to a unity vector:

```
float3 halfVector = normalize(lightDir + viewDir);
```

Then, we simply need to dot the vertex normal with this new half vector to get our main Specular value. After this, we just take it to a power of _SpecPower and multiply it by the Specular color variable. It's much lighter on the code and math, but still gives us a nice Specular highlight that will work for many real-time situations.

See also

The light models seen in this chapter are extremely simple; no real material is perfectly matte or perfectly specular. Moreover, it is not uncommon for complex materials such as clothing, wood, and skin to require knowledge of how light scatters in the layers beneath the surface. Use the following table to recap the different lighting models encountered so far:

Technique	Type	Light Intensity (I)
Lambertian	Diffuse	$I = N \cdot L$
Phong	Specular	$I = N \cdot L + (R \cdot V)^p$ $R = 2N \cdot (N \cdot L) - L$
BlinnPhong	Specular	$I = N \cdot L + (N \cdot H)^p$ $H = \dfrac{V + L}{|V + L|}$

There are other interesting models such as the Oren-Nayar lighting model for rough surfaces: https://en.wikipedia.org/wiki/Oren%E2%80%93Nayar_reflectance_model.

Creating an Anisotropic Specular type

Anisotropic is a type of Specular or reflection that simulates the directionality of grooves in a surface and modifies/stretches the Specular in the perpendicular direction. It is very useful when you want to simulate brushed metals, not a metal with a clear, smooth, and polished surface. Imagine the Specular that you see when you look at the data side of a CD or DVD or the way Specular is shaped at the bottom of a pot or pan. You will notice that if you carefully examine the surface, there is a direction to the grooves, usually in the way the metal was brushed. When you apply a Specular to this surface, you get a Specular stretched in the perpendicular direction.

This recipe will introduce you to the concept of augmenting your Specular highlights to achieve different types of brushed surfaces. In future recipes, we will look at the ways in which we can use the concepts of this recipe to achieve other effects, such as stretched reflections and hair, but here, you are going to learn the fundamentals of the technique first. We will be using this shader as a reference for our own custom Anisotropic Shader: `http://wiki.unity3d.com/index.php?title=Anisotropic_Highlight_Shader`. The following diagram shows examples of different types of Specular effects that you can achieve using Anisotropic Shaders in Unity:

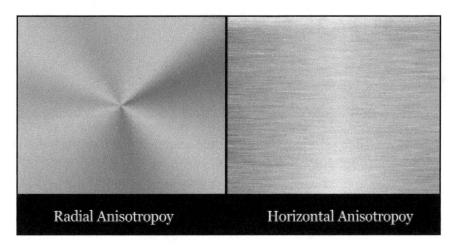

Radial Anisotropoy   Horizontal Anisotropoy

Getting ready

Let's start this recipe by creating a shader, its material, and some lights for our scene:

1. Create a new scene with some objects and lights so that we can visually debug our shader. In this case, we will be using some capsules, a sphere, and a cylinder.

2. Then create a new shader and material, and hook them up to your objects:

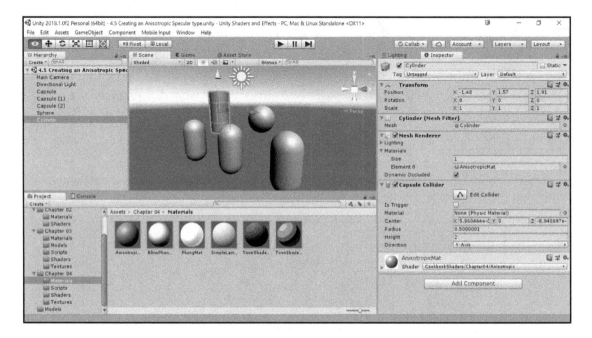

3. Lastly, we will need some sort of normal map that will indicate the directionality of our Anisotropic Specular highlight.

4. The following screenshot shows the Anisotropy normal map we will be using for this recipe. It is available from this book's support page at `https://www.packtpub.com/books/content/support`:

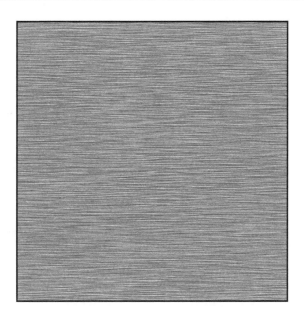

How to do it...

To create an Anisotropic effect, we need to make the following changes to the shader previously created:

1. We first need to remove the old properties and then add the properties that we are going to need for our shader. These will allow a lot of artistic control over the final appearance of the surface:

```
Properties
{
    _MainTint ("Diffuse Tint", Color) = (1,1,1,1)
    _MainTex ("Base (RGB)", 2D) = "white" {}
    _SpecularColor ("Specular Color", Color) = (1,1,1,1)
    _Specular ("Specular Amount", Range(0,1)) = 0.5
    _SpecPower ("Specular Power", Range(0,1)) = 0.5
    _AnisoDir ("Anisotropic Direction", 2D) = "" {}
    _AnisoOffset ("Anisotropic Offset", Range(-1,1)) = -0.2
}
```

2. We then need to make the connection between our `Properties` block and our `SubShader{}` block so that we can use the data being provided by the `Properties` block:

```
sampler2D _MainTex;
sampler2D _AnisoDir;
float4 _MainTint;
float4 _SpecularColor;
float _AnisoOffset;
float _Specular;
float _SpecPower;
```

3. Now we can create our `Lighting` function that will produce the correct Anisotropic effect on our surface. We will use the following code for this:

```
fixed4 LightingAnisotropic(SurfaceAnisoOutput s, fixed3
  lightDir, half3 viewDir, fixed atten)
{
  fixed3 halfVector = normalize(normalize(lightDir) +
    normalize(viewDir));
  float NdotL = saturate(dot(s.Normal, lightDir));

  fixed HdotA = dot(normalize(s.Normal + s.AnisoDirection),
    halfVector);  float aniso = max(0, sin(radians((HdotA +
_AnisoOffset) *
    180)));  float spec = saturate(pow(aniso, s.Gloss * 128) *
    s.Specular);

  fixed4 c;
  c.rgb = ((s.Albedo * _LightColor0.rgb * NdotL) +
    (_LightColor0.rgb * _SpecularColor.rgb * spec)) *
    atten;
  c.a = s.Alpha;
  return c;
}
```

4. In order to use this new `Lighting` function, we need to tell the subshader's `#pragma` statement to look for it instead of using one of the built-in `Lighting` functions:

```
CGPROGRAM
#pragma surface surf Anisotropic
```

5. We have also given the Anisotropic normal map its own UVs by declaring the following code in the `struct Input`. This isn't entirely necessary as we could just use the UVs from the main texture, but this gives us independent control over the tiling of our brushed metal effect so that we can scale it to any size we want:

```
struct Input
{
  float2 uv_MainTex;
  float2 uv_AnisoDir;
};
```

6. We also need to add the `struct SurfaceAnisoOutput`:

```
struct SurfaceAnisoOutput
{
  fixed3 Albedo;
  fixed3 Normal;
  fixed3 Emission;
  fixed3 AnisoDirection;
  half Specular;
  fixed Gloss;
  fixed Alpha;
};
```

7. Finally, we need to use the `surf()` function to pass the correct data to our `Lighting` function. Hence, we will get the per-pixel information from our Anisotropic normal map and set our Specular parameters as follows:

```
void surf(Input IN, inout SurfaceAnisoOutput o)
{
  half4 c = tex2D(_MainTex, IN.uv_MainTex) * _MainTint;
  float3 anisoTex = UnpackNormal(tex2D(_AnisoDir,
    IN.uv_AnisoDir));

  o.AnisoDirection = anisoTex;
  o.Specular = _Specular;
  o.Gloss = _SpecPower;
  o.Albedo = c.rgb;
  o.Alpha = c.a;
}
```

8. Save your script and return to the Unity editor. Select the `AnisotropicMat` material and assign the **Anisotropic Direction** property to the texture we talked about in the *Getting ready* section of this recipe. Afterward, adjust the Anisotopic `Offset` property using the slider and notice the changes.

The Anisotropic normal map allows us to give the surface direction and helps us disperse the Specular highlight around the surface. The following screenshot demonstrates the result of our Anisotropic Shader:

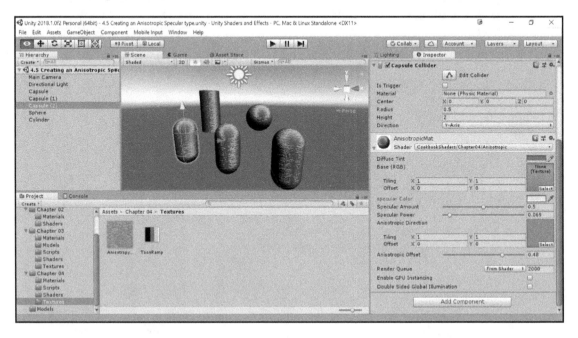

How it works...

Let's break down this shader into its core components and explain why we are getting the effect. We will mostly be covering the custom Lighting function here, as the rest of the shader should be pretty self-explanatory at this point.

We first start by declaring our own `SurfaceAnisoOutput struct`. We need to do this in order to get the per-pixel information from the Anisotropic normal map, and the only way we can do this in a Surface Shader is to use a `tex2D()` function in the `surf()` function. The following code shows the custom surface output structure used in our shader:

```
struct SurfaceAnisoOutput
{
    fixed3 Albedo;
    fixed3 Normal;
    fixed3 Emission;
    fixed3 AnisoDirection;
    half Specular;
```

```
    fixed Gloss;
    fixed Alpha;
};
```

We can use the `SurfaceAnisoOutput` struct as a way of interacting between the Lighting function and the surface function. In our case, we are storing the per-pixel texture information in the variable called `anisoTex` in our `surf()` function and then passing this data to the `SurfaceAnisoOutput` struct by storing it in the `AnisoDirection` variable. Once we have this, we can use the per-pixel information in the `Lighting` function using `s.AnisoDirection`.

With this data connection set up, we can move on to our actual lighting calculations. This begins by getting the usual out of the way, the half vector, so that we don't have to do the full reflection calculation and diffuse lighting, which is the vertex normal dotted with the light vector or direction. This is done in Cg with the following lines:

```
fixed3 halfVector = normalize(normalize(lightDir) +
                    normalize(viewDir));
float NdotL = saturate(dot(s.Normal, lightDir));
```

Then, we start the actual modification to the Specular to get the right look. We first dot the normalized sum of the vertex normal and per-pixel vectors from our Anisotropic normal map with the `halfVector` calculated in the previous step. This gives us a float value that gives a value of 1 as the surface normal, which is modified by the Anisotropic normal map as it becomes parallel with `halfVector` and 0 as it is perpendicular. Finally, we modify this value with a `sin()` function so that we can basically get a darker middle highlight and ultimately a ring effect based on `halfVector`. All the previously mentioned operations are summarized in the following two lines of Cg code:

```
fixed HdotA = dot(normalize(s.Normal + s.AnisoDirection),
                halfVector);
float aniso = max(0, sin(radians((HdotA + _AnisoOffset) * 180)));
```

Finally, we scale the effect of the `aniso` value by taking it to a power of `s.Gloss`, and then globally decrease its strength by multiplying it by `s.Specular`:

```
float spec = saturate(pow(aniso, s.Gloss * 128) * s.Specular);
```

This effect is great for creating more advanced metal type surfaces, especially the ones that are brushed and appear to have directionality to them. It also works well for hair or any sort of soft surface with directionality to it. The following screenshot shows the result of displaying the final Anisotropic lighting calculation:

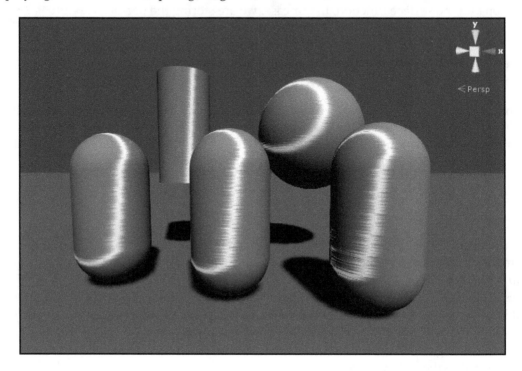

5
Physically-Based Rendering

Introduced in Unity 5, PBR is a shading model that seeks to render graphics in a way that acts in a similar manner to how light works in the real world. Previous chapters have repeatedly mentioned it without revealing too much about it. If you want to understand not only how PBR works, but how to make the most out of it, this is the chapter you should read. In this chapter, you will learn the following recipes:

- Understanding the metallic setup
- Adding transparency to PBR
- Creating mirrors and reflective surfaces
- Baking lights in your scene

Introduction

All the lighting models encountered in `Chapter 4`, *Understanding Lighting Models*, were very primitive descriptions of how light behaves. The most important aspect during their making was *efficiency*. Real-time shading is expensive, and techniques such as Lambertian or BlinnPhong are a compromise between computational cost and realism.

Having a more powerful GPU has allowed us to write progressively more sophisticated lighting models and rendering engines, with the aim of simulating how light actually behaves. This is, in a nutshell, the philosophy behind PBR. As the name suggests, it tries to get as close as possible to the physics behind the processes that give a unique look at each material. Despite this, the term PBR has been widely used in marketing campaigns and is more of a synonym for **state-of-the-art rendering** rather than a well-defined technique.

Unity implements PBR in two main ways:

- The first is a completely new lighting model (called Standard). Surface Shaders allow developers to specify the physical properties of a material, but they do not impose actual physical constraints on them. PBR fills this by gap using a lighting model that enforces principles of physics such as **energy conservation** (an object cannot reflect more light than the amount it receives), **microsurface scattering** (rough surfaces reflect light more erratically compared to smooth ones), **Fresnel reflectance** (specular reflections appear at grazing angles), and **surface occlusion** (the darkening of corners and other geometries that are hard to light). All these aspects, and many others, are used to calculate the standard lighting model.
- The second aspect that makes PBR so realistic is called **Global Illumination** (**GI**) and is the simulation of physically-based light transport. It means that objects are not drawn in the scene as if they were separate entities. They all contribute to the final rendering as light can reflect on them before hitting something else. This aspect is not captured in the shaders themselves, but is an essential part of how the rendering engine works. Unfortunately, accurately simulating how light rays actually bounce over surfaces in real time is beyond the capabilities of modern GPUs. Unity makes some clever optimizations that allow us to retain visual fidelity without sacrificing performance. Some of the most advanced techniques (such as reflections), however, require user input.

All of these aspects will be covered in this chapter. It is important to remember that PBR and GI do not automatically guarantee that your game will be photorealistic. Achieving photorealism is a very challenging task and, like every art, it requires great expertise and exceptional skills.

Understanding the metallic setup

Unity provides three different types of PBR shaders; they are referred to in the drop-down menu of the material's **Inspector** tab as **Standard**, **Standard (Roughness Setup)**, and **Standard (Specular setup)**. The main difference is that **Standard** and **Standard (Roughness Setup)** expose the **Metallic** property, but **Standard** contains a **Smoothness** property while the second replaces **Smoothness** with **Roughness**. **Standard (Specular setup)** contains **Smoothness**, but replaces the **Metallic** property with **Specular**. **Smoothness** and **Roughness** are opposites of each other, so a 1 **Smoothness** means 0 **Roughness** and vice versa. You can generally get the same result no matter which shader you use, so it mostly comes down to personal preference.

These setups represent different ways in which you can initialize PBR materials. One of the concepts that has driven PBR is the ability to provide meaningful, physically-related properties that artists and developers can tweak and play with. The properties of some materials are easier to represent, indicating how *metallic* they are. For others, it is more important to specify how they reflect lights directly through its **specularity**. This recipe will show you how to use the **metallic setup** effectively. It's important to remember that the metallic workflow is not just for metallic materials; it is a way of defining how materials will look according to how metallic or non-metallic their surface is. Despite being presented as two different types of shaders, both **Metallic** and **Specular** setups are generally equally expressive. As shown in the Unity documentation at `http://docs.unity3d.com/Manual/StandardShaderMetallicVsSpecular.html` and mentioned earlier, the same materials can usually be recreated with both setups (see the following screenshot):

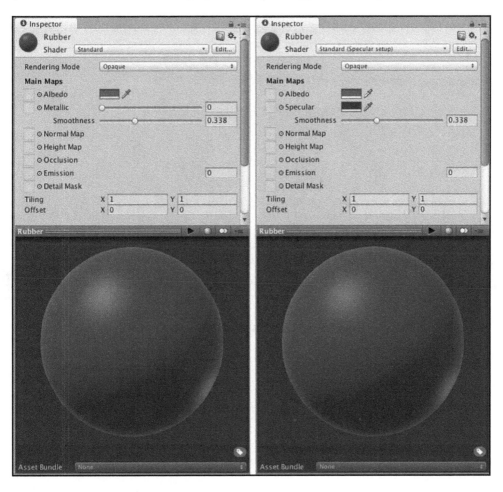

Getting ready

This recipe will use the Standard Shader, so there is no need to create a new one. The steps to start the recipe are as follows:

1. Create a new material (`MetallicMat`).

2. From its **Inspector**, make sure that **Standard** is selected from its **Shader** drop-down menu.

3. You will also need a textured 3D model. Our basic character we've been using previously will work perfectly. Drag and drop it into the scene. Afterward, drag and drop the `MetallicMat` material onto each of the parts of the character. Also, assign the texture for the material to the **Albedo** property:

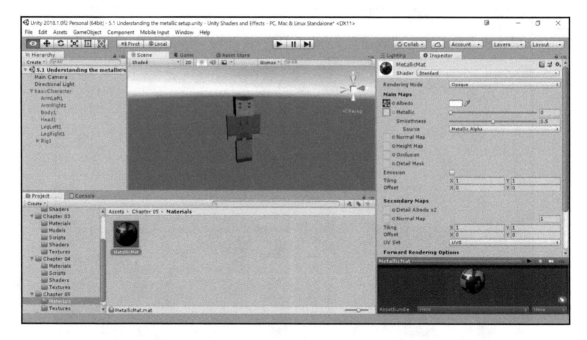

How to do it...

There are two main textures that need to be configured in the Standard Shader: **Albedo** and **Metallic**. To use the metallic workflow effectively, we need to initialize these maps correctly:

1. The **Albedo** map should be initialized with the unlit texture of the 3D model.

2. To create the **Metallic** map, start by duplicating the file for your **Albedo** map. You can do this by selecting the map from the **Project** tab and pressing *Ctrl + D*.

3. Use white (#ffffff) to color the regions of the map that correspond to materials that are made of pure metal. Use black (#000000) for all the other colors. Shades of grey should be used for dusty, weathered, or worn-out metal surfaces, rust, scratched paint, and so on. As a matter of fact, Unity uses only the red channel to store the metallic value; the green and blue ones are ignored.

4. Use the alpha channel of the image to provide information about the **Smoothness** of the material:

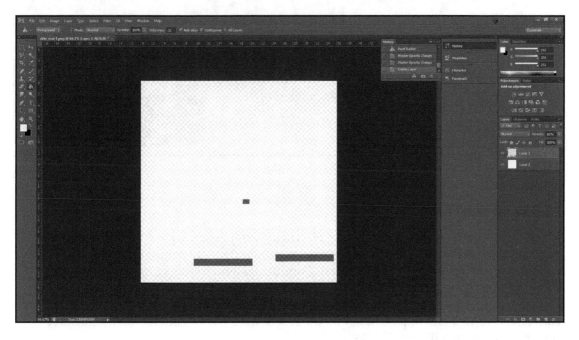

An example of a Metallic map opened in Photoshop

For our simple character, the belt and the little ends of the hoodie are the only parts we need to be metallic. I've also made the opacity around 55% for the main character, with the belt having a higher opacity of 80%:

5. Assign the **Metallic** map to the material. The **Metallic** slider will disappear as these two properties are now controlled by the map. You may use the **Smoothness** slider to provide a modifier on the map you've provided:

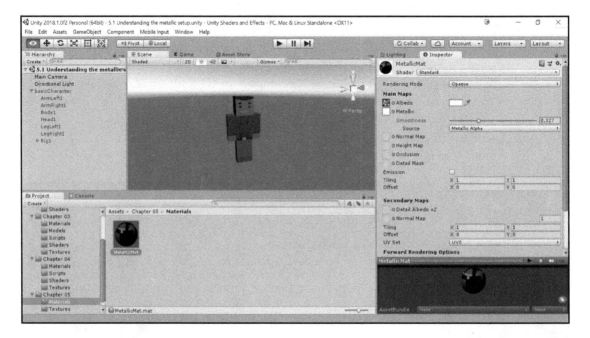

How it works...

Metals are known for the conducting of electricity; light is in the form of electromagnetic waves, meaning that almost all metals behave in a similar way compared to non-conductors (often referred as **insulators**). Conductors tend to reflect most photons (70-100%), resulting in high reflectance. The remaining light is absorbed, rather than diffused, suggesting that conductors have a very dark diffuse component. Insulators, conversely, have a low reflectance (4%); the rest of the light is scattered on the surface, contributing to their diffused looks.

In the Standard Shader, purely metallic materials have dark diffuse components, and the color of their specular reflections is determined by the **Albedo** map. Conversely, the diffuse component of purely non-metallic materials is determined by the **Albedo** map; the color of their specular highlights is determined by the color of the incoming light. Following these principles allows the metallic workflow to combine the **Albedo** and specular into the **Albedo** map, enforcing physically-accurate behaviors. This also allows for saving more space, resulting in a significant speed increase at the expenses of reduced control over the look of your materials.

See also

For more information about the metallic setup, you can refer to these links:

- **Calibration chart**: How to calibrate a metallic material (`http://blogs.unity3d.com/wp-content/uploads/2014/11/UnityMetallicChart.png`)
- **Material chart**: How to initialize the Standard Shader parameters for common materials (`http://docs.unity3d.com/Manual/StandardShaderMaterialCharts.html`)
- **Quixel MEGASCANS**: A vast library of materials, including textures and PBR parameters (`https://megascans.se/`)
- **PBR Texture Conversion**: How traditional shaders can be converted to PBR shaders (`http://www.marmoset.co/toolbag/learn/pbr-conversion`)
- **Substance Designer**: A node-based software to work with PBR (`https://www.allegorithmic.com/products/substance-designer`)
- **The Theory of Physically-Based Rendering**: A complete guide about PBR (`https://www.allegorithmic.com/pbr-guide`)

Adding transparency to PBR

Transparency is such an important aspect in games that the Standard Shader supports three different ways of doing it. This recipe is useful if you need to have realistic materials with transparent or semi-transparent properties. Glasses, bottles, windows, and crystals are good candidates for PBR transparent shaders. This is because you can still have all the realism introduced by PBR with the addition of a transparent or translucent effect. If you need transparency for something different, such as UI elements or pixel art, there are more efficient alternatives that are explored in the *Creating a transparent material* recipe in `Chapter 3, Surface Shaders and Texture Mapping`.

In order to have a transparent standard material, changing the alpha channel of its **Albedo** color property is not enough. Unless you properly set its **Rendering Mode**, your material will not appear transparent.

Getting ready

This recipe will use the Standard Shader, so there is no need to create a new one:

1. Create a new material (`TransparencyMat`).
2. Make sure that the **Shader** property is set to either **Standard** or **Standard (Specular setup)** from the material's **Inspector** tab.
3. Assign the newly created material to the 3D object that you want to be transparent:

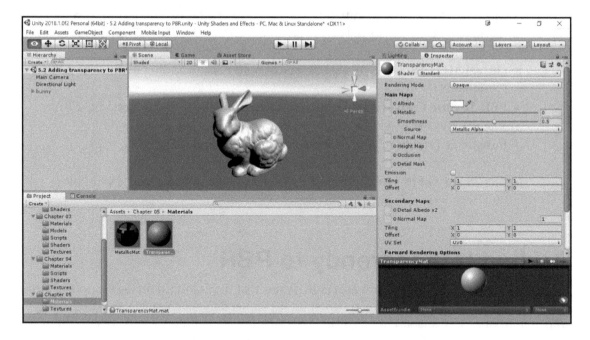

How to do it...

The Standard Shader provides three different types of transparencies. Despite being very similar, they have subtle differences and fit in different contexts.

Semi-transparent materials

Some materials such as clear plastics, crystal, and glass are semi-transparent. This means that they both require all the realistic effects of PBR (such as specular highlights and Fresnel refraction and reflection), but allow the geometry behind an object with the material attached to be seen. If this is what you need, perform the following steps:

1. From the material's **Inspector** tab, set **Rendering Mode** to **Transparent**.
2. The amount of transparency is determined by the alpha channel of the **Albedo** color or the **Albedo** map (if any). If you click on the box to the right of the **Albedo** section, you'll bring up a **Color** menu. Adjusting the **A** channel will make the item more visible or less visible:

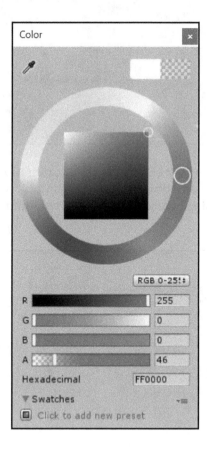

3. Setting the **A** channel to 44 provides the following effect:

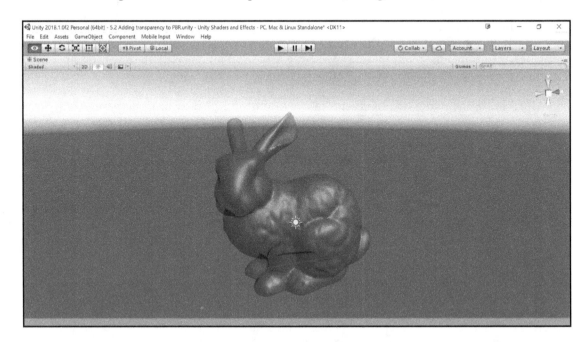

4. The following screenshot shows the Unity calibration scene with four different highly polished plastic spheres. From left to right, their transparency is increasing. The last sphere is fully transparent, but retains all the added effects of PBR:

The Unity Calibration Scene can be downloaded for free from the Asset Store at `https://www.assetstore.unity3d.com/en/#!/content/25422`.

The **Transparent** rendering mode is perfect for windows, bottles, gems, and headsets.

You should notice that many transparent materials don't usually project shadows. On top of this, the **Metallic** and **Smoothness** properties of a material can interfere with the transparency effect. A mirror-like surface can have the alpha set to zero, but if it reflects all the incoming light, it won't appear transparent.

Fading objects

Sometimes, you want an object to fully disappear with a fading effect. In this case, specular reflections and Fresnel refraction and reflection should disappear as well. When a fading object is fully transparent, it should also be invisible. To do this, perform the following steps:

1. From the material's **Inspector** tab, set **Rendering Mode** to **Fade**.
2. As before, use the alpha channel of the **Albedo** color or map to determine the final transparency:

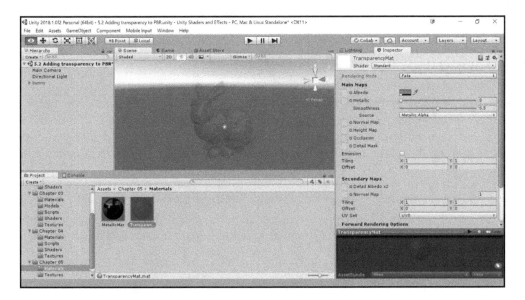

3. The following screenshot shows four fading spheres. It is clear from the screenshot that the PBR effects fade with the sphere as well. As you can see in the following image, the last one on the right is almost invisible:

4. This rendering mode works best for non-realistic objects, such as holograms, laser rays, faux lights, ghosts, and particle effects.

Solid geometries with holes

Most of the materials encountered in a game are solid, meaning that they don't allow light to pass through them. At the same time, many objects have a very complex (yet flat) geometry. Modeling leaves and grass with 3D objects is often overkilled. A more efficient approach is to use a quad (rectangle) with a leaf texture. While the leaf itself is solid, the rest of the texture should be fully transparent. If this is what you want, then perform the following steps:

1. From the material's **Inspector** tab, set **Rendering Mode** to **Cutout**.
2. Use the **Alpha Cutoff** slider to determine the cutoff threshold. All the pixels in the **Albedo** map with an alpha value equal to or less than **Alpha Cutoff** will be hidden.

The following image, taken from the *Unity Official Tutorials* on PBR (`https://www.youtube.com/watch?v=fD_ho_ofY6A`), shows you how the effect of the **Cutout** rendering mode can be used to create a hole in the geometry:

It's worth noticing that **Cutout** does not allow the back of the geometry to be seen. In the previous example, you could not see the inner volume of the sphere. If you require such an effect, you need to create your own shader and make sure that the back geometry is not culled.

See also

- As mentioned previously, some of the examples in this recipe have been created using the Unity **Shader Calibration Scene**, which is freely available in the Asset Store at `https://www.assetstore.unity3d.com/en/#!/content/25422`.
- More information about **Albedo** and **Transparency** can be found at `http://docs.unity3d.com/Manual/StandardShaderMaterialParameterAlbedoColor.html`.

Creating mirrors and reflective surfaces

Specular materials reflect lights when objects are viewed from certain angles. Unfortunately, even the Fresnel reflection, which is one of the most accurate models, does not correctly reflect lights from nearby objects. The lighting models examined in the previous chapters took into account only light sources, but ignored light that is reflected from other surfaces. With what you've learned about shaders so far, making a mirror is simply not possible.

Global illumination makes this possible by providing PBR shaders with information about their surroundings. This allows objects to have not just specular highlights, but also real reflections, which depend on the other objects around them. Real-time reflections are very costly and require manual setting up and tweaking in order to work. When done properly, they can be used to create mirror-like surfaces, as seen in the following diagram:

Getting ready

This recipe will not feature any new shader. Quite the opposite; most of the work is done directly in the editor. Perform the following steps:

1. Create a new scene.

2. Create a quad (**GameObject** | **3D Object** | **Quad**), which will serve as a mirror. I've rotated it to -65 in the Y axis to make it easy to see.

3. Create a new material (`MirrorMat`) and attach it to the mirror.

4. Place the quad in a scene with other objects.

5. Create a new reflection probe from **GameObject** | **Light** | **Reflection Probe** and place it in front of the quad:

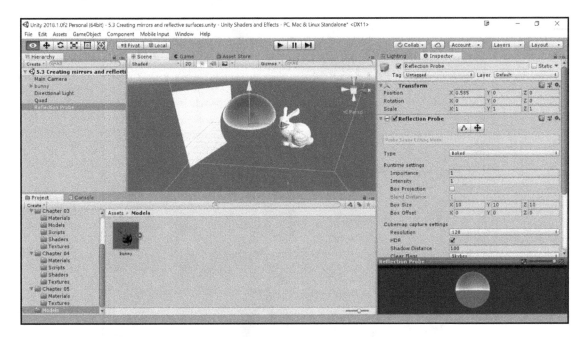

How to do it...

If the preceding steps have been followed correctly, you should have a quad in the middle of your scene, close to a reflection probe. In order to make it in a mirror, some changes need to be made:

1. Change the shader of the material to **Standard** and its **Rendering Mode** to **Opaque**.

2. Change its **Metallic** and **Smoothness** properties to one. You should see the material reflecting the sky more clearly.

3. Select the reflection probe and change its **Size** and **Probe Origin** until it is in front of the quad and it encloses all the objects that you want to reflect.

4. To make the item more clear under the **Cubemap capture settings**, change the **Resolution** to 2048.

5. Finally, change its **Type** to **Realtime** and the **Refresh Mode** to **Every frame**. Also, make sure that **Culling Mask** is set to **Everything**.

6. Your reflection probe should be configured, as shown in the following screenshot:

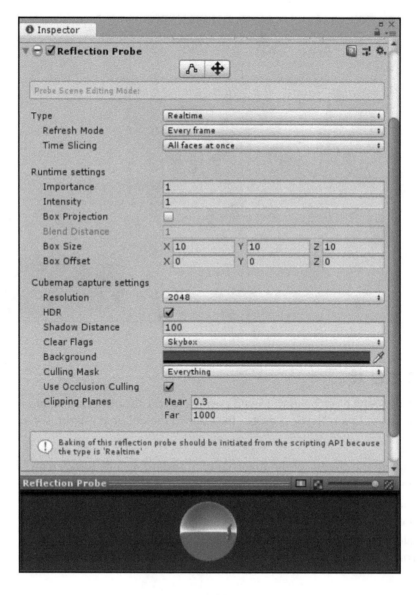

7. Using these settings, you should see something similar to this:

You may notice that the bunny seems larger in the reflection rather than what's beside it. If your probe is used for a real mirror, you should check the **Box Projection** flag (in this example, setting the box size to 1, 1, 1 does a pretty good job of looking like a mirror). If it is used for other reflective surfaces, such as shiny pieces of metal or glass tables, you can uncheck it.

How it works...

When a shader wants information about its surroundings, it is usually provided in a structure called **cube maps**. They have been briefly mentioned in Chapter 2, *Creating Your First Shader*, as one of the shader property types, among Color, 2D, Float, and Vector. Loosely speaking, cube maps are the 3D equivalent of 2D textures; they represent a 360-degree view of the world, as seen from a center point.

Unity previews cube maps with a spherical projection, as seen in the following diagram:

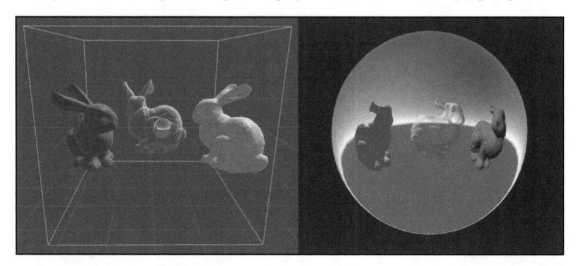

When cube maps are attached with a camera, they are referred to as **skyboxes**, as they are used to provide a way to reflect the sky. They can be used to reflect geometries that are not in the actual scene, such as nebulae, clouds, and stars.

The reason why they are called cube maps is because of the way they are created: a cube map is made up of six different textures, each one attached to the face of a cube. You can create a cube map manually or delegate it to a **reflection probe**. You can imagine a reflection probe as a collection of six cameras, creating a 360-degree mapping of the surrounding area. This also gives you an idea as to why probes are so expensive. By creating one in our scene, we allow Unity to know which objects are around the mirror. If you need more reflective surfaces, you can add multiple probes. You need no further action for the reflection probes to work. The Standard Shaders will use them automatically.

You should notice that when they are set to **Realtime**, they render their cube map at the beginning of every frame. There is a trick to make this faster; if you know that part of the geometry that you want to reflect does not move, you can bake the reflection. This means that Unity can calculate the reflection before starting the game, allowing more precise (and computationally expensive) calculations. In order to do this, your reflection probe must be set to **Baked** and will work only for objects that are flagged as **Static**. Static objects cannot move or change, which makes them perfect for terrain, buildings, and props. Every time a static object is moved, Unity will regenerate the cube maps for its baked reflection probes. This might take a few minutes to several hours.

You can mix **Realtime** and **Baked** probes to increase the realism of your game. Baked probes will provide very high-quality reflections, environmental reflections, while the real-time ones can be used to move objects such as cars or mirrors. The *Baking lights in your scene* section will explain in detail how light baking works.

See also

If you are interested in learning more about reflection probes, you should check these links:

- Unity manual about the Reflection Probe: `http://docs.unity3d.com/Manual/class-ReflectionProbe.html`
- Box projection and other advanced Reflection Probe settings: `https://docs.unity3d.com/Manual/AdvancedRefProbe.html`

Baking lights in your scene

Rendering lighting is a very expensive process. Even with state-of-the-art GPUs, accurately calculating the **light transport** (which is how light bounces between surfaces) can take hours. In order to make this process feasible for games, real-time rendering is essential. Modern engines compromise between realism and efficiency; most of the computation is done beforehand in a process called **light baking**. This recipe will explain how light baking works and how you can get the most out of it.

Getting ready

Light baking requires you to have a scene ready. It should have geometries and, obviously, lights. For this recipe, we will rely on Unity's standard features so there is no need to create additional shaders or materials. We will be reusing the map that we used previously in `Chapter 1`, *Post Processing Stack*. For better control, you might want to access the **Lighting** window. If you don't see it, select **Window | Lighting | Settings** from the menu and dock it where it is more convenient for you.

How to do it...

Light baking requires some manual configuration. There are three essential, yet independent, steps that you need to take.

Configuring the static geometry

These steps must be followed for the configuration:

1. Identify all the objects in your scene that do not change position, size, and material. Possible candidates are buildings, walls, terrain, props, trees, and others. In our case, it will be all of the objects aside from the `FPSController` and its children.

2. Select these objects and check the **Static** box from the **Inspector** tab, as shown in the following screenshot. If any of the selected objects have children, Unity will ask if you want them to be considered static as well. If they meet the requirements (fixed position, size, and material), select **Yes, change children** in the pop-up box:

> If a light qualifies as a static object but illuminates non-static geometry, make sure that its **Baking** property is set to **Mixed**. If it will affect only static objects, set it to **Baked**.

Configuring the light probes

There are objects in your game that will move, such as the main character, enemies, and the other **non-playable characters** (**NPCs**). If they enter a static region that is illuminated, you might want to surround it with light probes. To do this, follow the given steps:

1. From the menu, navigate to **GameObject** | **Light** | **Light Probe Group**. A new object called **Light Probe Group** will appear in **Hierarchy**.

2. Once selected, eight interconnected spheres will appear. Click and move them around the scene so that they enclose the static region in which your characters can enter. The following screenshot shows an example of how light probes can be used to enclose the volume of a static office space:

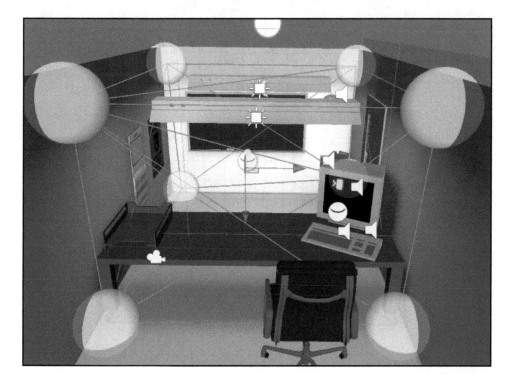

For our example, it would just be the center area the player is able to enter:

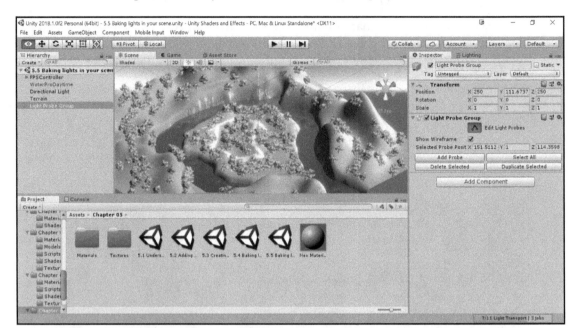

3. Select the moving objects that will enter the light probe region.
4. From their **Inspector**, expand their **renderer component** (usually **Mesh Renderer**) and make sure that **Light Probes** is not set to **Off checked** (see the following screenshot):

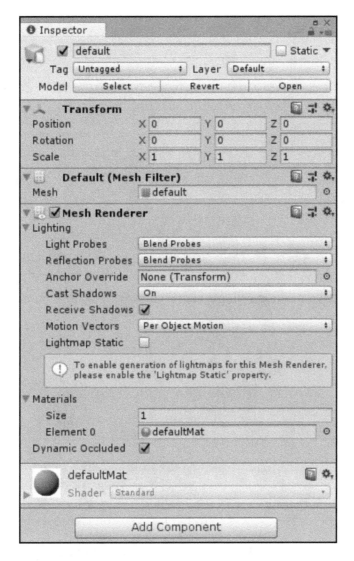

Deciding where and when to use light probes is a critical problem; more information about this can be found in the *How it works...* section for this recipe.

Baking the lights

To bake the lights, follow the given steps:

1. First, select the lights you'd like to bake. Confirm from the **Inspector** tab that the **Mode** is set to **Baked** in the **Light** component:

2. To finally bake the lights, open the **Lighting** window by going to **Window** | **Lighting** | **Settings**. Once there, select the **Global Maps** tab.

3. If the **Auto Generate** checkbox is enabled, Unity will automatically execute the baking process in the background. If not, click on **Generate Lighting**.

Light baking can take several hours even for a relatively small scene. If you are constantly moving static objects or lights, Unity will restart the process from scratch, causing a severe slowdown in the editor. You can uncheck the **Auto** checkbox from the **Lighting** | **Lightmaps** | **Settings** tab to prevent this so that you can decide when to start the process manually.

How it works...

The most complicated part of rendering is the light transport. During this phase, the GPU calculates how the rays of light bounce between objects. If an object and its lights don't move, this calculation can be done only once as it will never change during the game. Flagging an object as **Static** is how to tell Unity that such an optimization can be made.

Loosely speaking, light baking refers to the process of calculating the global illumination of a static object and saving it in what is called a **lightmap**. Once baking is completed, lightmaps can be seen in the **Global Maps** tab of the **Lighting** window:

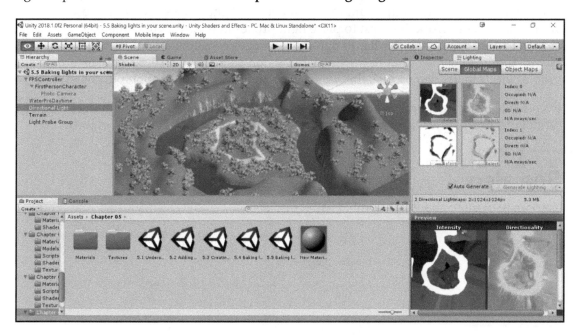

Light baking comes at a great expense: memory. Every static surface is, in fact, retextured so that it already includes its lighting condition. Let's imagine that you have a forest of trees, all sharing the same texture. Once they are made static, each tree will have its very own texture. Light baking not only increases the size of your game, but can take a lot of texture memory if used indiscriminately.

The second aspect introduced in this recipe is **light probing**. Light baking produces extremely high-quality results for static geometries, but does not work on moving objects. If your character is entering a static region, it can look somehow *detached* from the environment. Its shading will not match the surroundings, resulting in an aesthetically unpleasant result. Other objects, such as **skinned mesh renderers**, will not receive global illumination even if made static. Baking lights in real-time is not possible, although light probes offer an effective alternative. Every light probe samples the global illumination at a specific point in space. A light probe group can sample several points in space, allowing the interpolation of global illumination within a specific volume. This allows us to cast a better light on moving objects, even despite the fact that global illumination has been calculated only for a few points. It is important to remember that light probes need to enclose a volume in order to work. It is best to place light probes in regions where there is a sudden change in light conditions. Similar to lightmaps, probes consume memory and should be placed wisely; remember that they exist only for non-static geometry. Since there are no visible objects in the demoscene, this was done purely for demonstration purposes.

Even while using light probes, there are a few aspects that Unity's global illumination cannot capture. Non-static objects, for instance, cannot reflect light on other objects.

See also

You can read more about light probes at `http://docs.unity3d.com/Manual/LightProbes.html`.

6
Vertex Functions

The term shader originates from the fact that Cg has been used mainly to simulate realistic lighting conditions (shadows) on 3D models. Despite this, shaders are now much more than that. They not only define the way the objects are going to look, they can also redefine their shapes entirely. If you want to learn how to manipulate the geometry of a 3D object via shaders, this is the chapter for you.

In this chapter, you will learn the following recipes:

- Accessing a vertex color in a Surface Shader
- Animating vertices in a Surface Shader
- Extruding your models
- Implementing a snow shader
- Implementing a volumetric explosion

Introduction

In Chapter 2, *Creating Your First Shader*, we explained that 3D models are not just a collection of triangles. Each vertex can contain data that is essential to render the model itself correctly. This chapter will explore how to access this information in order to use it in a shader. We will also explore in detail how the geometry of an object can be deformed simply using Cg code.

Accessing a vertex color in a Surface Shader

Let's begin this chapter by taking a look at how we can access the information of a model's vertex using the vertex function in a Surface Shader. This will arm us with the knowledge to start utilizing the elements contained within a model's vertex in order to create really useful and visually appealing effects.

A vertex in a vertex function can return information about itself that we need to be aware of. You can actually retrieve the vertices' normal directions as a float3 value and the position of the vertex as float3, and you can even store color values in each vertex and return that color as float4. This is what we will take a look at in this recipe. We need to see how to store color information and retrieve this stored color information inside each vertex of a Surface Shader.

Getting ready

In order to write this shader, we need to prepare a few assets.

In order to view the colors of a vertex, we need to have a model that has had color applied to its vertices. While you could use Unity to apply colors, you would have to write a tool to allow an individual to apply the colors or write some scripts to achieve the color application.

In the case of this recipe, you can use a 3D modeling tool such as Maya or Blender to apply the colors to our model. There is a model available in the example code provided with the book in the Chapter 06 | Models folder (VertexColorObject.fbx) that you can obtain at the book's *Support* page at https://www.packtpub.com/books/content/support.

The following steps will set us up to create this Vertex Shader:

1. Create a new scene and place the imported model (VertexColorObject) in the scene.
2. Create a new **Shader** (SimpleVertexColor) and **Material** (SimpleVertexColorMat).
3. When completed, assign the shader to the material and then the material to the imported model.

Your scene should now look similar to the following screenshot:

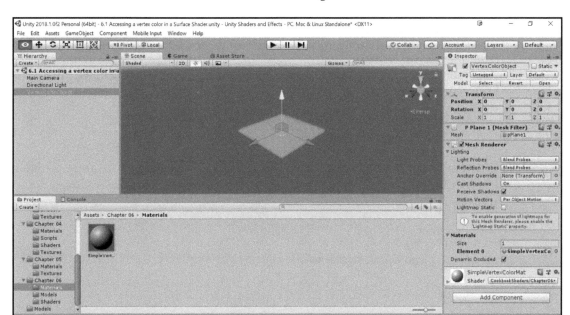

How to do it...

With our scene, shader, and material created and ready to go, we can begin to write the code for our shader. Launch the shader by double-clicking on it in the **Project** tab in the Unity editor. Perform the following steps:

1. As we are creating a very simple shader, we will not need to include any properties in our `Properties` block. We will still include a `Global Color Tint`, just to stay consistent with the other shaders in this book. Enter the following code in the `Properties` block of your shader:

```
Properties
{
    _MainTint("Global Color Tint", Color) = (1,1,1,1)
}
```

2. This next step tells Unity that we will be including a vertex function in our shader:

```
CGPROGRAM
#pragma surface surf Lambert vertex:vert
```

3. As usual, if we have included properties in our Properties block, we must make sure to create a corresponding variable in our CGPROGRAM statement. Enter the following code just below the #pragma statement:

```
float4 _MainTint;
```

4. We now turn our attention to the Input struct. We need to add a new variable in order for our surf() function to access the data given to us by our vert() function:

```
struct Input
{
    float2 uv_MainTex;
    float4 vertColor;
};
```

5. Now we can write our simple vert() function to gain access to the colors stored in each vertex of our mesh:

```
void vert(inout appdata_full v, out Input o)
{
    UNITY_INITIALIZE_OUTPUT(Input,o);
    o.vertColor = v.color;
}
```

6. Finally, we can use the vertex color data from our Input struct to be assigned to the o.Albedo parameters in the built-in SurfaceOutput struct:

```
void surf (Input IN, inout SurfaceOutput o)
{
    o.Albedo = IN.vertColor.rgb * _MainTint.rgb;
}
```

7. With our code completed, we can now re-enter the Unity editor and let the shader compile. If all goes well, you should see something similar to the following screenshot:

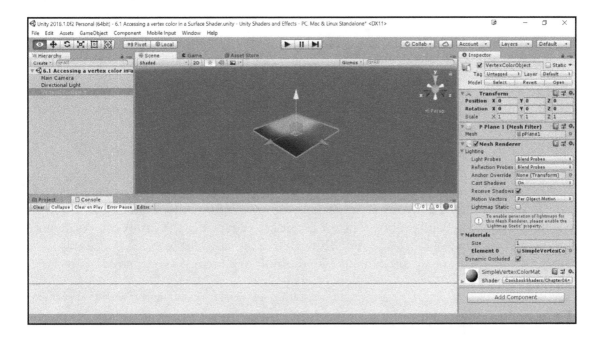

How it works...

Unity provides us with a way to access the vertex information of the model to which a shader is attached. This gives us the power to modify things such as the vertices' position and color. With this recipe, we have imported a mesh from Maya (though just about any 3D software application can be used), where vertex colors were added to Verts. You'll notice that by importing the model, the default material will not display the vertex colors. We actually have to write a shader to extract the vertex color and display it on the surface of the model. Unity provides us with a lot of built-in functionality when using Surface Shaders, which makes the process of extracting this vertex information quick and efficient.

Our first task is to tell Unity that we will be using a vertex function when creating our shader. We do this by adding the vertex:vert parameter to the #pragma statement of CGPROGRAM. This automatically makes Unity look for a vertex function named vert() when it goes to compile the shader. If it doesn't find one, Unity will throw a compiling error and ask you to add a vert() function to your shader.

This brings us to our next step. We have to actually code the vert() function, as seen in *step 5*. We first use a built-in macro to make sure that the 0 variable is initialized to 0 if it doesn't have anything that is a requirement if you are targeting DirectX 11 or above.

For more information on the macro, as well as all of the other macros that ShaderLab has to offer, check out: `https://docs.unity3d.com/Manual/SL-BuiltinMacros.html`.

By having this function, we can access the built-in data struct called `appdata_full`. This built-in struct is where the vertex information is stored. So, we then extract the vertex color information by passing it to our `Input struct` by adding the code, `o.vertColor = v.color`.

The o variable represents our `Input struct` and the v variable is our `appdata_full vertex` data. In this case, we are simply taking the color information from the `appdata_full` struct and putting it in our `Input struct`. Once the vertex color is in our Input struct, we can use it in our `surf()` function. In the case of this recipe, we simply apply the color to the o.Albedo parameter to the built-in `SurfaceOutput` struct.

There's more...

You can also access the fourth component from the `vert` color data. If you notice, the `vertColor` variable we declared in the `Input struct` is of the `float4` type. This means that we are also passing the alpha value of the vertex colors. Knowing this, you can use it to your advantage for the purpose of storing a fourth vertex color to perform effects such as transparency or giving yourself one more mask to blend two textures. It's really up to you and your production to determine if you really need to use the fourth component, but it is worth mentioning here.

Animating vertices in a Surface Shader

Now that we know how to access data on a per-vertex basis, let's expand our knowledge set to include other types of data and the position of a vertex.

Using a vertex function, we can access the position of each vertex in a mesh. This allows us to actually modify each individual vertex while the shader does the processing.

In this recipe, we will create a shader that will allow us to modify the positions of each vertex on a mesh with a sine wave. This technique can be used to create animations for objects such as flags or waves on an ocean.

Getting ready

Let's gather our assets together so that we can create the code for our Vertex Shader:

1. Create a new scene and place a plane mesh in the center of the scene (**GameObject** | **3D Objects** | **Plane**).

The `Plane` object created may seem to be a single quad but, in fact, has 121 verts, which we are going to be moving. Using a quad would provide unexpected results. To check for yourself, select the `Plane` object and, under the **Plane (Mesh Filter)** component, double-click on the **Mesh** property.

2. Create a new shader (`VertexAnimation`) and material (`VertexAnimationMat`).
3. Finally, assign the shader to the material and the material to the plane mesh.

Your scene should look similar to the following screenshot:

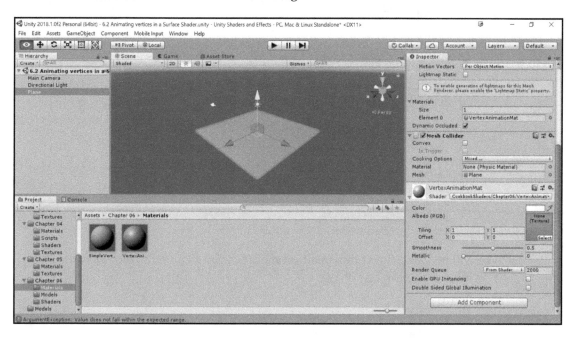

How to do it...

With our scene ready to go, let's double-click on our newly created shader to open it in the code editor:

1. Let's begin with our shader and populate the `Properties` block:

```
Properties
{
  _MainTex ("Base (RGB)", 2D) = "white" {}
  _tintAmount ("Tint Amount", Range(0,1)) = 0.5
  _ColorA ("Color A", Color) = (1,1,1,1)
  _ColorB ("Color B", Color) = (1,1,1,1)
  _Speed ("Wave Speed", Range(0.1, 80)) = 5
  _Frequency ("Wave Frequency", Range(0, 5)) = 2
  _Amplitude ("Wave Amplitude", Range(-1, 1)) = 1
}
```

2. We now need to tell Unity that we are going to be using a vertex function by adding the following to the `#pragma` statement:

```
CGPROGRAM
#pragma surface surf Lambert vertex:vert
```

3. In order to access the values that have been given to us by our properties, we need to declare a corresponding variable in our `CGPROGRAM` block:

```
sampler2D _MainTex;
float4 _ColorA;
float4 _ColorB;
float _tintAmount;
float _Speed;
float _Frequency;
float _Amplitude;
float _OffsetVal;
```

4. We will be using the vertex position modification as a `vert` color as well. This will allow us to tint our object:

```
struct Input
{
  float2 uv_MainTex;
  float3 vertColor;
}
```

5. At this point, we can perform our vertex modification using a sine wave and vertex function. Enter the following code after the `Input struct`:

```
void vert(inout appdata_full v, out Input o)
{
  UNITY_INITIALIZE_OUTPUT(Input,o);
  float time = _Time * _Speed;
  float waveValueA = sin(time + v.vertex.x * _Frequency) *
_Amplitude;

  v.vertex.xyz = float3(v.vertex.x, v.vertex.y + waveValueA,
v.vertex.z);
  v.normal = normalize(float3(v.normal.x + waveValueA,
v.normal.y, v.normal.z));
  o.vertColor = float3(waveValueA,waveValueA,waveValueA);
}
```

6. Finally, we complete our shader by performing a `lerp()` function between two colors so that we can tint the peaks and valleys of our new mesh, modified by our vertex function:

```
void surf (Input IN, inout SurfaceOutput o)
{
  half4 c = tex2D (_MainTex, IN.uv_MainTex);
  float3 tintColor = lerp(_ColorA, _ColorB, IN.vertColor).rgb;
  o.Albedo = c.rgb * (tintColor * _tintAmount);
  o.Alpha = c.a;
}
```

7. After completing the code for your shader, switch back to Unity and let the shader compile. Once compiled, select the **Material** and assign the **Base (RGB) Texture** to the `UV Checker` material that is included in `Chapter 6 | Textures` folder of this book's example code.

8. From there, assign **Color A** and **Color B** to different colors. After the changes, you should see something similar to the following screenshot:

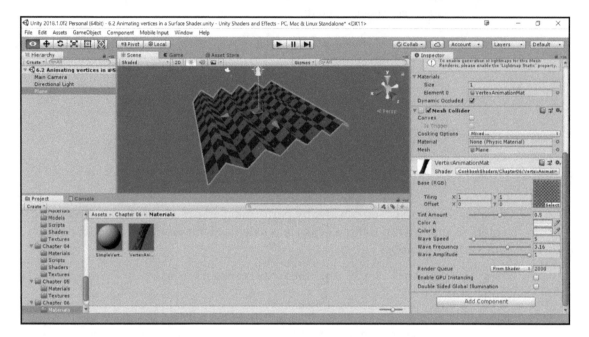

How it works...

This particular shader uses the same concept from the last recipe, except that this time, we are modifying the positions of the vertices in the mesh. This is really useful if you don't want to rig up simple objects, such as a flag, and then animate them using a skeleton structure or hierarchy of transforms.

We simply create a sine wave value using the `sin()` function that is built into the Cg language. After calculating this value, we add it to the *y* value of each vertex position, creating a wave-like effect.

We also modified the normal on the mesh just to give it more realistic shading based on the sine wave value.

You will see how easy it is to perform more complex vertex effects by utilizing the built-in vertex parameters that Surface Shaders give us.

Extruding your models

One of the biggest problems in games is repetition. Creating new content is a time-consuming task, and when you have to face thousands of enemies, chances are that they will all look the same. A relatively cheap technique to add variation to your models is using a shader that alters its basic geometry. This recipe will show you a technique called **normal extrusion**, which can be used to create a chubbier or skinnier version of a model, as shown in the following screenshot of a soldier from the Unity camp demo:

For ease of use, I have provided a prefab of the solider in the example code for this book under the `Chapter 6 | Prefabs` folder.

Getting ready

For this recipe, you need to have access to the shader used by the model that you want to alter. Once you have it, we duplicate it so that we can edit it safely. It can be done as follows:

1. Find the shader your model is using and, once selected, duplicate it by pressing *Ctrl + D*. If it is just using the Standard Shader, as in this example, it is also possible to just create a new Standard Material such as normal, and the Albedo map will automatically transfer over. Either way, rename this new shader `NormalExtrusion`.

2. Duplicate the original material of the model and assign the cloned shader to it.

3. Assign the new material to your model (`NormalExtrusionMat`) and start editing it.

In order for this effect to work, your model should have **normals**.

How to do it...

To create this effect, start by modifying the duplicated shader:

1. Let's start by adding a property to our shader, which will be used to modulate its extrusion. The range presented here goes from -0.0001 to 0.0001, but you might have to adjust this according to your own needs:

   ```
   _Amount ("Extrusion Amount", Range(-0.0001, 0.0001)) = 0
   ```

2. Couple the property with its respective variable:

   ```
   float _Amount;
   ```

3. Change the `#pragma` directive so that it now uses a vertex modifier. You can do this by adding `vertex:function_name` at the end of it. In our case, we have called the `vert:` function:

   ```
   #pragma surface surf Standard vertex:vert
   ```

4. Add the following vertex modifier:

   ```
   void vert (inout appdata_full v)
   {
       v.vertex.xyz += v.normal * _Amount;
   }
   ```

5. The shader is now ready; you can use the Extrusion Amount slider in the material's **Inspector** tab to make your model skinnier or chubbier. Also, feel free to create a clone of the material in order to have different extrusion amounts for each character:

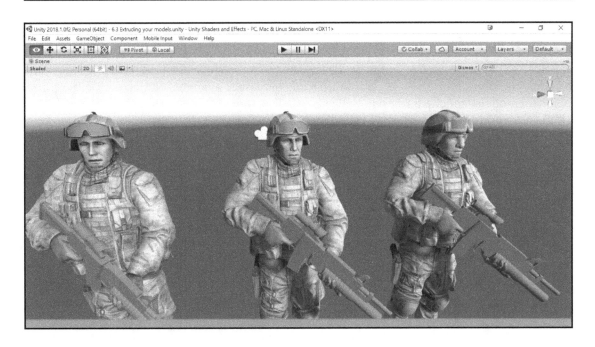

How it works...

Surface Shaders work in two steps. In all the previous chapters, we only explored its last one: the surface function. There is another function that can be used: the vertex modifier. It takes the data structure of a vertex (which is usually called `appdata_full`) and applies a transformation to it. This gives us the freedom to do virtually anything with the geometry of our model. We signal to the GPU that such a function exists by adding `vertex:vert` to the `#pragma` directive of the Surface Shader. You can refer to `Chapter 7`, *Fragment Shaders and Grab Passes*, to learn how vertex modifiers can be defined in a Vertex and Fragment Shader instead.

One of the most simple yet effective techniques that can be used to alter the geometry of a model is called normal extrusion. It works by projecting a vertex along its normal direction. This is done by the following line of code:

```
v.vertex.xyz += v.normal * _Amount;
```

The position of a vertex is displaced by `_Amount` units toward the vertex normal. If `_Amount` gets too high, the results can be quite unpleasant. With smaller values, however, you can add a lot of variation to your models.

There's more...

If you have multiple enemies and want each one to have its own weight, you have to create a different material for each one of them. This is necessary as materials are normally shared between models and changing one will change all of them. There are several ways in which you can do this; the quickest one is to create a script that automatically does it for you. The following script, once attached to an object with a `Renderer`, will duplicate its first material and set the _Amount property automatically:

```
using UnityEngine;
public class NormalExtruder : MonoBehaviour {
  [Range(-0.0001f, 0.0001f)]
  public float amount = 0;
  // Use this for initialization
  void Start ()
  {
    Material material = GetComponent<Renderer>().sharedMaterial;
    Material newMaterial = new Material(material);
    newMaterial.SetFloat("_Amount", amount);
    GetComponent<Renderer>().material = newMaterial;
  }
}
```

Adding extrusion maps

This technique can actually be improved even further. We can add an extra texture (or use the alpha channel of the main one) to indicate the amount of extrusion. This allows for much better control over which parts are raised or lowered. The following code shows you how it is possible to achieve such an effect (the main difference from what we've done before is in bold):

```
Shader "CookbookShaders/Chapter06/Normal Extrusion Map"
{
  Properties
  {
    _MainTex("Texture", 2D) = "white" {}
    _ExtrusionTex("Extrusion map", 2D) = "white" {}
    _ Amount("Extrusion Amount", Range(-0.0001, 0.0001)) = 0
  }
  SubShader
  {
    Tags{ "RenderType" = "Opaque" }

    CGPROGRAM
```

```
#pragma surface surf Standard vertex:vert
struct Input
{
    float2 uv_MainTex;
};

float _Amount;

sampler2D _ExtrusionTex;
void vert(inout appdata_full v)
{
    float4 tex = tex2Dlod (_ExtrusionTex, float4(v.texcoord.xy,0,0));
    float extrusion = tex.r * 2 - 1;
    v.vertex.xyz += v.normal * _Amount * extrusion;
}

sampler2D _MainTex;
void surf(Input IN, inout SurfaceOutputStandard o)
{
    float4 tex = tex2D(_ExtrusionTex, IN.uv_MainTex);
    float extrusion = abs(tex.r * 2 - 1);

    o.Albedo = tex2D(_MainTex, IN.uv_MainTex).rgb;
    o.Albedo = lerp(o.Albedo.rgb, float3(0, 0,0), extrusion * _Amount
                    / 0.0001 * 1.1);
}
ENDCG
}

    Fallback "Diffuse"
}
```

The red channel of `_ExtrusionTex` is used as a multiplying coefficient for normal extrusion. A value of `0.5` leaves the model unaffected; darker or lighter shades are used to extrude vertices inward or outward, respectively. You should note that in order to sample a texture within a vertex modifier, `tex2Dlod` should be used instead of `tex2D`.

In shaders, color channels go from zero to one, although sometimes you need to represent negative values as well (such as inward extrusion). When this is the case, treat `0.5` as zero; consider having smaller values as negative and higher values as positive. This is exactly what happens with normals, which are usually encoded in RGB textures. The `UnpackNormal()` function is used to map a value in the range (0,1) on the range (-1,+1). Mathematically speaking, this is equivalent to `tex.r * 2 -1`.

Extrusion maps are perfect for zombifying characters by shrinking the skin to highlight the shape of the bones underneath. The following screenshot shows you how a healthy soldier can be transformed into a corpse using just a shader and extrusion map. Compared to the previous example, you may notice how the clothing is unaffected. The shader used in the following screenshot also darkens the extruded regions to give an even more emaciated look to the soldier:

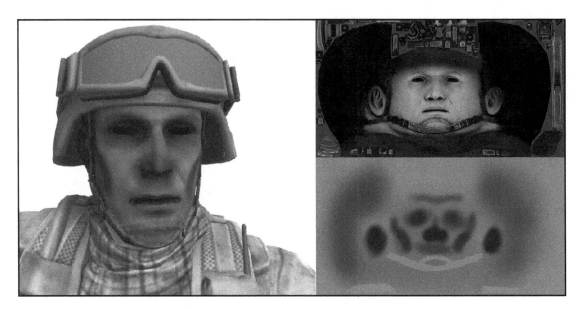

Implementing a snow shader

The simulation of snow has always been a challenge in games. The vast majority of games simply include snow directly in the model's texture so that their tops look white. However, what if one of these objects starts rotating? Snow is not just a lick of paint on a surface; it is a proper accumulation of material and should be treated as such. This recipe shows you how to give a snowy look to your models using just a shader.

This effect is achieved in two steps. First, white is used for all the triangles facing the sky. Second, their vertices are extruded to simulate the effect of snow accumulation. You can see the result in the following screenshot:

 Keep in mind that this recipe does not aim to create a photorealistic snow effect. It provides a good starting point, but it is up to the artist to create the right textures and find the right parameters to make it fit your game.

Getting ready

This effect is purely based on shaders. We will need the following:

1. Create a new shader for the snow effect (SnowShader).
2. Create a new material for the shader (SnowMat).

3. Assign the newly created material to the object that you want to be snowy and assign a color so it's easier to tell where the snow is:

How to do it...

To create a snowy effect, open your shader and make the following changes:

1. Replace the properties of the shader with the following ones:

```
_Color("Main Color", Color) = (1.0,1.0,1.0,1.0)
_MainTex("Base (RGB)", 2D) = "white" {}
_Bump("Bump", 2D) = "bump" {}
_Snow("Level of snow", Range(1, -1)) = 1
_SnowColor("Color of snow", Color) = (1.0,1.0,1.0,1.0)
_SnowDirection("Direction of snow", Vector) = (0,1,0)
_SnowDepth("Depth of snow", Range(0,1)) = 0
```

2. Complete them with their relative variables:

```
sampler2D _MainTex;
sampler2D _Bump;
float _Snow;
float4 _SnowColor;
float4 _Color;
float4 _SnowDirection;
float _SnowDepth;
```

3. Replace the Input structure with the following one:

```
struct Input
{
   float2 uv_MainTex;
   float2 uv_Bump;
   float3 worldNormal;
   INTERNAL_DATA
};
```

4. Replace the surface function with the following one. It will color the snowy parts of the model white:

```
void surf(Input IN, inout SurfaceOutputStandard o)
{
   half4 c = tex2D(_MainTex, IN.uv_MainTex);

   o.Normal = UnpackNormal(tex2D(_Bump, IN.uv_Bump));
   if (dot(WorldNormalVector(IN, o.Normal), _SnowDirection.xyz)
       >= _Snow)
   {
   o.Albedo = _SnowColor.rgb;
   }
   else
   {
   o.Albedo = c.rgb * _Color;
   }
   o.Alpha = 1;
}
```

5. Configure the #pragma directive so that it uses vertex modifiers:

```
#pragma surface surf Standard vertex:vert
```

6. Add the following vertex modifiers, which extrude the vertices covered in snow:

```
void vert(inout appdata_full v)
{
  float4 sn = mul(UNITY_MATRIX_IT_MV, _SnowDirection);

  if (dot(v.normal, sn.xyz) >= _Snow)
  {
    v.vertex.xyz += (sn.xyz + v.normal) * _SnowDepth * _Snow;
  }
}
```

7. You can now use the material's **Inspector** tab to select how much of your model is going to be covered and how thick the snow should be:

How it works...

This shader works in two steps:

- Coloring the surface
- Altering the geometry.

Coloring the surface

The first step alters the color of the triangles that are facing the sky. It affects all the triangles with a normal direction similar to _SnowDirection. As seen before in Chapter 3, *Understanding Lighting Models,* comparing unit vectors can be done using the **dot product**. When two vectors are orthogonal, their dot product is zero; it is one (or minus one) when they are parallel to each other. The _Snow property is used to decide how aligned they should be in order to be considered as facing the sky.

If you look closely at the surface function, you can see that we are not dotting the normal and snow direction directly. This is because they are usually defined in a different space. The snow direction is expressed in world coordinates, while the object normals are usually relative to the model itself. If we rotate the model, its normals will not change, which is not what we want. To fix this, we need to convert the normals from their object coordinates to world coordinates. This is done with the WorldNormalVector() function, as seen in the following code:

```
if (dot(WorldNormalVector(IN, o.Normal), _SnowDirection.xyz) >=
  _Snow)
{
  o.Albedo = _SnowColor.rgb;
}
else
{
  o.Albedo = c.rgb * _Color;
}
```

This shader simply colors the model white; a more advanced one should initialize the SurfaceOutputStandard structure with textures and parameters from a realistic snow material.

Altering the geometry

The second effect of this shader alters the geometry to simulate the accumulation of snow. Firstly, we identify which triangles have been colored white by testing the same condition used in the surface function. This time, unfortunately, we cannot rely on WorldNormalVector() as the SurfaceOutputStandard structure is not yet initialized in the vertex modifier. We use this other method instead, which converts _SnowDirection to object coordinates:

```
float4 sn = mul(UNITY_MATRIX_IT_MV, _SnowDirection);
```

Then, we can extrude the geometry to simulate the accumulation of snow:

```
if (dot(v.normal, sn.xyz) >= _Snow)
{
    v.vertex.xyz += (sn.xyz + v.normal) * _SnowDepth * _Snow;
}
```

Once again, this is a very basic effect. You could use a texture map to control the accumulation of snow more precisely or give a peculiar, uneven look.

See also

If you need high-quality snow effects and props for your game, you can also check these resources on the Unity Asset Store:

- **Winter Suite ($30)**: A much more sophisticated version of the snow shader presented in this recipe can be found at https://www.assetstore.unity3d.com/en/#!/content/13927.
- **Winter Pack ($60)**: A very realistic set of props and materials for snowy environments can be found at https://www.assetstore.unity3d.com/en/#!/content/13316.

Implementing a volumetric explosion

The art of game development is a clever trade-off between realism and efficiency. This is particularly true for explosions; they are at the heart of many games, yet the physics behind them is often beyond the computational power of modern machines. Explosions are, essentially, nothing more than very hot balls of gas; hence, the only way to correctly simulate them is by integrating a fluid simulation into your game. As you can imagine, this is unfeasible for a runtime application, and many games simulate them simply with particles. When an object explodes, it is common to simply instantiate fire, smoke, and debris particles so that, together, they can achieve believable results. This approach, unfortunately, is not very realistic and is easy to spot. There is an intermediate technique that can be used to achieve a much more realistic effect: volumetric explosions. The idea behind this concept is that explosions are not treated like a bunch of particles; they are evolving 3D objects, not just flat 2D textures.

Getting ready

Complete this recipe with the following steps:

1. Create a new shader for this effect (VolumetricExplosion).
2. Create a new material to host the shader (VolumetricExplosionMat).
3. Attach the material to a sphere. You can create one directly from the editor, navigating to **GameObject** | **3D Object** | **Sphere**:

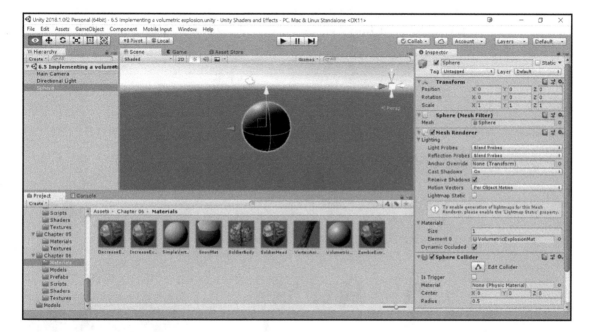

 This recipe works well with the standard Unity Sphere, but if you need big explosions, you might need to use a high-poly sphere. In fact, a vertex function can only modify the vertices of a mesh. All the other points will be interpolated using the positions of the nearby vertices. Fewer vertices means a lower resolution for your explosions.

4. For this recipe, you will also need a ramp texture that has, in a gradient, all the colors your explosions will have. You can create a texture like the following screenshot using GIMP or Photoshop:

You can find this image (`explosionRamp`) in `Chapter 6 | Textures` folder in the example code provided with this book.

5. Once you have the picture, import it to Unity. Then, from its **Inspector**, make sure that **Filter Mode** is set to **Bilinear** and the **Wrap Mode** to **Clamp**. These two settings make sure that the ramp texture is sampled smoothly.

6. Lastly, you will need a noisy texture. You can search on the internet for freely available noise textures. The most commonly used ones are generated using Perlin noise. I have included an example in `Chapter 6 | Textures` folder for your use:

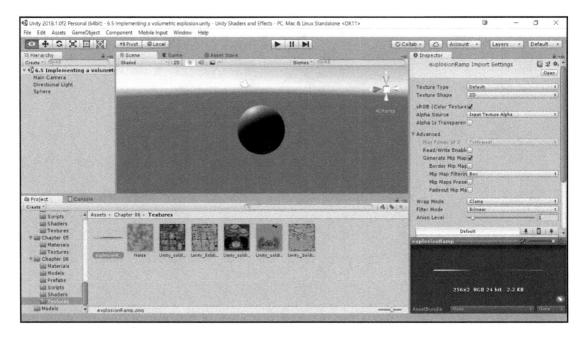

How to do it...

This effect works in two steps: a vertex function to change the geometry, and a surface function to give it the right color. The steps are as follows:

1. Remove the current properties and add the following properties to the shader:

```
Properties
{
    _RampTex("Color Ramp", 2D) = "white" {}
    _RampOffset("Ramp offset", Range(-0.5,0.5))= 0
    _NoiseTex("Noise Texture", 2D) = "gray" {}
    _Period("Period", Range(0,1)) = 0.5
    _Amount("_Amount", Range(0, 1.0)) = 0.1
    _ClipRange("ClipRange", Range(0,1)) = 1
}
```

2. Add their relative variables so that the Cg code of the shader can actually access them:

```
sampler2D _RampTex;
half _RampOffset;

sampler2D _NoiseTex;
float _Period;

half _Amount;
half _ClipRange;
```

3. Change the `Input` structure so that it receives the UV data of the ramp texture:

```
struct Input
{
    float2 uv_NoiseTex;
};
```

4. Add the following vertex function:

```
void vert(inout appdata_full v) {
    float3 disp = tex2Dlod(_NoiseTex, float4(v.texcoord.xy,0,0));
    float time = sin(_Time[3] *_Period + disp.r*10);
    v.vertex.xyz += v.normal * disp.r * _Amount * time;
}
```

5. Add the following surface function:

```
void surf(Input IN, inout SurfaceOutput o)
{
    float3 noise = tex2D(_NoiseTex, IN.uv_NoiseTex);

    float n = saturate(noise.r + _RampOffset);

    clip(_ClipRange - n);

    half4 c = tex2D(_RampTex, float2(n,0.5));

    o.Albedo = c.rgb;
    o.Emission = c.rgb*c.a;
}
```

6. We specify the vertex function in the `#pragma` directive, adding the `nolightmap` parameter to prevent Unity from adding realistic lighting to our explosion:

```
#pragma surface surf Lambert vertex:vert nolightmap
```

7. The last step is selecting the material and, from its **Inspector**, attaching the two textures in the relative slots:

8. This is animated material, meaning that it evolves over time. You can watch the material changing in the editor by clicking on **Animated Materials** from the **Scene** window:

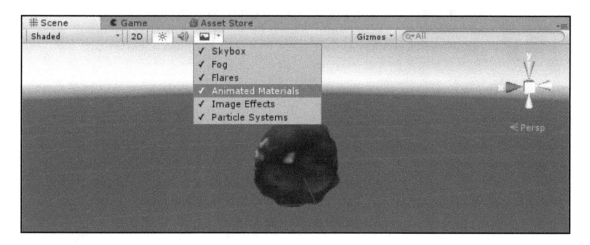

How it works...

If you are reading this recipe, you should already be familiar with how Surface Shaders and vertex modifiers work. The main idea behind this effect is to alter the geometry of the sphere in a seemingly chaotic way, exactly as it happens in a real explosion. The following screenshot shows you what such an explosion will look like inside the editor. You can see that the original mesh has been heavily deformed:

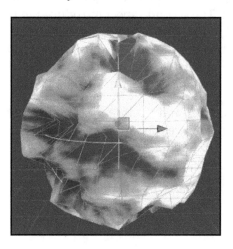

The vertex function is a variant of the technique called normal extrusion introduced in the *Extruding your models* recipe of this chapter. The difference here is that the amount of extrusion is determined both by the time and noise texture.

 When you need a random number in Unity, you can rely on the `Random.Range()` function. There is no standard way to get random numbers in a shader, so the easiest way is to sample a noise texture.

There is no standard way to do this, so take this as an example only:

```
float time = sin(_Time[3] *_Period + disp.r*10);
```

The built-in `_Time[3]` variable is used to get the current time from within the shader, and the red channel of the `disp.r` noise texture is used to make sure that each vertex moves independently. The `sin()` function makes the vertices go up and down, simulating the chaotic behavior of an explosion. Then, the normal extrusion takes place:

```
v.vertex.xyz += v.normal * disp.r * _Amount * time;
```

You should play with these numbers and variables until you find a pattern of movement that you are happy with.

The last part of the effect is achieved by the surface function. Here, the noise texture is used to sample a random color from the ramp texture. However, there are two more aspects that are worth noting. The first one is the introduction of _RampOffset. Its usage forces the explosion to sample colors from the left or right side of the texture. With positive values, the surface of the explosion tends to show more grey tones—exactly what happens when it is dissolving. You can use _RampOffset to determine how much fire or smoke there should be in your explosion. The second aspect introduced in the surface function is the usage of `clip()`. What `clip()` does is it clips (removes) pixels from the rendering pipeline. When invoked with a negative value, the current pixel is not drawn. This effect is controlled by _ClipRange, which determines which pixels of the volumetric explosions are going to be transparent.

By controlling both _RampOffset and _ClipRange, you have full control and can determine how the explosion behaves and dissolves.

There's more...

The shader presented in this recipe makes a sphere look like an explosion. If you really want to use it, you should couple it with some scripts in order to get the most out of it. The best thing to do is to create an explosion object and make it into a prefab so that you can reuse it every time you need to. You can do this by dragging the sphere back into the **Project** window. Once it is done, you can create as many explosions as you want using the `Instantiate()` function.

It is worth noticing, however, that all the objects with the same material share the same look. If you have multiple explosions at the same time, they should not use the same material. When you are instantiating a new explosion, you should also duplicate its material. You can do this easily with this piece of code:

```
GameObject explosion = Instantiate(explosionPrefab) as GameObject;
Renderer renderer = explosion.GetComponent<Renderer>();
Material material = new Material(renderer.sharedMaterial);
renderer.material = material;
```

Lastly, if you are going to use this shader in a realistic way, you should attach a script to it that changes its size, `_RampOffset`, and `_ClipRange` according to the type of explosion that you want to recreate.

See also

- Much more can be done to make explosions realistic. The approach presented in this recipe only creates an empty shell; inside it, the explosion is actually empty.
- An easy trick to improve this is to create particles inside it. However, you can only go so far with this.
- The short movie, *The Butterfly Effect* (http://unity3d.com/pages/butterfly), created by Unity Technologies in collaboration with Passion Pictures and Nvidia, is the perfect example.
- It is based on the same concept of altering the geometry of a sphere, but it renders it with a technique called **volume ray casting**.

- In a nutshell, it renders the geometry as if it's full. You can see an example in the following screenshot:

- If you are looking for high-quality explosions, check out Pyro Technix (`https://www.assetstore.unity3d.com/en/#!/content/16925`) in the Asset Store. It includes volumetric explosions and couples them with realistic shockwaves.

7
Fragment Shaders and Grab Passes

So far, we have relied on Surface Shaders. They have been designed to simplify the way shader coding works, providing meaningful tools for artists. If we want to push our knowledge of shaders further, we need to venture into the territory of Vertex and Fragment Shaders.

In this chapter, you will learn the following recipes:

- Understanding Vertex and Fragment Shaders
- Using grab passes to draw behind objects
- Implementing a Glass Shader
- Implementing a Water Shader for 2D games

Introduction

Compared to Surface Shaders, Vertex and Fragment Shaders come with little to no information about the physical properties that determine how light reflects on surfaces. What they lack in expressivity, they compensate for with power: Vertex and Fragment Shaders are not limited by physical constraints and are perfect for non-photorealistic effects. This chapter will focus on a technique called the **grab pass**, which allows these shaders to simulate deformations.

Understanding Vertex and Fragment Shaders

The best way to understand how Vertex and Fragment Shaders work is by creating one yourself. This recipe will show you how to write one of these shaders, which will simply apply a texture to a model and multiply it by a given color, as shown in the following screenshot:

Notice how it works similarly to how the Multiply filter in Photoshop works. That's because we will be doing the same calculation done there!

The shader presented here is very simple, and it will be used as a starting base for all the other Vertex and Fragment Shaders.

Getting ready

For this recipe, we will need a new shader. Follow these steps:

1. Create a new shader (`Multiply`).

2. Create a new material (`MultiplyMat`) and assign the shader to it.

3. Bring the soldier prefab from the `Chapter 06 | Prefabs` folder into the scene, and attach the new material to the prefab's head. The head can be found in the `Soldier` child of the `Soldier` object.

4. From there, in the **Inspector** tab, scroll down to the **Skinned Mesh Renderer** component and, under **Materials**, set **Element 0** to the new materials. Lastly, in the `Albedo (RGB)` property, drag and drop the `Unity_soldier_Head_DIF_01` texture. The following screenshot should help demonstrate what we are looking for:

How to do it...

In all the previous chapters, we have always been able to refit Surface Shaders. This is not the case any more, as Surface and Fragment Shaders are structurally different. We will need to implement the following changes:

1. Delete all the properties of the shader, replacing them with the following:

```
Properties
{
 _Color ("Color", Color) = (1,0,0,1)
 _MainTex ("Albedo (RGB)", 2D) = "white" {}
}
```

2. Delete all the code in the SubShader block and replace it with this:

```
SubShader
{
 Pass
 {
 CGPROGRAM

 #pragma vertex vert
 #pragma fragment frag

 half4 _Color;
 sampler2D _MainTex;

 struct vertInput
 {
 float4 pos : POSITION;
 float2 texcoord : TEXCOORD0;
 };

 struct vertOutput
 {
 float4 pos : SV_POSITION;
 float2 texcoord : TEXCOORD0;
 };

 vertOutput vert(vertInput input)
 {
 vertOutput o;
 o.pos = mul(UNITY_MATRIX_MVP, input.pos);
 o.texcoord = input.texcoord;
 return o;
 }
```

```
half4 frag(vertOutput output) : COLOR
{
half4 mainColour = tex2D(_MainTex, output.texcoord);
return mainColour * _Color;
}

ENDCG
}
}
FallBack "Diffuse"
```

3. Save your shader script and return to the Unity editor. Once finished, modify the **Color** property of the `MultiplyMat` material and see that we get the result we are looking for:

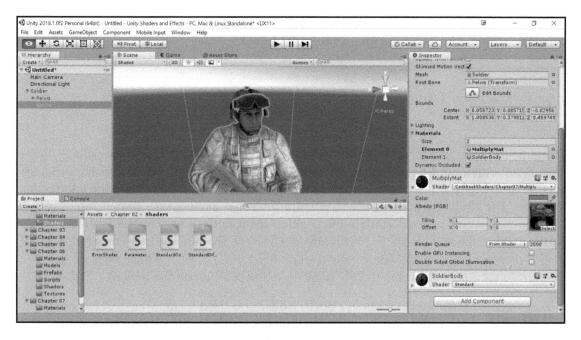

This will also be the base for all future Vertex and Fragment Shaders.

How it works...

As the name suggests, Vertex and Fragment Shaders work in two steps. The model is first passed through a vertex function; the result is then inputted to a Fragment function. Both these functions are assigned using #pragma directives:

```
#pragma vertex vert
#pragma fragment frag
```

In this case, they are simply called vert and frag.

Conceptually speaking, fragments are closely related to pixels; the term fragment is often used to refer to the collection of data necessary to draw a pixel. This is also why Vertex and Fragment Shaders are often called **Pixel Shaders**.

The vertex function takes the input data in a structure that is defined as vertInput in the shader:

```
struct vertInput
{
  float4 pos : POSITION;
  float2 texcoord : TEXCOORD0;
};
```

Its name is totally arbitrary, but its content is not. Each field of the struct must be decorated with a **binding semantic**. This is a feature of Cg that allows us to mark variables so that they will be initialized with certain data, such as normal vectors and the vertex position. The binding semantic, POSITION, indicates that when vertInput is inputted to the vertex function, pos will contain the position of the current vertex. This is similar to the vertex field of the appdata_full structure in a Surface Shader. The main difference is that pos is represented in model coordinates (relative to the 3D object), which we need to convert to view coordinates manually (relative to the position on the screen).

 The vertex function in a Surface Shader is used to alter the geometry of the model only. In a Vertex and Fragment Shader, instead, the vertex function is necessary to project the coordinates of the model to the screen.

The mathematics behind this conversion is beyond the scope of this chapter. However, this transformation can be achieved by using the `UnityObjectToClipPos` function, which will take a point from object space to the camera's clip space in homogeneous coordinates. This is done by multiplying by the **model-view-projection matrix**, and it is essential to find the position of a vertex on the screen:

```
vertOutput o;
o.pos = UnityObjectToClipPos(input.pos);
```

 For more information on this and other helper functions that ShaderLab has built-in, check out `https://docs.unity3d.com/Manual/SL-BuiltinFunctions.html`.

The other piece of information initialized is `textcoord`, which uses the `TEXCOORD0` binding semantics to get the UV data of the first texture. No further processing is required, and this value can be passed directly to the fragment function (`frag`):

```
o.texcoord = input.texcoord;
```

While Unity will initialize `vertInput` for us, we are responsible for the initialization of `vertOutput`. Despite this, its fields still need to be decorated with binding semantics:

```
struct vertOutput
{
    float4 pos : SV_POSITION;
    float2 texcoord : TEXCOORD0;
};
```

Once the vertex function has initialized `vertOutput`, the structure is passed to the fragment function (`frag`). This samples the main texture of the model and multiplies it by the color provided.

As you can see, the Vertex and Fragment Shader have no knowledge of the physical properties of the material. This means that the material does not have the same effect by light sources, and it does not have data regarding how light reflects to create bumped surfaces compared to a Surface Shader; it works closer to the architecture of the graphics GPU.

There's more...

One of the most confusing aspects of Vertex and Fragment Shaders is binding semantics. There are many others that you can use, and their meanings depend on context.

Input semantics

The binding semantics in the following table can be used in `vertInput`, which is the structure that Unity provides to the vertex function. The fields decorated with this semantics will be initialized automatically:

Binding semantics	Description
`POSITION, SV_POSITION`	The position of a vertex in world coordinates (object space)
`NORMAL`	The normal of a vertex, relative to the world (not to the camera)
`COLOR, COLOR0, DIFFUSE,` `SV_TARGET`	The color information stored in the vertex
`COLOR1, SPECULAR`	The secondary color information stored in the vertex (usually the specular)
`TEXCOORD0, TEXCOORD1, ...,` `TEXCOORDi`	The i-th UV data stored in the vertex

Output semantics

When binding, semantics are used in `vertOutput`; they do not automatically guarantee that fields will be initialized. Quite the opposite; it's our responsibility to do so. The compiler will do its best to ensure that the fields are initialized with the right data:

Binding semantics	Description
`POSITION, SV_POSITION, HPOS`	The position of a vertex in camera coordinates (clip space, from zero to one for each dimension)
`COLOR, COLOR0, COL0, COL,` `SV_TARGET`	The front primary color
`COLOR1, COL1`	The front secondary color
`TEXCOORD0, TEXCOORD1, ...,` `TEXCOORDi, TEXi`	The i-th UV data stored in the vertex

WPOS	The position, in pixels, in the window (origin in the lower left corner)

If, for any reason, you need a field that will contain a different type of data, you can decorate it with one of the many TEXCOORD data available. The compiler will not allow fields to be left undecorated.

See also

You can refer to the NVIDIA Reference Manual to check the other binding semantics that are available in Cg:

```
http://developer.download.nvidia.com/cg/Cg_3.1/Cg-3.1_April2012_
ReferenceManual.pdf
```

Using the grab pass to draw behind objects

In the *Adding transparency to PBR* recipe of Chapter 5, *Physically-Based Rendering*, we have seen how a material can be made transparent. Even if a transparent material can draw over a scene, it cannot change what has been drawn underneath it. This means that those Transparent Shaders cannot create distortions such as the ones typically seen in glass or water. In order to simulate them, we need to introduce another technique called a grab pass. This allows us to access what has been drawn on-screen so far, so that a shader can use it (or alter it) with no restrictions. To learn how to use grab passes, we will create a material that grabs what's rendered behind it and draws it again on the screen. It's a shader that, paradoxically, uses several operations to show no changes at all.

Getting ready

This recipe requires the following operations:

1. Create a shader (GrabShader) that we will initialize later.
2. Create a material (GrabMat) to host the shader.

3. Attach the material to a flat piece of geometry, such as a quad. Place it in front of some other object so that you cannot see through it. The quad will appear transparent as soon as the shader is complete:

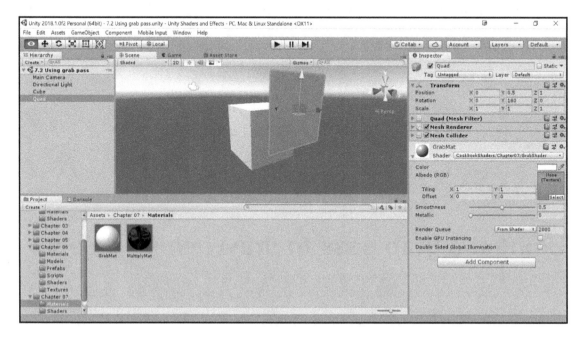

How to do it...

To use a grab pass, you need to follow these steps:

1. Remove the `Properties` section, and the `Input` section; this shader will not use any of them.

2. In the `SubShader` section, remove everything, and add the following to ensure the object is treated as being `Transparent`:

   ```
   Tags{ "Queue" = "Transparent" }
   ```

3. Then, below that, add a grab pass:

   ```
   GrabPass{ }
   ```

4. After the `GrabPass`, we will need to add this extra pass:

```
Pass
{
  CGPROGRAM
  #pragma vertex vert
  #pragma fragment frag

  #include "UnityCG.cginc"
  sampler2D _GrabTexture;

  struct vertInput
  {
    float4 vertex : POSITION;
  };

  struct vertOutput
  {
    float4 vertex : POSITION;
    float4 uvgrab : TEXCOORD1;
  };

  // Vertex function
  vertOutput vert(vertInput v)
  {
    vertOutput o;
    o.vertex = mul(UNITY_MATRIX_MVP, v.vertex);
    o.uvgrab = ComputeGrabScreenPos(o.vertex);
    return o;
  }
  // Fragment function
  half4 frag(vertOutput i) : COLOR
  {
    fixed4 col = tex2Dproj(_GrabTexture,
UNITY_PROJ_COORD(i.uvgrab));
    return col + half4(0.5,0,0,0);
  }
  ENDCG
}
```

5. Save your script and return to the Unity editor. Upon getting back, you should notice your material now works the way you intend it to:

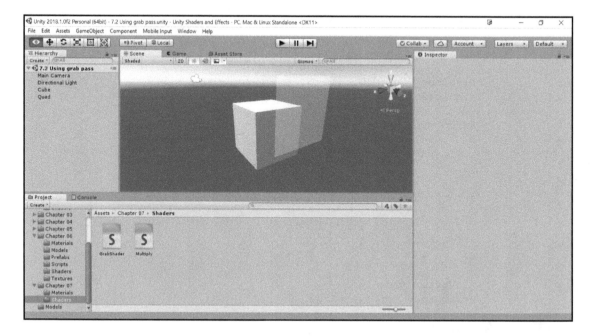

How it works...

This recipe not only introduces grab passes, but also Vertex and Fragment Shaders; for this reason, we have to analyze the shader in detail.

So far, all the code has always been placed directly in the SubShader section. This is because our previous shaders required only a single pass. This time, two passes are required. The first one is the GrabPass{}, which is defined simply by GrabPass{}. The rest of the code is placed in the second pass, which is contained in a Pass block.

The second pass is not structurally different from the shader shown in the first recipe of this chapter; we use the vertex function, `vert`, to get the position of the vertex, and then we give it a color in the Fragment function frag. The difference is that vert calculates another important detail: the UV data for the `GrabPass{}`. The `GrabPass{}` automatically creates a texture that can be referred to as follows:

```
sampler2D _GrabTexture;
```

In order to sample this texture, we need its UV data. The `ComputeGrabScreenPos` function returns data that we can use later to sample the grab texture correctly. This is done in the Fragment Shader using the following line:

```
fixed4 col = tex2Dproj(_GrabTexture, UNITY_PROJ_COORD(i.uvgrab));
```

This is the standard way in which a texture is grabbed and applied to the screen in its correct position. If everything has been done correctly, this shader will simply clone what has been rendered behind the geometry. We will see in the following recipes how this technique can be used to create materials such as water and glass.

There's more...

Every time you use a material with `GrabPass{}`, Unity will have to render the screen to a texture. This operation is very expensive and limits the number of `GrabPass` instances that you can use in a game. Cg offers a slightly different variation:

```
GrabPass {"TextureName"}
```

This line not only allows you to give a name to the texture, but also shares the texture with all the materials that have a `GrabPass` called `TextureName`. This means that if you have ten materials, Unity will only do a single `GrabPass` and share the texture with all of them. The main problem of this technique is that it doesn't allow for effects that can be stacked. If you are creating a glass with this technique, you won't be able to have two glasses one after the other.

Implementing a Glass Shader

Glass is a very complicated material; it should not be a surprise that other chapters have already created shaders to simulate it in the *Adding transparency to PBR* recipe of Chapter 5, *Physically-Based Rendering*. We already know how to make our glasses semi-transparent to show the objects behind it perfectly and that works for a number of applications. However, most glasses are not perfect. For instance, if you look through a stain glass window you may notice distortions or deformations when you look through them. This recipe will teach you how to achieve that effect. The idea behind this effect is to use a Vertex and Fragment Shader with a GrabPass, and then sample the grab texture with a little change to its UV data to create a distortion. You can see the effect in the following screenshot, using the glass-stained textures from the Unity Standard Assets:

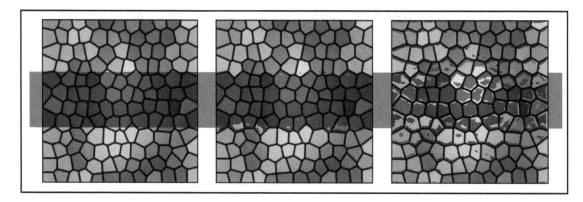

Getting ready

The setup for this recipe is similar to the one presented previously in Chapter 6, *Vertex Functions*:

1. Create a new Vertex and Fragment Shader. You can start by copying the one used in the previous recipe, *Using the grab pass to draw behind objects*, as a base by selecting it and hitting *Ctrl+D* to duplicate it. Once duplicated, change its name to WindowShader.

2. Create a material that will use the shader (WindowMat).

3. Assign the material to a quad or another flat geometry that will simulate your glass.

4. Place some objects behind it so that you can see the distortion effect:

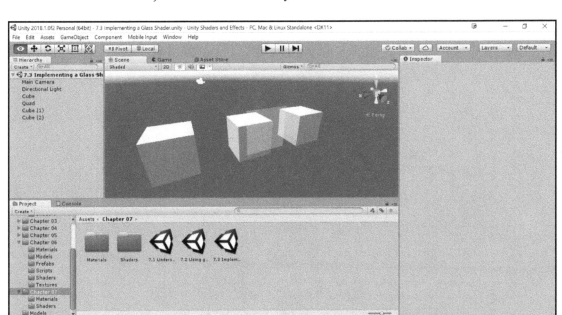

How to do it...

Let's start by editing the Vertex and Fragment Shaders:

1. Create a `Properties` block with these items in it:

```
Properties
{
    _MainTex("Base (RGB) Trans (A)", 2D) = "white" {}
    _Colour("Colour", Color) = (1,1,1,1)
    _BumpMap("Noise text", 2D) = "bump" {}
    _Magnitude("Magnitude", Range(0,1)) = 0.05
}
```

2. Add their variables in the second pass:

```
sampler2D _MainTex;
fixed4 _Colour;

sampler2D _BumpMap;
float _Magnitude;
```

3. Add the texture information to the input and output structures:

```
float2 texcoord : TEXCOORD0;
```

4. Transfer the UV data from the input to the output structure:

```
// Vertex function
vertOutput vert(vertInput v)
{
    vertOutput o;
    o.vertex = UnityObjectToClipPos(v.vertex);
    o.uvgrab = ComputeGrabScreenPos(o.vertex);
    o.texcoord = v.texcoord;
    return o;
}
```

5. Use the following Fragment function:

```
half4 frag(vertOutput i) : COLOR
{
    half4 mainColour = tex2D(_MainTex, i.texcoord);
    half4 bump = tex2D(_BumpMap, i.texcoord);
    half2 distortion = UnpackNormal(bump).rg;

    i.uvgrab.xy += distortion * _Magnitude;

    fixed4 col = tex2Dproj(_GrabTexture, UNITY_PROJ_COORD(i.uvgrab));
    return col * mainColour * _Colour;
}
```

6. This material is transparent, so it changes its tags in the `SubShader` block:

```
Tags{ "Queue" = "Transparent" "IgnoreProjector" = "True"
"RenderType" =
    "Opaque" }
```

7. What's left now is to set the texture for the glass, and for a normal map to displace the grab texture:

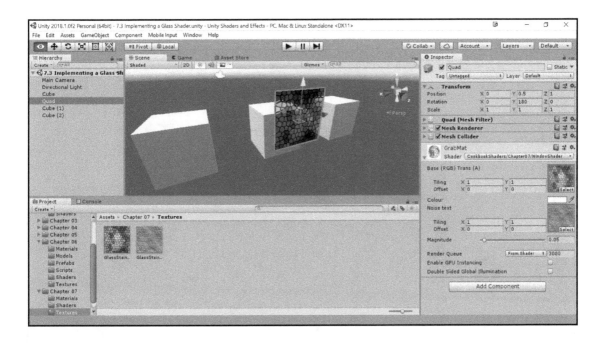

How it works...

The core that this shader uses is a grab pass to take what has already been rendered on the screen. The part where the distortion takes place is in the Fragment function. Here, a normal map is unpacked and used to offset the UV data of the grab texture:

```
half4 bump = tex2D(_BumpMap, i.texcoord);
half2 distortion = UnpackNormal(bump).rg;

i.uvgrab.xy += distortion * _Magnitude;
```

The _Magnitude slider is used to determine how strong the effect is:

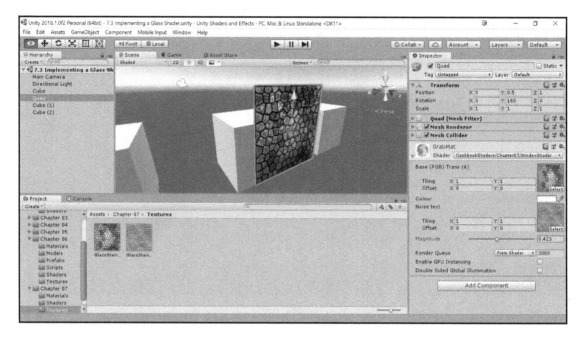

There's more...

This effect is very generic; it grabs the screen and creates a distortion based on a normal map. There is no reason why it shouldn't be used to simulate more interesting things. Many games use distortions around explosions or other sci-fi devices. This material can be applied to a sphere and, with a different normal map, it would simulate the heat wave of an explosion perfectly.

Implementing a Water Shader for 2D games

The Glass Shader introduced in the previous recipe is static; its distortion never changes. It takes just a few changes to convert it to an animated material, making it perfect for 2D games that feature water. This uses a similar technique to the one shown in `Chapter 6`, *Vertex Functions*, in the recipe entitled *Animating Vertices in a Surface Shader*:

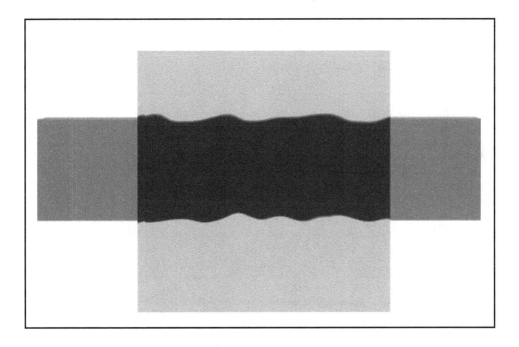

Getting ready

This recipe is based on the Vertex and Fragment Shaders described in the *Using the grab pass to draw behind objects* recipe, as it will rely heavily on GrabPass.

1. Create a new Vertex and Fragment Shader. You can start by copying the one used in the previous recipe, *Using the grab pass to draw behind objects*, as a base by selecting it and hitting *Ctrl+D* to duplicate it. Once duplicated, change its name to WaterShader.

2. Create a material that will use the shader (WaterMat).

3. Assign the material to a flat geometry that will represent your 2D water. In order for this effect to work, you should have something rendered behind it so that you can see the water-like displacement:

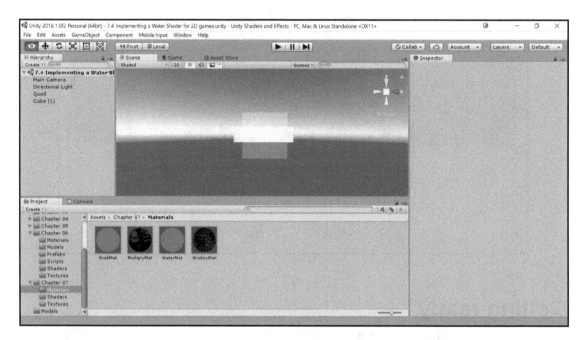

4. This recipe requires a noise texture, which is used to get pseudo-random values. It is important that you choose a seamless noise texture, such as the ones generated by tileable 2D Perlin noise, as shown in the following screenshot. This ensures that when the material is applied to a large object, you will not see any discontinuity. In order for this effect to work, the texture has to be imported in Repeat mode. If you want a smooth and continuous look for your water, you should also set it to Bilinear from Inspector. These settings ensure that the texture is sampled correctly from the shader:

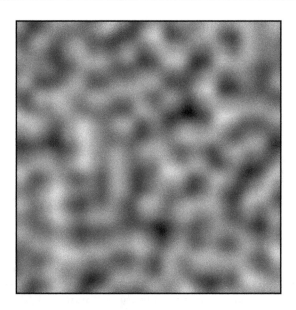

 You can find an example noise texture in `Chapter 6 | Textures` folder of the book's example code.

How to do it...

To create this animated effect, you can start by refitting the shader. Follow these steps:

1. Add the following properties:

```
_NoiseTex("Noise text", 2D) = "white" {}
_Colour ("Colour", Color) = (1,1,1,1)
_Period ("Period", Range(0,50)) = 1
_Magnitude ("Magnitude", Range(0,0.5)) = 0.05
_Scale ("Scale", Range(0,10)) = 1
```

2. Add their respective variables to the second pass of the shader:

```
sampler2D _NoiseTex;
fixed4 _Colour;

float _Period;
float _Magnitude;
float _Scale;
```

3. Define the following input and output structures for the vertex function:

```
struct vertInput
{
   float4 vertex : POSITION;
   fixed4 color : COLOR;
   float2 texcoord : TEXCOORD0;
};

struct vertOutput
{
   float4 vertex : POSITION;
   fixed4 color : COLOR;
   float2 texcoord : TEXCOORD0;
   float4 worldPos : TEXCOORD1;
   float4 uvgrab : TEXCOORD2;
};
```

4. This shader needs to know the exact position of the space of every fragment. To do this, update the vertex function to the following:

```
// Vertex function
vertOutput vert (vertInput v)
{
   vertOutput o;
   o.vertex = UnityObjectToClipPos(v.vertex);
   o.color = v.color;
   o.texcoord = v.texcoord;

   o.worldPos = mul(unity_ObjectToWorld, v.vertex);
   o.uvgrab = ComputeGrabScreenPos(o.vertex);
   return o;
}
```

5. Use the following Fragment function:

```
fixed4 frag (vertOutput i) : COLOR
{
   float sinT = sin(_Time.w / _Period);

   float distX = tex2D(_NoiseTex, i.worldPos.xy / _Scale +
float2(sinT,
      0) ).r - 0.5;
   float distY = tex2D(_NoiseTex, i.worldPos.xy / _Scale + float2(0,
      sinT) ).r - 0.5;

   float2 distortion = float2(distX, distY);
   i.uvgrab.xy += distortion * _Magnitude;
```

```
    fixed4 col = tex2Dproj( _GrabTexture,
UNITY_PROJ_COORD(i.uvgrab));
    return col * _Colour;
}
```

6. Save your script and return to the Unity editor. Afterward, select your Water Material (`WatMat`)and apply the noise texture. Afterward, tweak the properties in the Water Material and notice how it modifies the things behind it.

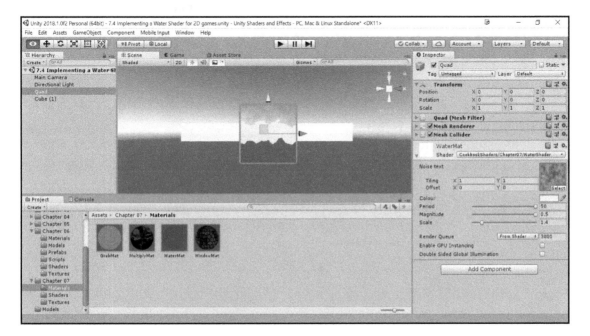

How it works...

This shader is very similar to the one introduced in the *Implementing a Glass Shader* recipe. The major difference is that this is an animated material; the displacement is not generated from a normal map, but takes into account the current time in order to create a constant animation. The code that displaces the UV data of the grab texture seems quite complicated; let's try to understand how it has been generated. The idea behind it is that a sinusoid function is used to make the water oscillate. This effect needs to evolve over time; to achieve this effect, the distortion generated by the shader depends on the current time that is retrieved with the built-in variable, _Time. The _Period variable determines the period of the sinusoid, which means how fast the waves appear:

```
float2 distortion = float2( sin(_Time.w/_Period),
    sin(_Time.w/_Period) ) - 0.5;
```

The problem with this code is that you have the same displacement on the X and Y axes; as a result, the entire grab texture will rotate in a circular motion, which looks nothing like water. We obviously need to add some randomness to this.

The most common way to add random behaviors to shaders is by including a noise texture. The problem now is to find a way to sample the texture at seemingly random positions. The best way to avoid seeing an obvious sinusoid pattern is to use the sine waves as an offset in the UV data of the _NoiseTex texture:

```
float sinT = sin(_Time.w / _Period);
float2 distortion = float2(
    tex2D(_NoiseTex, i.texcoord / _Scale + float2(sinT, 0) ).r - 0.5,
    tex2D(_NoiseTex, i.texcoord / _Scale + float2(0, sinT) ).r - 0.5
);
```

The _Scale variable determines the size of the waves. This solution is closer to the final version but has a severe issue—if the water quad moves, the UV data follows it and you can see the water waves following the material rather than being anchored to the background. To solve this, we need to use the world position of the current fragment as the initial position for the UV data:

```
float sinT = sin(_Time.w / _Period);
float2 distortion = float2(
    tex2D(_NoiseTex, i.worldPos.xy / _Scale + float2(sinT, 0) ).r - 0.5,
    tex2D(_NoiseTex, i.worldPos.xy / _Scale + float2(0, sinT) ).r - 0.5
);
i.uvgrab.xy += distortion * _Magnitude;
```

The result is a pleasant, seamless distortion, which doesn't move in any clear direction.

We can also improve the readability of the code by breaking apart the distortion into smaller steps:

```
float sinT = sin(_Time.w / _Period);

float distX = tex2D(_NoiseTex, i.worldPos.xy / _Scale +
    float2(sinT, 0) ).r - 0.5;
float distY = tex2D(_NoiseTex, i.worldPos.xy / _Scale +
    float2(0, sinT) ).r - 0.5;

float2 distortion = float2(distX, distY);
i.uvgrab.xy += distortion * _Magnitude;
```

That is what you should see in the final result.

 As happens with all these special effects, there is no perfect solution. This recipe shows you a technique to create water-like distortion, but you are encouraged to play with it until you find an effect that fits the aesthetics of your game.

Mobile Shader Adjustment

8

In the next two chapters, we are going to take a look at making the shaders that we write in a performance-friendly manner for different platforms. We won't be talking about any one platform specifically, but we are going to break down the elements of shaders we can adjust in order to make them more optimized for mobiles and efficient on any platform in general. These techniques range from understanding what Unity offers in terms of built-in variables that reduce the overhead of the shaders memory to learning about ways in which we can make our own shader code more efficient. This chapter will cover the following recipes:

- Techniques to make shaders more efficient
- Profiling your shaders
- Modifying our shaders for mobile

Introduction

Learning the art of optimizing your shaders will come up in just about any game project that you work on. There will always come a point in any production where a shader needs to be optimized, or maybe it needs to use fewer textures but produces the same effect. As a technical artist or shader programmer, you have to understand these core fundamentals to optimize your shaders so that you can increase the performance of your game while still achieving the same visual fidelity. Having this knowledge can also help in setting the way in which you write your shader from the start. For instance, by knowing that the game built using your shader will be played on a mobile device, we can automatically set all our `Lighting` functions to use a half-vector as the view direction or set all of our float variable types to fixed or half so as to reduce the amountof memory used. These, and many other techniques, all contribute to your shaders running efficiently on your target hardware. Let's begin our journey and start learning how to optimize our shaders.

Techniques to make shaders more efficient

What is a cheap shader? When first asked the question, it might be a little tough to answer, as there are many elements that go into making a more efficient shader. It could be the amount of memory used up by your variables. It could be the amount of textures the shader is using. It could also be that our shader is working fine, but we can actually produce the same visual effect with half the amount of data by reducing the amount of code we are using or data we are creating. We are going to explore a few of these techniques in this recipe and show how they can be combined to make your shader fast and efficient but still produce the high-quality visuals everyone expects from games today, whether on a mobile or PC.

Getting ready

In order to get this recipe started, we need to gather a few resources together. So, let's perform the following tasks:

1. Create a new scene and fill it with a simple sphere object and single directional light.
2. Create a new shader (`OptimizedShader01`) and material (`OptimizedShader01Mat`) and assign the shader to the material.
3. We then need to assign the material we just created to our sphere object in our new scene:

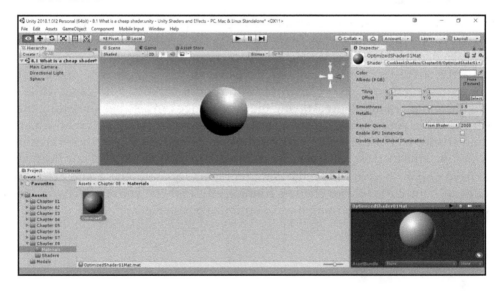

4. Finally, modify the shader so that it uses a diffuse texture and normal map and includes your own custom `Lighting` function.

```
Properties
{
   _MainTex ("Base (RGB)", 2D) = "white" {}
   _NormalMap ("Normal Map", 2D) = "bump" {}
}
SubShader
{
   Tags { "RenderType"="Opaque" }
   LOD 200
   CGPROGRAM
   #pragma surface surf SimpleLambert

   sampler2D _MainTex;
   sampler2D _NormalMap;

   struct Input
   {
      float2 uv_MainTex;
      float2 uv_NormalMap;
   };
   inline float4 LightingSimpleLambert (SurfaceOutput s,
                                        float3 lightDir,
                                        float atten)
   {
    float diff = max (0, dot (s.Normal, lightDir));
    float4 c;
    c.rgb = s.Albedo * _LightColor0.rgb * (diff * atten * 2);
    c.a = s.Alpha;
    return c;
   }

   void surf (Input IN, inout SurfaceOutput o)
   {
      fixed4 c = tex2D (_MainTex, IN.uv_MainTex);
      o.Albedo = c.rgb;
      o.Alpha = c.a;
      o.Normal = UnpackNormal(tex2D(_NormalMap, IN.uv_NormalMap));
   }
   ENDCG
}
FallBack "Diffuse"
```

5. Lastly, assign a base and normal map to your material (I used the `MudRockey` texture included in the assets for `Chapter 1`, *Post Processing Stack*). You should now have a setup similar to the following screenshot.

6. This setup will allow us to take a look at some of the basic concepts that go into optimizing shaders using Surface Shaders in Unity:

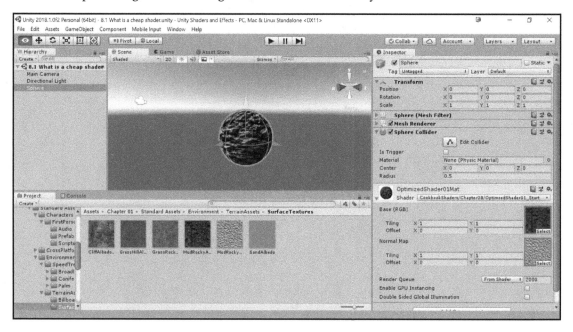

How to do it...

We are going to build a simple `DiffuseShader` to take a look at a few ways in which you can optimize your shaders in general.

First, we'll optimize our variable types so that they use less memory when they are processing data:

1. Let's begin with the `struct Input` in our shader. Currently, our UVs are being stored in a variable of the `float2` type.

2. Remember that floats provide the highest form of precision at a full 32 bits of memory. This is needed for complex trigonometry or exponents, but if you can handle less precision, it's much better to use either a half or a fixed instead. The half type provides up to 3 digits of precision using half the size, or 16 bits of memory. That means we can have a `half2` with the same amount of memory of a single float. We need to change this to use `half2` instead:

```
struct Input
{
    half2 uv_MainTex;
    half2 uv_NormalMap;
};
```

3. We can then move to our `Lighting` function and reduce the variables' memory footprint by changing their types to the following:

```
inline fixed4 LightingSimpleLambert (SurfaceOutput s, fixed3
lightDir, fixed atten)
{
    fixed diff = max (0, dot(s.Normal, lightDir));
    fixed4 c;
    c.rgb = s.Albedo * _LightColor0.rgb * (diff * atten * 2);
    c.a = s.Alpha;
    return c;
}
```

4. In this case, we are using the lowest precision type of `fixed`, which is only 11 bits as compared to the `float` type's 32. This is useful for simple calculations such as color or texture data, which is perfect for this particular case.

In case you'd like a refresher on the fixed type as well as all of the other types we are using, please check out `Chapter 2`, *Creating Your First Shader*, or look at `https://docs.unity3d.com/Manual/SL-DataTypesAndPrecision.html`.

5. Finally, we can complete this optimization pass by updating the variables in our `surf()` function. Since we're using texture data, it's fine for us to use a `fixed4` here instead:

```
void surf (Input IN, inout SurfaceOutput o)
{
  fixed4 c = tex2D (_MainTex, IN.uv_MainTex);
  o.Albedo = c.rgb;
  o.Alpha = c.a;
  o.Normal = UnpackNormal(tex2D(_NormalMap, IN.uv_NormalMap));
}
```

6. Now that we have our variables optimized, we are going to take advantage of a built-in `Lighting` function variable so that we can control how lights are processed by this shader. By doing this, we can greatly reduce the number of lights the shader processes. Modify the `#pragma` statement in your shader with the following code:

```
CGPROGRAM
#pragma surface surf SimpleLambert noforwardadd
```

7. We can optimize this further by sharing UVs between the normal map and diffuse texture. To do this, we simply change the UV lookup in our `UnpackNormal()` function to use _MainTex UVs instead of the UVs of _NormalMap:

```
void surf (Input IN, inout SurfaceOutput o)
{
  fixed4 c = tex2D (_MainTex, IN.uv_MainTex);
  o.Albedo = c.rgb;
  o.Alpha = c.a;
  o.Normal = UnpackNormal(tex2D(_NormalMap, IN.uv_MainTex));
}
```

8. As we have removed the need for the normal map UVs, we need to make sure that we remove the normal map UV code from the `Input` struct:

```
struct Input
{
  half2 uv_MainTex;
};
```

9. Finally, we can further optimize this shader by telling the shader that it only works with certain renderers:

```
CGPROGRAM
#pragma surface surf SimpleLambert exclude_path:prepass
noforwardadd
```

The result of our optimization passes show us that we really don't notice a difference in the visual quality, but we have reduced the amount of time it takes for this shader to be drawn to the screen. You will learn about finding out how much time it takes for a shader to render in the next recipe, but the idea to focus on here is that we achieve the same result with fewer data. So keep this in mind when creating your shaders. The following screenshot shows us the final result of our shader:

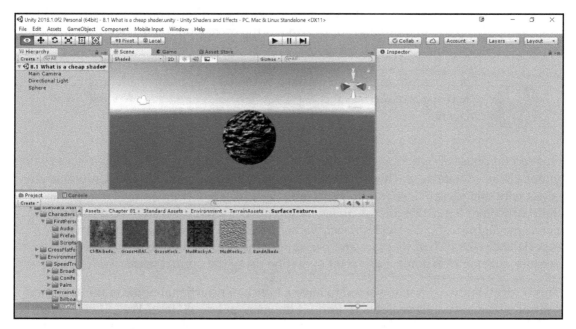

How it works...

Now that we have seen the ways in which we can optimize our shaders, let's dive in a bit deeper and really understand how all of these techniques work, why we should use them, and look at a couple of other techniques that you can try for yourself in your own shaders.

Let's first focus our attention on the size of the data each of our variables is storing when we declare them. If you are familiar with programming, then you will understand that you can declare values or variables with different sizes of types. This means that a float actually has a maximum size in memory. The following description will describe these variable types in much more detail:

- **Float**: A float is a full 32-bit precision value and is the slowest of the three different types we see here. It also has its corresponding values of `float2`, `float3`, and `float4`, which allow us to store multiple floats in one variable.
- **Half**: The half variable type is a reduced 16-bit floating point value and is suitable for store UV values and color values and much faster than using a float value. As with the float type, it has its corresponding values, which are `half2`, `half3`, and `half4`.
- **Fixed**: A fixed value is the smallest in size of the three types, but can be used for lighting calculations and colors and has the corresponding values of `fixed2`, `fixed3`, and `fixed4`.

For more information on working with array types for shaders, check out the *Using packed arrays* recipe from `Chapter 3`, *Surface Shaders and Texture Mapping*.

Our second phase of optimizing our simple shader was to declare the `noforwardadd` value to our `#pragma` statement. This is basically a switch that automatically tells Unity that any object with this particular shader receives only per-pixel light from a single directional light. Any other lights that are calculated by this shader will be forced to be processed as per-vertex lights using *spherical harmonic* values produced internally by Unity. This is especially obvious when we place another light in the scene to light our sphere object because our shader is doing a per-pixel operation using the normal map.

This is great, but what if you wanted to have a bunch of directional lights in the scene and control over which of these lights is used for the main per-pixel light? Well, if you notice, each light has a **Render Mode** drop-down. If you click on this drop-down, you will see a couple of flags that can be set. These are **Auto**, **Important**, and **Not Important**. By selecting a light, you can tell Unity that a light should be considered more as a per-pixel light than a per-vertex light, by setting its render mode to **Important** and vice versa. If you leave a light set to **Auto**, then you will let Unity decide the best course of action:

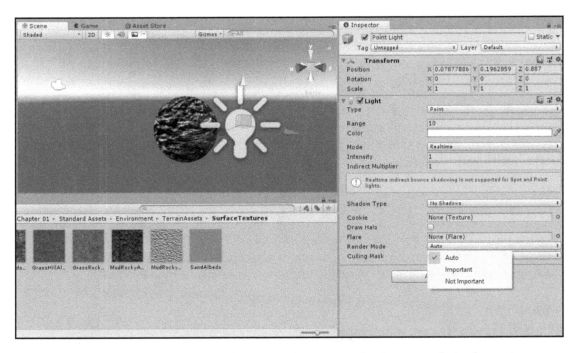

Place another light in your scene and remove the texture that is currently in the main texture for our shader. You will notice that the second point light does not react with the normal map, only the directional light that we created first. The concept here is that you save on per-pixel operations by just calculating all extra lights as vertex lights, and save performance by just calculating the main directional light as a per-pixel light. The following diagram visually demonstrates this concept as the point light is not reacting with the normal map:

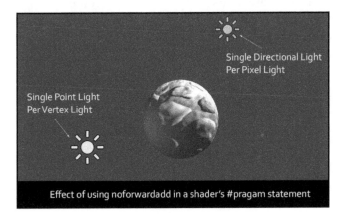

Finally, we did a bit of cleaning up and simply told the normal map texture to use the main texture's UV values, and we got rid of the line of code that pulled in a separate set of UV values specifically for the normal map. This is always a nice way to simplify your code and clean up any unwanted data.

We also declared `exclude_pass: prepass` in our `#pragma` statement so that this shader wouldn't accept any custom lighting from the deferred renderer. This means that we can really use this shader effectively in the forward renderer only, which is set in the main camera's settings.

By taking a bit of time, you will be amazed at how much a shader can be optimized. You have seen how we can pack grayscale textures into a single RGBA texture as well as use lookup textures to fake lighting. There are many ways in which a shader can be optimized, which is why it is always an ambiguous question to ask in the first place, but knowing these different optimization techniques, you can cater your shaders to your game and target platform, ultimately resulting in very streamlined shaders and a nice steady frame rate.

Profiling your shaders

Now that we know how we can reduce the overhead that our shaders might take, let's take a look at how to find problematic shaders in a scene where you might have a lot of shaders or a ton of objects, shaders, and scripts, all running at the same time. To find a single object or shader among a whole game can be quite daunting, but Unity provides us with its built-in **Profiler**. This allows us to actually see, on a frame-by-frame basis, what is happening in the game, and each item that is being used by the GPU and CPU.

Using the **Profiler**, we can isolate items such as shaders, geometry, and general rendering items using its interface to create blocks of profiling jobs. We can filter out items until we are looking at the performance of just a single object. This then lets us see the effects on the CPU and GPU that the object has while it is performing its functions at runtime.

Let's take a look through the different sections of the **Profiler** and learn how to debug our scenes and, most importantly, our shaders.

Getting ready

Let's use our **Profiler** by getting a few assets ready and launching the **Profiler** window:

1. Let's use the scene from the last recipe and launch the Unity **Profiler** from **Window** | **Profiler** or *Ctrl + 7*. Feel free to drag and drop or move it so you can see it well. I personally put it at the same spot as the **Inspector** tab.
2. Let's also duplicate our sphere a couple more times to see how that affects our rendering.
3. From the **Profiler** tab, click on the **Deep Profile** option to get additional information about the project and then play your game!

You should see something similar to the following image:

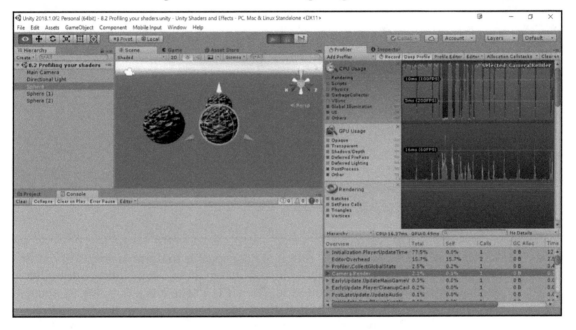

How to do it...

To use the **Profiler**, we will take a look at some of the UI elements of this window. Before we hit Play, let's take a look at how to get the information we need from the **Profiler**:

1. First, click on the larger blocks in the **Profiler** window called **GPU Usage**, **CPU Usage**, and **Rendering**. You will find these blocks on the left-hand side of the upper window:

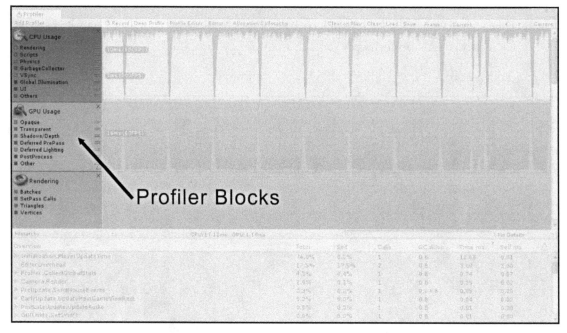

2. Using these blocks, we can see different data specific to those major functions of our game. The **CPU Usage** is showing us what most of our scripts are doing, as well as physics and overall rendering. The **GPU Usage** block is giving us detailed information about the elements that are specific to our lighting, shadows, and render queues. Finally, the **Rendering** block is giving us information about the drawcalls and amount of geometry we have in our scene at any one frame.

If you do not see the GPU Usage option, click on **Add Profiler** | **GPU**. It is possible that it may not show up if your graphics card drivers are not up to date.

By clicking on each of these blocks, we can isolate the type of data we see during our profiling session.

3. Now, click on the tiny colored blocks in one of these **Profile** blocks and hit Play, or *Ctrl + P*, to run the scene.

4. This lets us dive down even deeper into our profiling session so that we can filter out what is being reported back to us. While the scene is running, uncheck all of the boxes, except for **Opaque** in the **GPU Usage** block. Notice that we can now see just how much time is being used to render the objects that are set to the **Render Queue** of **Opaque**:

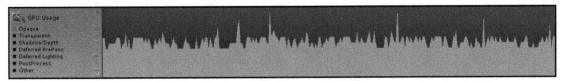

5. Another great function of the **Profiler** window is the action of clicking and dragging in the graph view.

6. This will automatically pause your game so that you can further analyze a certain spike in the graph to find out exactly which item is causing the performance problem. Click and drag around in the graph view to pause the game and see the effect of using this functionality:

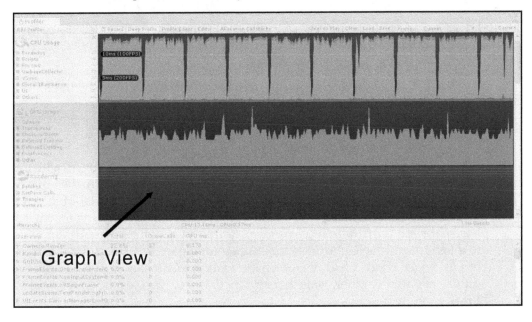

Graph View

7. Turning our attention now towards the lower half of the **Profiler** window, you will notice that there is a dropdown item available when we have the **GPU Block** selected. We can expand this to get even more detailed information about the current active profiling session and, in this case, more information about what the camera is currently rendering and how much time it is taking up:

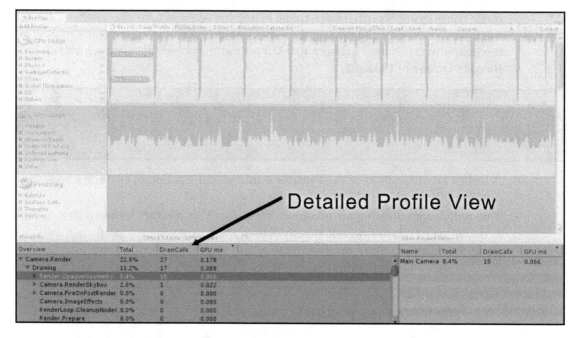

Detailed Profile View

> **TIP**
>
> If you click on the button that says **No Details** and changes the option to **Show Related Objects**, you can see what objects are being used in the functions being called.

8. This gives us a complete look at the inner workings of what Unity is processing in this particular frame. In this case, we can see that our three spheres with our optimized shader are taking roughly **0.066** milliseconds to draw to the screen, they are taking up fifteen drawcalls, and this process is taking **8.4%** of the GPU's time in every frame (the numbers will likely be different depending on what hardware you have for your computer). It's this type of information we can use to diagnose and solve performance issues with regard to shaders. Let's conduct a test to see the effects of adding one more texture to our shader and blending two diffuse textures together using a `lerp` function. You will see the effects in the **Profiler** pretty clearly.

9. Modify the `Properties` block of your shader with the following code to give us another texture to use:

```
Properties
{
  _MainTex ("Base (RGB)", 2D) = "white" {}
  _BlendTex("Blend Texture", 2D) = "white" {}
  _NormalMap ("Normal Map", 2D) = "bump" {}
}
```

10. Then let's feed our texture to `CGPROGRAM`:

```
sampler2D _MainTex;
sampler2D _NormalMap;
sampler2D _BlendTex;
```

11. Now it's time to update our `surf()` function accordingly so that we blend our diffuse textures together:

```
void surf (Input IN, inout SurfaceOutput o)
{
  fixed4 c = tex2D (_MainTex, IN.uv_MainTex);
  fixed4 blendTex = tex2D(_BlendTex, IN.uv_MainTex);

  c = lerp(c, blendTex, blendTex.r);

  o.Albedo = c.rgb;
  o.Alpha = c.a;
  o.Normal = UnpackNormal(tex2D(_NormalMap, IN.uv_MainTex));
}
```

Once you save your modifications in your shader and return to Unity's editor, we can run our game and see the increase in milliseconds of our new shader.

12. Attach a new texture inside of your `Blend Texture`:

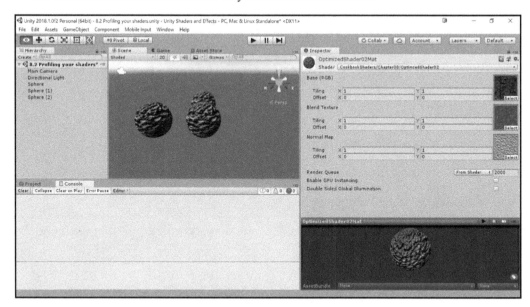

13. Press Play to start the game again with the **Profiler** turned on. Press Play once you have returned to Unity and let's take a look at the results in our **Profiler**:

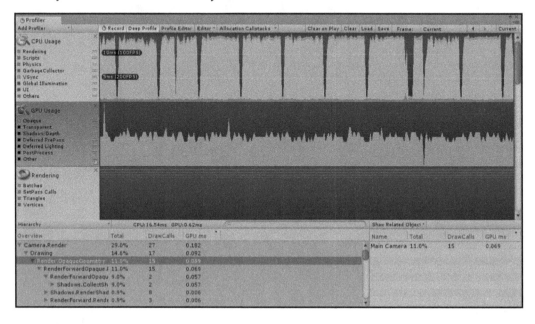

You can see now that the amount of time to render our **Opaque** Shaders in this scene is taking **0.069** milliseconds, up from **0.066** milliseconds. By adding another texture and using the `lerp()` function, we increased the render time for our spheres. While it's a small change, imagine having 20 shaders all working in different ways on different objects.

Using the information given here, you can pinpoint areas that are causing performance decreases more quickly and solve these issues using the techniques from the previous recipe.

How it works...

While it's completely out of the scope of this book to describe how this tool actually works internally, we can surmise that Unity has given us a way to view the computer's performance while our game is running. Basically, this window is tied very tightly to the CPU and GPU to give us real-time feedback of how much time is being taken for each of our scripts, objects, and render queues. Using this information, we have seen that we can track the efficiency of our shader writing to eliminate problem areas and code.

It's important to note that games running with the **Profiler** open, as well as from within the editor in general, will make the game slightly slower than it would be when compiled and running in a normal situation. You might even see the **Editor** in the **Profilers** list of CPU expenses.

There's more...

It is also possible to profile specifically for mobile platforms. Unity provides us with a couple of extra features when the Android or iOS build target is set in the **Build Settings**. We can actually get real-time information from our mobile devices while the game is running. This becomes very useful because you are able to profile directly on the device itself instead of profiling directly in your editor. To find out more about this process, refer to Unity's documentation at the following link:

`http://docs.unity3d.com/Documentation/Manual/MobileProfiling.html`.

Modifying our shaders for mobile

Now that we have seen quite a broad set of techniques for making really optimized shaders, let's take a look at writing a nice, high-quality shader targeted for a mobile device. It is actually quite easy to make a few adjustments to the shaders we have written so that they run faster on a mobile device. This includes elements such as using the `approxview` or `halfasview Lighting` function variables. We can also reduce the amount of textures we need and even apply better compression for the textures we are using. By the end of this recipe, we will have a nicely optimized normal-mapped, Specular Shader for use in our mobile games.

Getting ready

Before we begin, let's get a fresh new scene and fill it with some objects to apply our `MobileShader`:

1. Create a new scene and fill it with a default sphere and single directional light.
2. Create a new material (`MobileMat`) and shader (`MobileShader`), and assign the shader to the material.
3. Finally, assign the material to our sphere object in our scene.

When completed, you should have a scene similar to the one in the following screenshot:

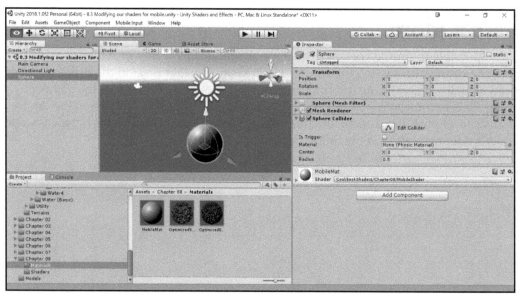

How to do it...

For this recipe, we will write a mobile-friendly shader from scratch and discuss the elements that make it more mobile friendly:

1. Let's first populate our `Properties` block with the textures required. In this case, we are going to use a single `_Diffuse` texture with the gloss map in its alpha channel, `Normal map`, and a slider for specular intensity:

   ```
   Properties
   {
     _Diffuse ("Base (RGB) Specular Amount (A)", 2D) = "white" {}
     _SpecIntensity ("Specular Width", Range(0.01, 1)) = 0.5
     _NormalMap ("Normal Map", 2D) = "bump"{}
   }
   ```

2. Our next task is to set up our `#pragma` declarations. This will simply turn certain features of the Surface Shader on and off, ultimately making the shader cheaper or more expensive:

   ```
   CGPROGRAM
   #pragma surface surf MobileBlinnPhong exclude_path:prepass
   nolightmap noforwardadd halfasview
   ```

   The highlighted line should be on one line.

3. Next, remove the `#pragma target 3.0` line, as we are not using any of the features of it.

4. We then need to make the connection between our `Properties` block and CGPROGRAM. This time, we are going to use the fixed variable type for our specular intensity slider in order to reduce its memory usage:

   ```
   sampler2D _Diffuse;
   sampler2D _NormalMap;
   fixed _SpecIntensity;
   ```

5. In order for us to map our textures to the surface of our object, we need to get some UVs. In this case, we are going to get only one set of UVs to keep the amount of data in our shader down to a minimum:

```
struct Input
{
  half2 uv_Diffuse;
};
```

6. The next step is to fill in our Lighting function using a few of the new input variables that are available to us when using the new #pragma declarations:

```
inline fixed4 LightingMobileBlinnPhong (SurfaceOutput s, fixed3
lightDir, fixed3 halfDir, fixed atten)
    {
      fixed diff = max (0, dot (s.Normal, lightDir));
      fixed nh = max (0, dot (s.Normal, halfDir));
      fixed spec = pow (nh, s.Specular*128) * s.Gloss;
      fixed4 c;
      c.rgb = (s.Albedo * _LightColor0.rgb * diff +
_LightColor0.rgb * spec) * (atten*2);
      c.a = 0.0;
      return c;
    }
```

7. Finally, we complete the shader by creating the surf() function and processing the final color of our surface:

```
void surf (Input IN, inout SurfaceOutput o)
{
  fixed4 diffuseTex = tex2D (_Diffuse, IN.uv_Diffuse);
  o.Albedo = diffuseTex.rgb;
  o.Gloss = diffuseTex.a;
  o.Alpha = 0.0;
  o.Specular = _SpecIntensity;
  o.Normal = UnpackNormal(tex2D(_NormalMap, IN.uv_Diffuse));
}
```

8. When finished with the code portion of this recipe, save your shader and return to the Unity editor to let the shader compile. If no errors occurred, assign some properties for the **Base** and **Normal Map** properties:

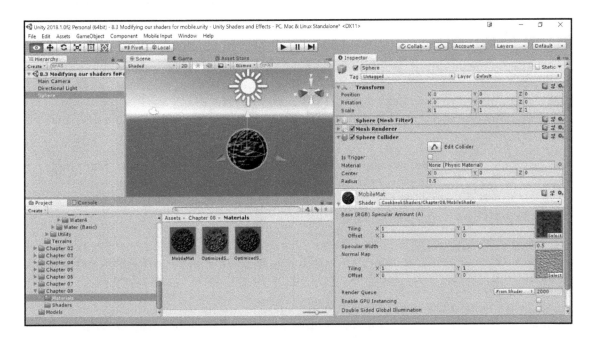

9. Add a few point lights and some copies of the new object and you should see a result similar to the following screenshot:

How it works...

So, let's begin the description of this shader by explaining what it does and doesn't do. First, it excludes the deferred lighting pass. This means that if you created a `Lighting` function that was connected to the deferred renderer's `prepass`, it wouldn't use that particular `Lighting` function and would look for the default `Lighting` function like the ones that we have been creating thus far in this book.

This particular shader does not support *lightmapping* by Unity's internal light-mapping system. This just keeps the shader from trying to find light maps for the object that the shader is attached to, making the shader more performance-friendly because it is not having to perform the lightmapping check.

We included the `noforwardadd` declaration so that we process only per-pixel textures with a single directional light. All other lights are forced to become per-vertex lights and will not be included in any per-pixel operations you might do in the `surf()` function.

Finally, we are using the `halfasview` declaration to tell Unity that we aren't going to use the main `viewDir` parameter found in a normal `Lighting` function. Instead, we are going to use the half vector as the view direction and process our specular with this. This becomes much faster for the shader to process as it will be done on a per-vertex basis. It isn't completely accurate when it comes to simulating specular in the real world, but visually, on a mobile device, it looks just fine and the shader is more optimized.

It's techniques like these that make a shader more efficient and cleaner, codewise. Always make sure that you are using only the data you need while weighing this against your target hardware and the visual quality that the game requires. In the end, a cocktail of these techniques is what ultimately makes up your shaders for your games.

Screen Effects with Unity Render Textures

9

In this chapter, you will learn the following recipes:

- Setting up the screen effects script system
- Using brightness, saturation, and contrast with screen effects
- Using basic Photoshop-like Blend modes with screen effects
- Using the Overlay Blend mode with screen effects

Introduction

One of the most impressive aspects of learning to write shaders is the process of creating your own screen effects, also known as post effects. With these screen effects, we can create stunning real-time images with Bloom, Motion Blur, HDR effects, and so on. Most modern games on the market today make heavy use of these screen effects for their depth of field effects, Bloom effects, and even color correction effects.

In `Chapter 1`, *Post Processing Stack*, we discussed how to use this with Unity's built-in Post Processing Stack, but in this chapter, you will learn how to build up the script system yourself. This system will give you the control to create many kinds of screen effects. We will cover `RenderTexture`, what the depth buffer is, and how to create effects that give you Photoshop-like control over the final rendered image of your game. By utilizing screen effects for your games, you not only round out your shader writing knowledge, but you will also have the power to create your own incredible real-time renders with Unity from scratch.

Setting up the screen effects script system

The process of creating screen effects is one in which we grab a full-screen image (or texture), use a shader to process its pixels on the GPU, and then send it back to Unity's renderer to apply it to the whole rendered image of the game. This allows us to perform per-pixel operations on the rendered image of the game in real time, giving us a more global artistic control.

Imagine if you had to go through and adjust each material on each object in your game to just adjust the contrast of the final look of your game. While not impossible, this would take a bit of labor to perform. By utilizing a screen effect, we can adjust the screen's final look as a whole, thereby giving us more Photoshop-like control over our game's final appearance.

In order to get a screen effect system up and running, we have to set up a single script to act as the courier of the game's current rendered image, or what Unity calls the RenderTexture. By utilizing this script to pass the RenderTexture to a shader, we can create a flexible system for establishing screen effects. For our first screen effect, we are going to create a very simple grayscale effect and make our game look black and white. Let's take a look at how this is done.

Getting ready

In order to get our screen effects system up and running, we need to create a few assets for our current Unity project. By doing this, we will set ourselves up for the steps in the following sections:

1. In the current project, create a new scene to work in.
2. Create a simple sphere in the scene and assign it a new material (I called mine RedMat). This new material can be anything, but for our example, we will make a simple red material using the Standard Shader.
3. Finally, create a new directional light and save the scene.
4. We need to create a new C# script and call it TestRenderImage.cs. For organization purposes, create a folder called Scripts from the **Project** tab to put it in.

With all of our assets ready, you should have a simple scene setup, which looks similar to the following screenshot:

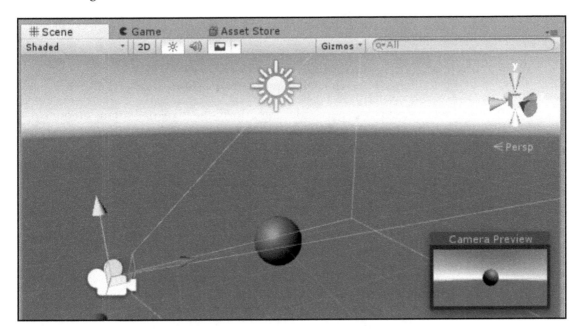

How to do it...

In order to make our grayscale screen effect work, we need a script and shader. So, we will complete these two new items here and fill them in with the appropriate code to produce our first screen effect. Our first task is to complete the C# script. This will get the whole system running. After this, we will complete the shader and see the results of our screen effect. Let's complete our script and shader with the following steps:

1. Open the `TestRenderImage.cs` C# script and begin by entering a few variables that we will need to store important objects and data. Enter the following code at the very top of the `TestRenderImage` class:

```
#region Variables
public Shader curShader;
public float greyscaleAmount = 1.0f;
private Material screenMat;
#endregion
```

2. In order for us to edit the screen effect in real time, when the Unity editor isn't playing, we need to enter the following line of code just above the declaration of the `TestRenderImage` class:

```
using UnityEngine;

[ExecuteInEditMode]
public class TestRenderImage : MonoBehaviour {
```

3. As our screen effect is using a shader to perform the pixel operations on our screen image, we have to create a material to run the shader. Without this, we can't access the properties of the shader. For this, we will create a C# property to check for a material, and create one if it doesn't find one. Enter the following code just after the declaration of the variables from *step 1*:

```
#region Properties
Material ScreenMat
{
    get
    {
        if (screenMat == null)
        {
            screenMat = new Material(curShader);
            screenMat.hideFlags = HideFlags.HideAndDontSave;
        }
        return screenMat;
    }
}
#endregion
```

4. We now want to set up some checks in our script to see if the current target platform that we are building the Unity game on actually supports image effects. If it doesn't find anything at the start of this script, then the script will disable itself:

```
void Start()
{
    if (!SystemInfo.supportsImageEffects)
    {
        enabled = false;
        return;
    }

    if (!curShader && !curShader.isSupported)
    {
        enabled = false;
```

```
        }
    }
```

5. To actually grab the rendered image from the Unity renderer, we need to make use of the following built-in function that Unity provides us, called `OnRenderImage()`. Enter the following code so that we can have access to the current `RenderTexture`:

```
void OnRenderImage(RenderTexture sourceTexture, RenderTexture
destTexture)
{
    if (curShader != null)
    {
        ScreenMat.SetFloat("_Luminosity", greyscaleAmount);

        Graphics.Blit(sourceTexture, destTexture, ScreenMat);
    }
    else
    {
        Graphics.Blit(sourceTexture, destTexture);
    }
}
```

6. Our screen effect has a variable called `grayScaleAmount` with which we can control how much grayscale we want for our final screen effect. So, in this case, we need to make the value go from 0 to 1, where 0 is no grayscale effect and 1 is a full grayscale effect. We will perform this operation in the `Update()` function, which will be called every frame while the game is running:

```
void Update ()
{
    greyscaleAmount = Mathf.Clamp(greyscaleAmount, 0.0f, 1.0f);
}
```

7. Finally, we complete our script by doing a little bit of clean-up on objects we created when the script started:

```
void OnDisable()
{
  if(screenMat)
  {
    DestroyImmediate(screenMat);
  }
}
```

8. At this point, we can now apply this script to the camera, if it compiled without errors, in Unity. Let's apply the `TestRenderImage.cs` script to our main camera in our scene. You should see the `grayScaleAmount` value and a field for a shader, but the script throws an error to the console window. It says that it is missing an instance to an object and so won't process appropriately. If you recall from *step 4*, we are doing some checks to see whether we have a shader and if the current platform supports the shader. As we haven't given the screen effect script a shader to work with, then the `curShader` variable is just null, which throws an error. Let's continue with our screen effects system by completing the shader.

9. Create a new shader called `ScreenGrayscale`. To begin our shader, we will populate our `Properties` with some variables so that we can send data to this shader:

```
Properties
{
  _MainTex ("Base (RGB)", 2D) = "white" {}
  _Luminosity("Luminosity", Range(0.0, 1)) = 1.0
}
```

10. Our shader is now going to utilize pure CG shader code instead of utilizing Unity's built-in Surface Shader code. This will make our screen effect more optimized as we need to work only with the pixels of the `RenderTexture`. So, we will delete everything inside of the `Pass` that was there before and create a new `Pass` block in our shader and fill it with some new `#pragma` statements that we haven't seen before:

```
SubShader
{
  Pass
  {
    CGPROGRAM
    #pragma vertex vert_img
    #pragma fragment frag
    #pragma fragmentoption ARB_precision_hint_fastest
    #include "UnityCG.cginc"
```

11. In order to access the data being sent to the shader from the Unity editor, we need to create the corresponding variables in our `CGPROGRAM`:

```
uniform sampler2D _MainTex;
fixed _Luminosity;
```

12. Finally, all we need to do is set up our pixel function, in this case called `frag()`. This is where the meat of the screen effect is. This function will process each pixel of the `RenderTexture` and return a new image to our `TestRenderImage.cs` script:

```
fixed4 frag(v2f_img i) : COLOR
{
  //Get the colors from the RenderTexture and the uv's
  //from the v2f_img struct
  fixed4 renderTex = tex2D(_MainTex, i.uv);
  //Apply the Luminosity values to our render texture
  float luminosity = 0.299 * renderTex.r + 0.587 * renderTex.g
+ 0.114 * renderTex.b;
  fixed4 finalColor = lerp(renderTex, luminosity, _Luminosity);
  renderTex.rgb = finalColor;

  return renderTex;
}
```

13. Lastly, change the `FallBack` line to the following:

```
FallBack off
```

14. The final shader should look as follows:

```
Shader "CookbookShaders/Chapter09/Grayscale"
{
  Properties
  {
    _MainTex ("Base (RGB)", 2D) = "white" {}
    _Luminosity("Luminosity", Range(0.0, 1)) = 1.0
  }

  SubShader
  {
    Pass
    {
      CGPROGRAM
      #pragma vertex vert_img
      #pragma fragment frag
      #pragma fragmentoption ARB_precision_hint_fastest
      #include "UnityCG.cginc"

      uniform sampler2D _MainTex;
      fixed _Luminosity;

      fixed4 frag(v2f_img i) : COLOR
```

```
        {
            //Get the colors from the RenderTexture and the uv's
            //from the v2f_img struct
            fixed4 renderTex = tex2D(_MainTex, i.uv);
            //Apply the Luminosity values to our render texture
            float luminosity = 0.299 * renderTex.r + 0.587 *
renderTex.g + 0.114 * renderTex.b;
            fixed4 finalColor = lerp(renderTex, luminosity,
_Luminosity);

            renderTex.rgb = finalColor;
            return renderTex;
        }
    ENDCG
    }
}
    FallBack off
}
```

Once the shader is complete, return to Unity and let it compile to see if any errors occurred. If not, assign the new shader to the `TestRenderImage.cs` script and change the value of the grayscale amount variable. You should see the game view go from a colored version of the game to a grayscale version of the game:

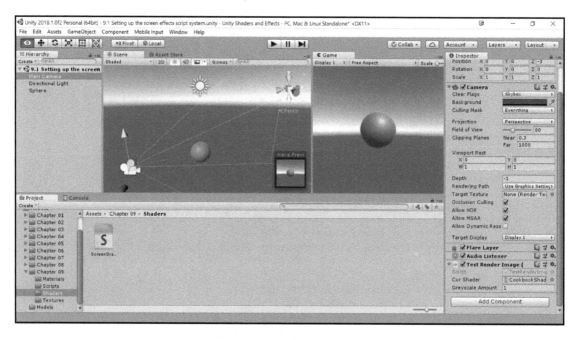

The following screenshot demonstrates this Screen Effect:

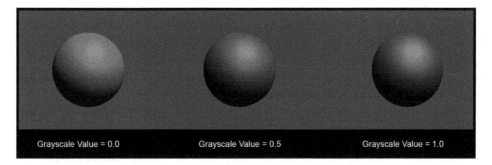

With this complete, we now have an easy way to test out new screen effect shaders without having to write our whole screen effect system over and over again. Let's dive in a little deeper and learn about what's going on with the RenderTexture and how it is processed throughout its existence.

How it works...

To get a screen effect up and running inside of Unity, we need to create a script and shader. The script drives the real-time update in the editor and is also responsible for capturing the RenderTexture from the main camera and passing it to the shader. Once the RenderTexture gets to the shader, we can use the shader to perform per-pixel operations.

At the start of the script, we perform a few checks to make sure that the current selected build platform actually supports screen effects and the shader itself. There are instances where a current platform will not support screen effects or the shader that we are using. So, the checks that we do in the Start() function ensure we don't get any errors if the platform doesn't support the screen system.

Once the script passes these checks, we initiate the screen effects system by calling the built-in OnRenderImage() function. This function is responsible for grabbing the renderTexture, giving it to the shader using the Graphics.Blit() function, and returning the processed image to the Unity renderer. You can find more information on these two functions at the following URLs:

- OnRenderImage: http://docs.unity3d.com/Documentation/ScriptReference/MonoBehaviour.OnRenderImage.html
- Graphics.Blit: http://docs.unity3d.com/Documentation/ScriptReference/Graphics.Blit.html

Once the current `RenderTexture` reaches the shader, the shader takes it, processes it through the `frag()` function, and returns the final color for each pixel.

You can see how powerful this becomes as it gives us Photoshop-like control over the final rendered image of our game. These screen effects work sequentially like Photoshop layers on top of what the camera sees. When you place these screen effects one after the other, they will be processed in that order. These are just the bare bones steps to get a screen effect working, but it is the core of how the screen effects system works.

There's more...

Now that we have our simple screen effect system up and running, let's take a look at some of the other useful information we can obtain from Unity's renderer:

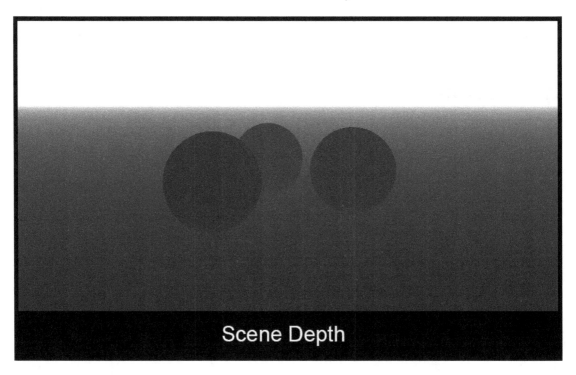

Scene Depth

We can actually get the depth of everything in our current game by turning on Unity's built-in **Depth** mode. Once this is turned on, we can use the depth information for a ton of different effects. Let's take a look at how this is done:

1. Duplicate the sphere we created twice and create a plane underneath:

2. Create a new shader by duplicating the `ScreenGreyscale` code by selecting it and pressing *Ctrl + D*. Once duplicated, rename the script to `SceneDepth`. Then double-click on this shader to open it in your script editor.

3. We will create the main texture (`_MainTex`) property and a property to control the power of the scene depth effect. Enter the following code in your shader:

```
Properties
{
    _MainTex ("Base (RGB)", 2D) = "white" {}
    _DepthPower("Depth Power", Range(0, 1)) = 1
}
```

4. Now we need to create the corresponding variables in our CGPROGRAM. We are going to add one more variable called _CameraDepthTexture. This is a built-in variable that Unity has provided us with through the use of the UnityCG.cginclude file. It gives us the depth information from the camera:

```
Pass
{
  CGPROGRAM
  #pragma vertex vert_img
  #pragma fragment frag
  #pragma fragmentoption ARB_precision_hint_fastest
  #include "UnityCG.cginc"

  uniform sampler2D _MainTex;
  fixed _DepthPower;
  sampler2D _CameraDepthTexture;
```

5. We will complete our depth shader by utilizing a couple of built-in functions that Unity provides us with, the UNITY_SAMPLE_DEPTH() and linear01Depth() functions. The first function actually gets the depth information from our _CameraDepthTexture and produces a single float value for each pixel. The Linear01Depth() function then makes sure that the values are within the 0-1 range by taking this final depth value to a power we can control, where the mid-value in the 0-1 range sits in the scene based off of the camera position:

```
fixed4 frag(v2f_img i) : COLOR
{
  //Get the colors from the RenderTexture and the uv's
  //from the v2f_img struct
  float depth = UNITY_SAMPLE_DEPTH(tex2D(_CameraDepthTexture,
i.uv.xy));
  depth = pow(Linear01Depth(depth), _DepthPower);

  return depth;
}
```

6. With our shader complete, let's turn our attention to the Unity editor and create a new script to work with. Select our TestRenderImage script and duplicate it. Name this new script RenderDepth and open it up in your script editor.

7. Update the script to have the same class name as we renamed it to in the previous step (RenderDepth):

```
using UnityEngine;

[ExecuteInEditMode]
public class RenderDepth : MonoBehaviour {
```

8. We need to add the depthPower variable to the script so that we can let users change the value in the editor:

```
#region Variables
public Shader curShader;
public float depthPower = 0.2f;
private Material screenMat;
#endregion
```

9. Our OnRenderImage() function then needs to be updated so that it is passing the right value to our shader:

```
void OnRenderImage(RenderTexture sourceTexture, RenderTexture destTexture)
{
    if (curShader != null)
    {
        ScreenMat.SetFloat("_DepthPower", depthPower);

        Graphics.Blit(sourceTexture, destTexture, ScreenMat);
    }
    else
    {
        Graphics.Blit(sourceTexture, destTexture);
    }
}
```

10. To complete our depth screen effect, we need to tell Unity to turn on the depth rendering in the current camera. This is done by simply setting the main camera's depthTextureMode:

```
void Update ()
{
    Camera.main.depthTextureMode = DepthTextureMode.Depth;
    depthPower = Mathf.Clamp(depthPower, 0, 1);
}
```

With all the code set up, save your script and shader and return to Unity to let them both compile. Afterward, select the **Main Camera**, right-click on the **TextRenderImage** component, and select **Remove Component**. Afterward, attach this new component to the object and drag and drop our new shader inside. If no errors are encountered, you should see a result similar to the following screenshot:

Here's an example of what we can get if we tweak the values even more:

Using brightness, saturation, and contrast with screen effects

Now that we have our screen effects system up and running, we can explore how to create more involved pixel operations to perform some of the more common screen effects found in games today.

Using a screen effect to adjust the overall final colors of your game is crucial in giving artists global control over the final look of the game. Techniques such as color adjustment sliders allow users to adjust the intensity of the reds, blues, and greens of the final rendered game. This concept is also used with techniques such as putting a certain tone of color over the whole screen, as seen in something like a sepia film effect.

For this particular recipe, we are going to cover some of the more core color adjustment operations we can perform on an image. These are brightness, saturation, and contrast. Learning how to code these color adjustments gives us a nice base from which we can learn the art of screen effects.

Getting ready

We will need to create a couple of new assets. We can utilize the same scene as our test scene, but we will need a new script and shader:

1. Create a new scene by going to **File | New Scene**.
2. Add a couple of new objects to the scene, set up some different colored diffuse materials, and randomly assign them to the new objects in the scene. This will give us a good range of colors to test with our new screen effect:

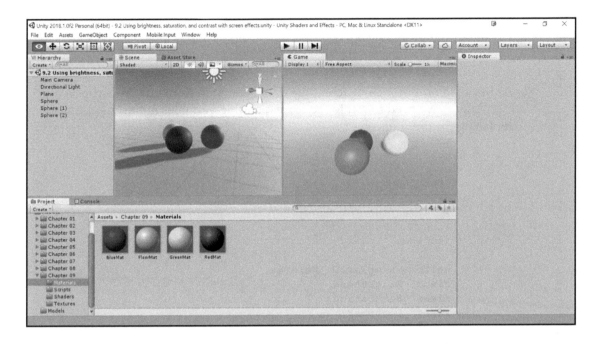

How to do it...

Now that we have completed our scene setup and created our new script and shader, we can begin to fill in the code necessary to achieve the brightness, saturation, and contrast screen effects. We will be focusing on just the pixel operation and variable setup for our script and shader, since getting a screen effect system up and running is described in the *Setting up the screen effects script system* recipe in this chapter:

1. Create a new shader by duplicating the `ScreenGreyscale` code by selecting it from the **Project** tab under the `Chapter 9 | Shaders` folder and pressing *Ctrl + D*. Once duplicated, rename the script to `ScreenBSC`. Then double-click on this shader to open it in your script editor.

2. Editing the shader first makes more sense so that we know what kind of variables we will need for our C# script. Let's begin by entering the appropriate properties for our brightness, saturation, and contrast effect. Remember that we need to keep the `_MainTex` property in our shader as this is the property that the `RenderTexture` targets when creating screen effects:

```
Properties
{
    _MainTex ("Base (RGB)", 2D) = "white" {}
```

```
_Brightness("Brightness", Range(0.0, 1)) = 1.0
_Saturation("Saturation", Range(0.0, 1)) = 1.0
_Contrast("Contrast", Range(0.0, 1)) = 1.0
}
```

3. As usual, in order for us to access the data coming in from our properties in our CGPROGRAM, we need to create the corresponding variables in the CGPROGRAM, replacing the previous ones:

```
Pass
{
  CGPROGRAM
  #pragma vertex vert_img
  #pragma fragment frag
  #pragma fragmentoption ARB_precision_hint_fastest
  #include "UnityCG.cginc"

  uniform sampler2D _MainTex;
  fixed _Brightness;
  fixed _Saturation;
  fixed _Contrast;
```

4. Now, we need to create the operations that will perform the brightness, saturation, and contrast effects. Enter the following new function in our shader, just above the frag() function:

```
float3 ContrastSaturationBrightness(float3 color, float brt,
float sat, float con)
{
  // Increase or decrease these values to
  //adjust r, g and b color channels separately
  float AvgLumR = 0.5;
  float AvgLumG = 0.5;
  float AvgLumB = 0.5;
//Luminance coefficients for getting lumoinance from the image
  float3 LuminanceCoeff = float3(0.2125, 0.7154, 0.0721);
  //Operation for brightness
  float3 AvgLumin = float3(AvgLumR, AvgLumG, AvgLumB);
  float3 brtColor = color * brt;
  float intensityf = dot(brtColor, LuminanceCoeff);
  float3 intensity = float3(intensityf, intensityf,
intensityf);
  //Operation for Saturation
  float3 satColor = lerp(intensity, brtColor, sat);
  //Operation for Contrast
  float3 conColor = lerp(AvgLumin, satColor, con);
  return conColor;
```

```
}
```

Don't worry if it doesn't make sense just yet; all the code will be explained in the *How it works* section of this recipe.

5. Finally, we just need to update our frag() function to actually use the ContrastSaturationBrightness() function. This will process all the pixels of our RenderTexture and pass it back to our script:

```
fixed4 frag(v2f_img i) : COLOR
{
    //Get the colors from the RenderTexture and the uv's
    //from the v2f_img struct
    fixed4 renderTex = tex2D(_MainTex, i.uv);
    //Apply the Brughtness, saturation, contrast operations
    renderTex.rgb = ContrastSaturationBrightness(renderTex.rgb,
                        _Brightness,
                        _Saturation,
                        _Contrast);
    return renderTex;
}
```

With the code entered in the shader, return to the Unity editor to let the new shader compile. If there are no errors, we can return to our code editor to work on our script. Let's begin by creating a couple of new lines of code that will send the proper data to our shader:

1. Now that the shader is finished, let's work on the script needed to make the effect show up. From the **Project** tab, go to the Chapter 9 | Scripts folder. Once there, select the TestRenderImage script and duplicate it by pressing *Ctrl + D*. Rename the newly created script to RenderBSC. Once renamed, double-click on it to enter your IDE of choice.

2. To modify our script, we need to rename the class to match our filename, RenderBSC:

```
[ExecuteInEditMode]
public class RenderBSC : MonoBehaviour {
```

3. Afterward, we need to add the proper variables that will drive the values of our screen effect. In this case, we will need a slider for brightness, a slider for saturation, and a slider for contrast:

```
#region Variables
public Shader curShader;
public float brightness = 1.0f;
public float saturation = 1.0f;
public float contrast = 1.0f;
private Material screenMat;
#endregion
```

4. With our variables set up, we now need to tell the script to send the values of the variables we created to the shader. We do this in the OnRenderImage() function:

```
void OnRenderImage(RenderTexture sourceTexture, RenderTexture
destTexture)
{
    if (curShader != null)
    {
        ScreenMat.SetFloat("_Brightness", brightness);
        ScreenMat.SetFloat("_Saturation", saturation);
        ScreenMat.SetFloat("_Contrast", contrast);

        Graphics.Blit(sourceTexture, destTexture, ScreenMat);
    }
    else
    {
        Graphics.Blit(sourceTexture, destTexture);
    }
}
```

5. Finally, all we need to do is clamp the values of the variables within a range that is reasonable. These clamp values are entirely preferential, so you can use whichever values you see fit:

```
void Update()
{
    brightness = Mathf.Clamp(brightness, 0.0f, 2.0f);
    saturation = Mathf.Clamp(saturation, 0.0f, 2.0f);
    contrast = Mathf.Clamp(contrast, 0.0f, 3.0f);
}
```

With the script completed and shader finished, we simply assign our script to our **Main Camera** and our shader to the script, and you should see the effects of brightness, saturation, and contrast by manipulating the property values:

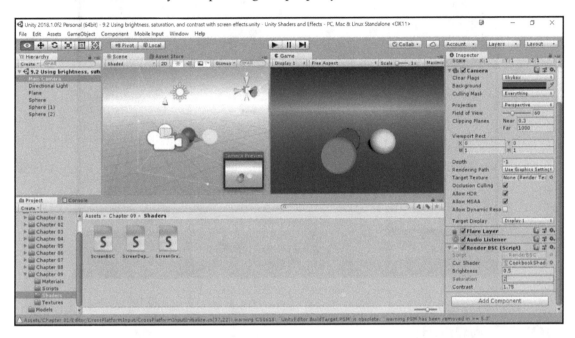

The following screenshot shows a result you can achieve with this screen effect:

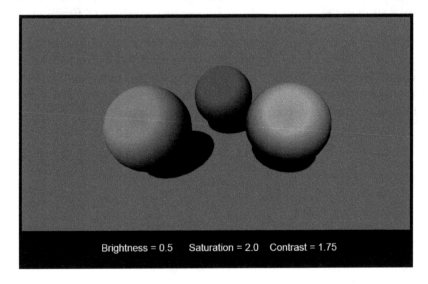

The following screenshot shows another example of what can be done by adjusting the colors of the render image:

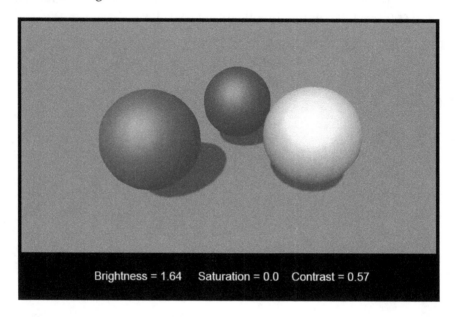

Brightness = 1.64   Saturation = 0.0   Contrast = 0.57

How it works...

Since we now know how the basic screen effects system works, let's just cover the per-pixel operations we created in the ContrastSaturationBrightness() function.

The function starts by taking a few arguments. The first and most important is the current RenderTexture. The other arguments simply adjust the overall effect of the screen effect and are represented by sliders in the screen effect's **Inspector** tab. Once the function receives the RenderTexture and the adjustment values, it declares a few constant values that we use to modify and compare against the original RenderTexture.

The `luminanceCoeff` variable stores the values that will give us the overall brightness of the current image. These coefficients are based on the CIE color matching functions and are pretty standard throughout the industry. We can find the overall brightness of the image by getting the dot product of the current image dotted with these luminance coefficients. Once we have the brightness, we simply use a couple of `lerp` functions to blend the grayscale version of the brightness operation and the original image, multiplied by the brightness value being passed into the function.

Screen effects such as this are crucial to achieving high-quality graphics for your games as they let you tweak the final look of your game without you having to edit each material in your current game scene.

Using basic Photoshop-like Blend modes with screen effects

The screen effects aren't just limited to adjusting the colors of a rendered image from our game. We can also use them to combine other images with our `RenderTexture`. This technique is no different than creating a new layer in Photoshop and choosing a **Blend** mode to blend two images together or, in our case, a texture with a `RenderTexture`. This becomes a very powerful technique as it gives the artists in a production environment a way to simulate their blending modes in the game rather than just in Photoshop.

For this particular recipe, we are going to take a look at some of the more common blend modes, such as **Multiply**, **Add**, and **Overlay**. You will see how simple it is to have the power of Photoshop **Blend** modes in your game.

Getting ready

To begin, we have to get our assets ready. So let's follow the next few steps to get our screen effects system up and running for our new **Blend** mode screen effect:

1. We will need another texture to perform our **Blend** mode effect. In this recipe, we will use a grunge-type texture. This will make the effect very obvious when we are testing it out.

2. The following screenshot is the grunge map used in the making of this effect. Finding a texture with enough detail and a nice range of grayscale values will make for a nice texture to test our new effect:

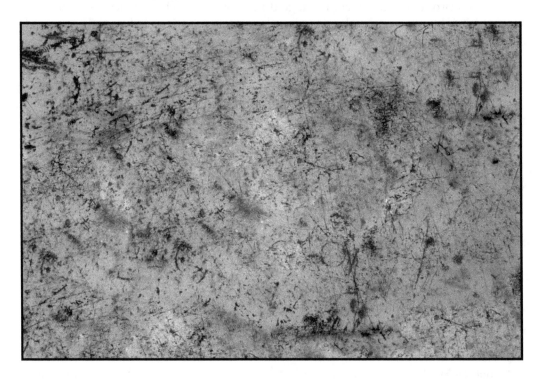

The preceding texture is available in the example code for this book in `Chapter 9 | Textures` folder.

How to do it...

The first **Blend** mode that we will implement is the **Multiply** blend mode as seen in Photoshop. Let's begin by modifying the code in our shader first:

1. Create a new shader by duplicating the `ScreenGreyscale` code by selecting it from the **Project** tab under the `Chapter 9 | Shaders` folder and pressing *Ctrl + D*. Once duplicated, rename the script to `ScreenBlendMode`. Then, double-click on this shader to open it in your script editor.

2. We need to add some new properties so that we have a texture to blend with and a slider for an opacity value. Enter the following code in your new shader:

```
Properties
{
  _MainTex ("Base (RGB)", 2D) = "white" {}
  _BlendTex ("Blend Texture", 2D) = "white"{}
  _Opacity ("Blend Opacity", Range(0,1)) = 1
}
```

3. Enter the corresponding variables in our CGPROGRAM so that we can access the data from our Properties block, replacing the previously created variables:

```
Pass
{
  CGPROGRAM
  #pragma vertex vert_img
  #pragma fragment frag
  #pragma fragmentoption ARB_precision_hint_fastest
  #include "UnityCG.cginc"

  uniform sampler2D _MainTex;
  uniform sampler2D _BlendTex;
  fixed _Opacity;
```

4. We modify our frag() function so that it performs the multiply operation on our two textures:

```
fixed4 frag(v2f_img i) : COLOR
{
  //Get the colors from the RenderTexture and the uv's
  //from the v2f_img struct
  fixed4 renderTex = tex2D(_MainTex, i.uv);
  fixed4 blendTex = tex2D(_BlendTex, i.uv);
  //Perform a multiply Blend mode
  fixed4 blendedMultiply = renderTex * blendTex;
  //Adjust amount of Blend Mode with a lerp
  renderTex = lerp(renderTex, blendedMultiply, _Opacity);
  return renderTex;
}
```

5. Save the shader and return to the Unity editor to let the new shader code compile and check for errors. If no errors occurred, then we can move on to creating our script file.

6. Now that the shader is finished, let's work on the script needed to make the effect show up. From the **Project** tab, go to the `Chapter 09 | Scripts` folder. Once there, select the `TestRenderImage` script and duplicate it by pressing *Ctrl + D*. Rename the newly created script to `RenderBlendMode`. Once renamed, double-click on it to enter your IDE of choice.

7. Our first step in modifying our script is to rename the class to match our filename, `RenderBlendMode`:

```
[ExecuteInEditMode]
public class RenderBlendMode : MonoBehaviour {
```

8. In our script file, we need to create the corresponding variables. We will need a texture so that we can assign one to the shader and a slider to adjust the final amount of the Blend mode we want to use:

```
#region Variables
public Shader curShader;
public Texture2D blendTexture;
public float blendOpacity = 1.0f;
private Material screenMat;
#endregion
```

9. We then need to send our variable data to the shader through the `OnRenderImage()` function:

```
void OnRenderImage(RenderTexture sourceTexture, RenderTexture
destTexture)
{
    if (curShader != null)
    {
        ScreenMat.SetTexture("_BlendTex", blendTexture);
        ScreenMat.SetFloat("_Opacity", blendOpacity);

        Graphics.Blit(sourceTexture, destTexture, ScreenMat);
    }
    else
    {
        Graphics.Blit(sourceTexture, destTexture);
    }
}
```

10. To complete the script, we simply fill in our `Update()` function so that we can clamp the value of the `blendOpacity` variable between a value of `0.0` and `1.0`:

```
void Update()
{
    blendOpacity = Mathf.Clamp(blendOpacity, 0.0f, 1.0f);
}
```

11. With this complete, we assign the screen effect script to our **Main Camera** (remove the previous `Render BSC` script if it is attached) and add our screen effect shader to our script so that it has a shader to use for the per-pixel operations. In order for the effect to be fully functional, the script and shader look for a texture. You can assign any texture to the **Texture** field in the **Inspector** for the screen effect script. Once this texture is in place, you will see the effect of multiplying this texture over the game's rendered screenshot:

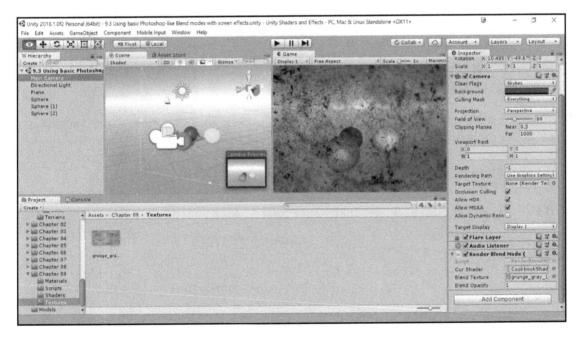

12. The following screenshot demonstrates the screen effect with a smaller `Blend Opacity` option:

Blend Mode = Multiply   Opacity = 0.5

With our first blend mode set up, we can begin to add a couple of simpler blend modes to get a better understanding of how easy it is to add more effects and really fine-tune the final result in your game. However, first let's break down what is happening here.

How it works...

Now we are starting to gain a ton of power and flexibility in our screen effects programming. I am sure that you are now starting to understand how much you can do with this simple system in Unity. We can literally replicate the effects of Photoshop layer blending modes in our game to give artists the flexibility they need to achieve high-quality graphics in a short amount of time.

With this particular recipe, we look at how to multiply two images together, add two images together, and perform a screen blending mode, using just a little bit of mathematics. When working with Blend modes, you have to think on a per-pixel level. For instance, when we are using the multiply blend mode, we literally take each pixel from the original `RenderTexture` and multiply it by each pixel of the Blend texture. The same goes for the add Blend mode. It is just a simple mathematical operation of adding each pixel from the source texture, or `RenderTexture`, to the Blend texture.

The screen Blend mode is definitely a bit more involved, but it is actually doing the same thing. It takes each image, `RenderTexture`, and Blend texture, inverts them, then multiplies them together, and inverts them again to achieve the final look. Just as Photoshop blends its textures together using blend modes, we can do the same with screen effects.

There's more...

Let's continue this recipe by adding a couple more blend modes to our screen effect:

1. In the screen effect shader, let's add the following code to our `frag()` function and change the value we are returning to our script. We will also need to comment out the multiply blend so that we don't return that as well:

```
fixed4 frag(v2f_img i) : COLOR
{
  //Get the colors from the RenderTexture and the uv's
  //from the v2f_img struct
  fixed4 renderTex = tex2D(_MainTex, i.uv);
  fixed4 blendTex = tex2D(_BlendTex, i.uv);
  //Perform a multiply Blend mode
  //fixed4 blendedMultiply = renderTex * blendTex;

  //Perform an additive Blend mode
  fixed4 blendedAdd = renderTex + blendTex;
  //Adjust amount of Blend Mode with a lerp
  renderTex = lerp(renderTex, blendedAdd, _Opacity);
  return renderTex;
}
```

2. Save the shader file in your IDE of choice and `MonoDevelop` and return to the Unity editor to let the shader compile. If no errors occurred, you should see a result similar to the following screenshot:

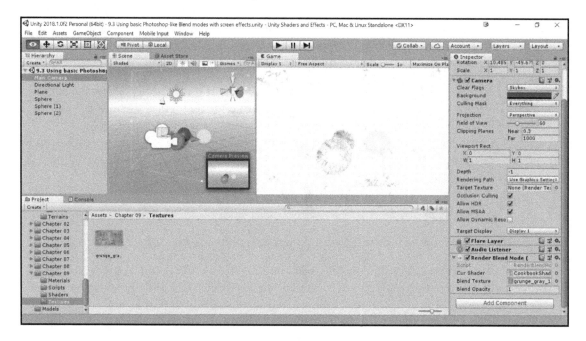

3. This is a simple add blending mode with a figure of `0.5` set for the `Blend Opacity`:

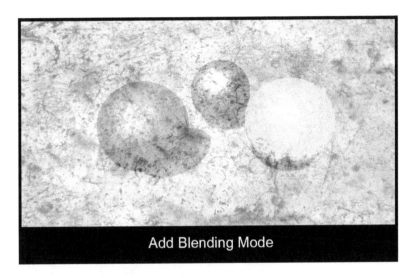

Add Blending Mode

As you can see, this has the opposite effect of multiply because we are adding the two images together.

4. Finally, let's add one more blend mode called a screen blend. This one is a little bit more involved, from a mathematical standpoint, but still simple to implement. Enter the following code in the `frag()` function of our shader:

```
fixed4 frag(v2f_img i) : COLOR
{
  //Get the colors from the RenderTexture and the uv's
  //from the v2f_img struct
  fixed4 renderTex = tex2D(_MainTex, i.uv);
  fixed4 blendTex = tex2D(_BlendTex, i.uv);
  //Perform a multiply Blend mode
  //fixed4 blendedMultiply = renderTex * blendTex;

  //Perform an additive Blend mode
  //fixed4 blendedAdd = renderTex + blendTex;

  //Perform screen blending mode
  fixed4 blendedScreen = (1.0 - ((1.0 - renderTex) * (1.0 -
blendTex)));
  //Adjust amount of Blend Mode with a lerp
  renderTex = lerp(renderTex, blendedScreen, _Opacity);
  return renderTex;
}
```

The following screenshot demonstrates the results of using a screen type Blend mode to blend two images together in a screen effect:

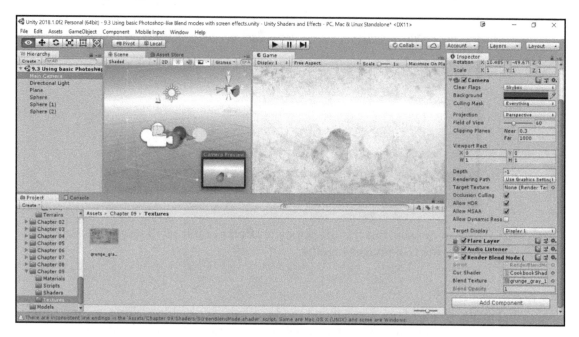

Here's a screenshot displaying the effect:

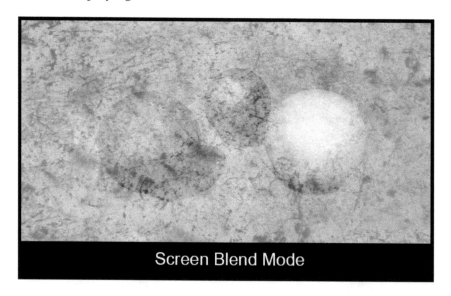

Using the Overlay Blend mode with screen effects

For our final recipe, we are going to take a look at another type of blend mode, the Overlay Blend mode. This blend mode actually makes use of some conditional statements that determine the final color of each pixel in each channel. So, the process of using this type of blend mode requires a bit more coding to work. Let's take a look at how this is done in the next few recipes.

How to do it...

To begin our Overlay Screen effect, we will need to get the code of our shader up and running without errors. We can then modify our script file to feed the correct data to the shader:

1. Create a new shader by duplicating the `ScreenGreyscale` code and selecting it from the **Project** tab under the `Chapter 9 | Shaders` folder and pressing *Ctrl + D*. Once duplicated, rename the script to `ScreenOverlay`. Then, double-click on this shader to open it in your script editor.

2. We first need to set up the properties in our `Properties` block. We will use the same properties from the previous few recipes in this chapter:

```
Properties
{
    _MainTex ("Base (RGB)", 2D) = "white" {}
    _BlendTex ("Blend Texture", 2D) = "white"{}
    _Opacity ("Blend Opacity", Range(0,1)) = 1
}
```

3. We then need to create the corresponding variables in our `CGPROGRAM`, removing the previously created ones:

```
Pass
{
    CGPROGRAM
    #pragma vertex vert_img
    #pragma fragment frag
    #pragma fragmentoption ARB_precision_hint_fastest
    #include "UnityCG.cginc"
    uniform sampler2D _MainTex;
    uniform sampler2D _BlendTex;
    fixed _Opacity;
```

4. In order for the Overlay Blend effect to work, we will have to process each pixel from each channel individually. To do this in a shader, we have to write a custom function that will take in a single channel, for instance, the red channel, and perform the overlay operation. Enter the following code in the shader just below the variable declarations:

```
fixed OverlayBlendMode(fixed basePixel, fixed blendPixel)
{
  if(basePixel < 0.5)
  {
    return (2.0 * basePixel * blendPixel);
  }
  else
  {
    return (1.0 - 2.0 * (1.0 - basePixel) * (1.0 -
blendPixel));
  }
}
```

5. We need to update our frag() function to process each channel of our textures in order to perform the blending:

```
fixed4 frag(v2f_img i) : COLOR
{
  //Get the colors from the RenderTexture and the uv's
  //from the v2f_img struct
  fixed4 renderTex = tex2D(_MainTex, i.uv);
  fixed4 blendTex = tex2D(_BlendTex, i.uv);
  fixed4 blendedImage = renderTex;
  blendedImage.r = OverlayBlendMode(renderTex.r, blendTex.r);
  blendedImage.g = OverlayBlendMode(renderTex.g, blendTex.g);
  blendedImage.b = OverlayBlendMode(renderTex.b, blendTex.b);
  //Adjust amount of Blend Mode with a lerp
  renderTex = lerp(renderTex, blendedImage, _Opacity);
  return renderTex;
}
```

6. With the code completed in the shader, our effect should be working. Save the shader and return to the Unity editor to let the shader compile. Our script is already set up; select the **Main Camera** object. From the **Project** tab, drag and drop the **ScreenOverlay** shader onto the Cur Shader property from the **Render Blend Mode** component in the **Inspector** tab. Once the shader compiles, you should see a result similar to the following screenshot:

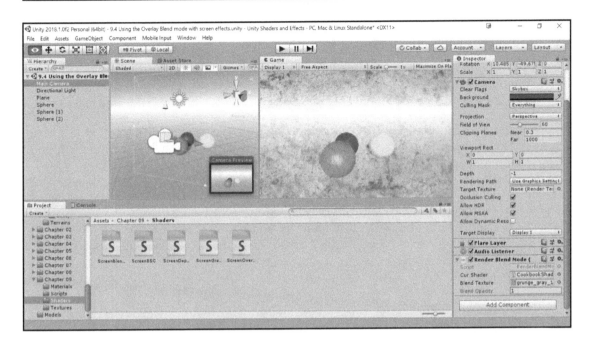

Here's a screenshot using a **Blend Opacity** of 0.5:

How it works...

Our overlay blend mode is definitely a lot more involved, but if you really break down the function, you will notice that it is simply a multiply blend mode and screen blend mode. In this case, we are doing a conditional check to apply one or the other blend mode to a pixel.

With this particular screen effect, when the overlay function receives a pixel, it checks to see whether it is less than 0.5. If it is, then we apply a modified multiply blend mode to that pixel; if it's not, then we apply a modified screen blend mode to the pixel. We do this for each pixel for each channel, giving us the final RGB pixel values for our screen effect.

As you can see, there are many things that can be done with screen effects. It really just depends on the platform and amount of memory you have allocated for screen effects. Usually, this is determined throughout the course of a game project, so have fun and get creative with your screen effects.

10
Gameplay and Screen Effects

When it comes to creating believable and immersive games, the material design is not the only aspect that we need to take into account. The overall feeling can be altered using screen effects. This is very common in movies, for instance, when colors are corrected in the post-production phase. You can implement these techniques in your games too, using the knowledge from `Chapter 9`, *Screen Effects with Unity Render Texture*. Two interesting effects are presented in this chapter; you can, however, adapt them to fit your needs and create your very own screen effect.

In this chapter, you will learn the following:

- Creating an old movie screen effect
- Creating a night vision screen effect

Introduction

If you are reading this book, you are most likely a person who has played a game or two in your time. One of the aspects of real-time games is the effect of immersing a player into a world to make it feel as if they were actually playing in the real world. More modern games make heavy use of screen effects to achieve this immersion.

With screen effects, we can turn the mood of a certain environment from calm to scary, just by changing the look of the screen. Imagine walking into a room that is contained within a level, then the game takes over and goes into a cinematic moment. Many modern games will turn on different screen effects to change the mood of the current moment. Understanding how to create effects triggered by gameplay is next in our journey about shader writing.

In this chapter, we are going to take a look at some of the more common gameplay screen effects. You are going to learn how to change the look of the game from normal to an old movie effect, and we are going to take a look at how many first-person shooter games apply their night vision effects to the screen. With each of these recipes, we are going to look at how to hook these up to game events so that they are turned on and off as the game's current presentation require.

Creating an old movie screen effect

Many games are set in different times. Some take place in fantasy worlds or future sci-fi worlds, and some even take place in the Old West, where film cameras were just being developed and the movies that people watched were black and white or sometimes tinted with what is called a **sepia effect**. The look is very distinct, and we are going to replicate this look using a screen effect in Unity.

There are a few steps to achieving this look; just to make the whole screen black and white or grayscale, we need to break down this effect into its component parts. If we analyze some reference footage of an old movie, we can begin to do this. Let's take a look at the following image and break down the elements that make up the old movie look:

We constructed this image using a few reference images found online. It is always a good idea to try and utilize Photoshop to construct images like this to aid you in creating a plan for your new screen effect. Performing this process not only tells us the elements we will have to code in, but it also gives us a quick way to see which blending modes work and how we will construct the layers of our screen effect.

Getting ready

Now that we know what we have to make, let's take a look at how each of the layers is combined to create the final effect and gather some resources for our shader and screen effect script:

- **Sepia tone**: This is a relatively simple effect to achieve, as we just need to bring all the pixel colors of the original render texture to a single color range. This is easily achieved using the luminance of the original image and adding a constant color. Our first layer will look like the following screenshot:

- **Vignette effect**: We can always see some sort of soft border around old films when they are being projected using an old movie projector. This is caused because the bulb that is used for the movie projector has more brightness in the middle than it does at the edges of the film. This effect is generally called the vignette effect and is the second layer in our screen effect. We can achieve this with an overlaid texture over the whole screen. The following screenshot demonstrates what this layer looks like, isolated as a texture:

- **Dust and scratches**: The third and final layer in our old movie screen effect is dust and scratches. This layer will utilize two different tiled textures, one for scratches and one for dust. The reason is that we will want to animate these two textures over time at different tiling rates. This will give the effect that the film is moving along and there are small scratches and dust on each frame of the old film. The following screenshot demonstrates this effect isolated to its own texture:

Let's get our screen effect system ready with the preceding textures. Perform the following steps:

1. Gather up a vignette texture and a dust and scratches texture, like the ones we just saw.

2. We will also need a scene for which we want to emulate the effect we're trying to build. I have created a sample scene that you can use in the `Chapter 10` folder of the example code, called `10.1 Starter Scene`:

3. Create a new shader by duplicating the `ScreenGrayscale` code; select it from the **Project** tab under the `Chapter 9 | Shaders` folder and press *Ctrl + D*. Once duplicated, rename the script to `ScreenOldFilm`. Then, drag and drop the script into the `Chapter 10 | Shaders` folder, creating it if needed.

4. Next, go to the `Chapter 9 | Scripts` folder and duplicate the `TestRenderImage` script. Rename the new file to `RenderOldFilm` and then drag and drop it into the `Chapter 10 | Scripts` folder, creating it if needed.

Finally, with our screen effect system up and running and our textures gathered, we can begin the process of recreating this old film effect.

How to do it...

Our individual layers for our old film screen effect are quite simple, but when combined, we get some very visually stunning effects. Let's run through how to construct the code for our script and shader, then we can step through each line of code and learn why things are working the way they are. At this point, you should have the screen effects system up and running, as we will not be covering how to set this up in this recipe.

1. We will begin by entering the code in our script. Our first step in modifying our script is to rename the class to match our filename, RenderOldFilm:

```
[ExecuteInEditMode]
public class RenderOldFilm : MonoBehaviour {
```

2. The first block of code that we will enter will define the variable that we want to expose to **Inspector**, in order to let the user of this effect adjust it as they see fit. We can also use our mocked-up Photoshop file as a reference when deciding what we will need to expose to the **Inspector** of this effect. Enter the following code in your effect script:

```
#region Variables
public Shader curShader; // old film shader

public float OldFilmEffectAmount = 1.0f;

public Color sepiaColor = Color.white;
public Texture2D vignetteTexture;
public float vignetteAmount = 1.0f;

public Texture2D scratchesTexture;
public float scratchesYSpeed = 10.0f;
public float scratchesXSpeed = 10.0f;

public Texture2D dustTexture;
public float dustYSpeed = 10.0f;
public float dustXSpeed = 10.0f;

private Material screenMat;
private float randomValue;
#endregion
```

3. Next, we need to fill in the contents of our `OnRenderImage()` function. Here, we will be passing the data from our variables to our shader so that the shader can then use this data in the processing of the render texture:

```
void OnRenderImage(RenderTexture sourceTexture, RenderTexture
destTexture)
{
    if (curShader != null)
    {
        ScreenMat.SetColor("_SepiaColor", sepiaColor);
        ScreenMat.SetFloat("_VignetteAmount", vignetteAmount);
        ScreenMat.SetFloat("_EffectAmount",
OldFilmEffectAmount);

        if (vignetteTexture)
        {
            ScreenMat.SetTexture("_VignetteTex",
vignetteTexture);
        }

        if (scratchesTexture)
        {
            ScreenMat.SetTexture("_ScratchesTex",
scratchesTexture);
            ScreenMat.SetFloat("_ScratchesYSpeed",
scratchesYSpeed);
            ScreenMat.SetFloat("_ScratchesXSpeed",
scratchesXSpeed);
        }

        if (dustTexture)
        {
            ScreenMat.SetTexture("_DustTex", dustTexture);
            ScreenMat.SetFloat("_dustYSpeed", dustYSpeed);
            ScreenMat.SetFloat("_dustXSpeed", dustXSpeed);
            ScreenMat.SetFloat("_RandomValue", randomValue);
        }

        Graphics.Blit(sourceTexture, destTexture, ScreenMat);
    }
    else
    {
        Graphics.Blit(sourceTexture, destTexture);
    }
}
```

4. To complete the script portion of this effect, we simply need to make sure that we clamp the values of the variables that need to have a clamped range instead of being any value:

```
void Update()
{
    vignetteAmount = Mathf.Clamp01(vignetteAmount);
    OldFilmEffectAmount = Mathf.Clamp(OldFilmEffectAmount, 0f,
1.5f);
    randomValue = Random.Range(-1f, 1f);
}
```

5. With our script complete, let's turn our attention to our shader file. We need to create the corresponding variables, which we created in our script in our shader. This will allow the script and shader to communicate with one another. Enter the following code in the Properties block of the shader:

```
Properties
{
    _MainTex ("Base (RGB)", 2D) = "white" {}
    _VignetteTex ("Vignette Texture", 2D) = "white"{}
    _ScratchesTex ("Scratches Texture", 2D) = "white"{}
    _DustTex ("Dust Texture", 2D) = "white"{}
    _SepiaColor ("Sepia Color", Color) = (1,1,1,1)
    _EffectAmount ("Old Film Effect Amount", Range(0,1)) = 1.0
    _VignetteAmount ("Vignette Opacity", Range(0,1)) = 1.0
    _ScratchesYSpeed ("Scratches Y Speed", Float) = 10.0
    _ScratchesXSpeed ("Scratches X Speed", Float) = 10.0
    _dustXSpeed ("Dust X Speed", Float) = 10.0
    _dustYSpeed ("Dust Y Speed", Float) = 10.0
    _RandomValue ("Random Value", Float) = 1.0
    _Contrast ("Contrast", Float) = 3.0

}
```

6. Then, as usual, we need to add these same variable names to our CGPROGRAM block so that the Properties block can communicate with the CGPROGRAM block:

```
Pass
{
  CGPROGRAM
  #pragma vertex vert_img
  #pragma fragment frag
  #pragma fragmentoption ARB_precision_hint_fastest
  #include "UnityCG.cginc"
  uniform sampler2D _MainTex;
  uniform sampler2D _VignetteTex;
  uniform sampler2D _ScratchesTex;
  uniform sampler2D _DustTex;
  fixed4 _SepiaColor;
  fixed _VignetteAmount;
  fixed _ScratchesYSpeed;
  fixed _ScratchesXSpeed;
  fixed _dustXSpeed;
  fixed _dustYSpeed;
  fixed _EffectAmount;
  fixed _RandomValue;
  fixed _Contrast;
```

7. Now, we simply fill in the guts of our frag() function so that we can process the pixels for our screen effect. To start with, let's get the render texture and vignette texture passed to us by the script:

```
fixed4 frag(v2f_img i) : COLOR
{
    //Get the colors from the RenderTexture and the uv's
    //from the v2f_img struct
    fixed4 renderTex = tex2D(_MainTex, i.uv);
    //Get the pixels from the Vignette Texture
    fixed4 vignetteTex = tex2D(_VignetteTex, i.uv);
```

8. We then need to add the process for the dust and scratches by entering the following code:

```
//Process the Scratches UV and pixels
half2 scratchesUV = half2(i.uv.x + (_RandomValue * _SinTime.z *
_ScratchesXSpeed), i.uv.y + (_Time.x * _ScratchesYSpeed));
fixed4 scratchesTex = tex2D(_ScratchesTex, scratchesUV);
//Process the Dust UV and pixels
half2 dustUV = half2(i.uv.x + (_RandomValue * (_SinTime.z *
_dustXSpeed)), i.uv.y + (_RandomValue * (_SinTime.z *
_dustYSpeed)));
fixed4 dustTex = tex2D(_DustTex, dustUV);
```

9. The sepia tone process is next on our list:

```
// get the luminosity values from the render texture using the
YIQ values.
fixed lum = dot (fixed3(0.299, 0.587, 0.114), renderTex.rgb);
//Add the constant color to the lum values
fixed4 finalColor = lum + lerp(_SepiaColor, _SepiaColor +
  fixed4(0.1f,0.1f,0.1f,1.0f), _RandomValue);
finalColor = pow(finalColor, _Contrast);
```

10. Finally, we combine all of our layers and colors and return the final screen effect texture:

```
//Create a constant white color we can use to adjust opacity
of effects
  fixed3 constantWhite = fixed3(1,1,1);
  //Composite together the different layers to create finsl
Screen Effect
  finalColor = lerp(finalColor, finalColor * vignetteTex,
_VignetteAmount);
  finalColor.rgb *= lerp(scratchesTex, constantWhite,
(_RandomValue));
  finalColor.rgb *= lerp(dustTex.rgb, constantWhite,
(_RandomValue * _SinTime.z));
  finalColor = lerp(renderTex, finalColor, _EffectAmount);
  return finalColor;
}
```

11. With all of our code entered and no errors, return to the Unity editor and add the RenderOldFilm component to the MainCamera in our example scene. From there, drag and drop our shader into the **Cur Shader** property. Afterward, under **Sepia Color**, assign a brown color like the following:

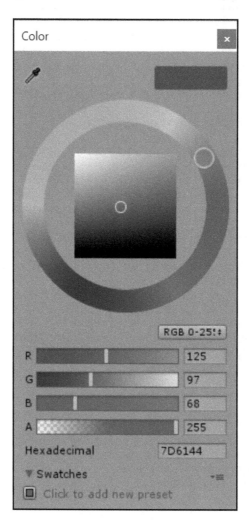

12. Afterward, assign each of the textures given to the appropriate property. You should then notice something similar to the following on the screen:

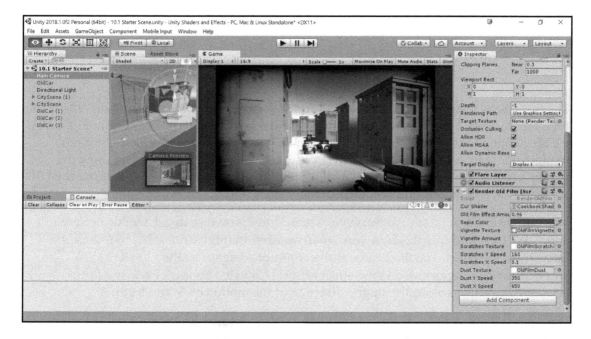

13. Also, make sure to hit Play in the Unity Editor to see the full extent of the effects of the dust and scratches and the slight image shift that we gave the screen effect.

How it works...

Now, let's walk through each of the layers in this screen effect, break down why each of the lines of code is working the way it is, and get more insight about how we can add more to this screen effect.

Now that our old film screen effect is working, let's step through the lines of code in our `frag()` function, as all the other code should be pretty self-explanatory at this point in the book.

Just like our Photoshop layers, our shader is processing each layer and then compositing them together, so while we go through each layer, try to imagine how the layers in Photoshop work. Keeping this concept in mind always helps when developing new screen effects.

Here, we have the first set of lines of code in our `frag()` function:

```
fixed4 frag(v2f_img i) : COLOR
{
    //Get the colors from the RenderTexture and the uv's
    //from the v2f_img struct
    fixed4 renderTex = tex2D(_MainTex, i.uv);
    //Get the pixels from the Vignette Texture
    fixed4 vignetteTex = tex2D(_VignetteTex, i.uv);
```

The first line of code, just after the `frag()` function declaration, is the definition of how the UVs should work for our main render texture or the actual rendered frame of our game. As we are looking to fake the effect of an old film style, we want to adjust the UVs of our render texture in every frame, such that they flicker. This flickering simulates how the winding of the film's projector is just a bit off. This tells us that we need to animate the UVs and this is what this first line of code is doing.

We used the built-in `_SinTime` variable, which Unity provides, to get a value between –1 and 1. We then multiply this by a very small number, in this case, `0.005`, to reduce the intensity of the effect. The final value is then multiplied again by the `_RandomValue` variable, which we generated in the effect script. This value bounces back and forth between –1 and 1 to basically flip the direction of the motion back and forth.

Once our UVs are built and stored in the `renderTexUV` variable, we can sample the render texture using a `tex2D()` function. This operation then gives us our final render texture, which we can use to process further in the rest of the shader.

Moving on to the last line in the previous image, we simply do a straight sample of the vignette texture using the `tex2D()` function. We don't need to use the animated UVs we already created, as the vignette texture will be tied to the motion of the camera itself and not to the flickering of the camera film.

The following code snippet illustrates the second set of lines of code in our `frag()` function:

```
//Process the Scratches UV and pixels
half2 scratchesUV = half2(i.uv.x + (_RandomValue * _SinTime.z *
_ScratchesXSpeed),
        i.uv.y + (_Time.x * _ScratchesYSpeed));
fixed4 scratchesTex = tex2D(_ScratchesTex, scratchesUV);
//Process the Dust UV and pixels
half2 dustUV = half2(i.uv.x + (_RandomValue * (_SinTime.z * _dustXSpeed)),
        i.uv.y + (_RandomValue * (_SinTime.z * _dustYSpeed)));
fixed4 dustTex = tex2D(_DustTex, dustUV);
```

These lines of code are almost exactly like the previous lines of code, in which we need to generate unique animated UV values to modify the position of our screen effect layers. We simply use the built-in _SinTime value to get a value between −1 and 1, multiply it by our random value, and then by another multiplier to adjust the overall speed of the animation. Once these UV values are generated, we can then sample our dust and scratches texture using these new animated values.

Our next set of code handles the creation of the colorizing effect for our old film screen effect. The following code snippet demonstrates these lines:

```
// get the luminosity values from the render texture using the YIQ values
fixed lum = dot (fixed3(0.299, 0.587, 0.114), renderTex.rgb);
//Add the constant color to the lum values
fixed4 finalColor = lum + lerp(_SepiaColor, _SepiaColor +
    fixed4(0.1f,0.1f,0.1f,1.0f), _RandomValue);
```

With this set of code, we are creating the actual color tinting of the entire render texture. To accomplish this, we first need to turn the render texture into the grayscale version of itself. To do this, we can use the luminosity values given to us by the YIQ values. YIQ values are the color space used by the NTSC color TV system. Each letter in YIQ actually stores color constants that are used by TVs to adjust the color for readability.

While it is not necessary to actually know the reasons for this color scale, it should be known that the Y value in YIQ is the constant luminance value for any image. So, we can generate a grayscale image of our render texture by taking each pixel of the render texture and dotting it with our luminance values. This is what the first line in this set is doing.

Once we have the luminance values, we can simply add the color we want to tint the image with. This color is passed from our script to our shader, then to our CGPROGRAM block, where we can add it to our grayscale render to texture. Once completed, we will have a perfectly tinted image.

Finally, we create the blending between each of our layers in our screen effect. The following code snippet shows the set of code we are looking at:

```
//Create a constant white color we can use to adjust opacity of effects
fixed3 constantWhite = fixed3(1,1,1);
//Composite together the different layers to create finsl Screen Effect
finalColor = lerp(finalColor, finalColor * vignetteTex, _VignetteAmount);
finalColor.rgb *= lerp(scratchesTex, constantWhite, (_RandomValue));
finalColor.rgb *= lerp(dustTex.rgb, constantWhite, (_RandomValue *
_SinTime.z));
finalColor = lerp(renderTex, finalColor, _EffectAmount);
return finalColor
```

Our last set of code is relatively simple and doesn't really need a ton of explanation. In short, it is simply multiplying all the layers together to reach our final result. Just like we multiplied our layers together in Photoshop, we multiply them together in our shader. Each layer is processed through a lerp() function so that we can adjust the opacity of each layer, which gives more artistic control over the final effect. The more tweaks one can offer, the better when it comes to screen effects.

See also

For more information on the YIQ values, refer to the following links:

- http://en.wikipedia.org/wiki/YIQ
- http://www.blackice.com/colorspaceYIQ.htm

Creating a night vision screen effect

Our next screen effect is definitely a more popular one. The night vision screen effect is seen in *Call of Duty: Modern Warfare, Halo,* and just about any first-person shooter out in the market today. It is the effect of brightening the whole image using that very distinct lime-green color.

In order to achieve our night vision effect, we need to break down our effect using Photoshop. It is a simple process of finding some reference images online and composing a layered image to see what kind of blending modes you will need or in which order we will need to combine our layers. The following screenshot shows the result of performing just this process in Photoshop:

Let's begin to break down our rough Photoshop composite image into its component parts so that we can better understand the assets we will have to gather. In the next recipe, we will cover the process of doing this.

Getting ready

Let's begin this screen effect by again breaking down our effect into its component layers. Using Photoshop, we can construct a layered image to better illustrate how we can go about capturing the effect of night vision:

- **Tinted green**: Our first layer in our screen effect is the iconic green color, found in just about every night vision image. This will give our effect that signature night vision look, as shown in the following screenshot:

- **Scan lines**: To increase the effect of this being a new type of display for the player, we include scan lines over the top of our tinted layer. For this, we will use a texture created in Photoshop and let the user tile it so that the scan lines can be bigger or smaller.

- **Noise**: Our next layer is a simple noise texture that we tile over the tinted image and scan lines to break up the image and add even more detail to our effect. This layer simply emphasizes that digital read-out look:

- **Vignette**: The last layer in our night vision effect is the vignette. If you look at the night vision effect in *Call of Duty: Modern Warfare*, you will notice that it uses a vignette that fakes the effect of looking down a scope. We will do that for this screen effect:

Let's create a screen effect system by gathering our textures. Perform the following steps:

1. Gather up a vignette texture, noise texture, and scan line texture, like the ones we just saw. Like before, I have these textures available in the book's example code under the Chapter 10 | Textures folder.

2. Find a sample scene to make it easy to see the effect of the shader. I will be using the same scene as in the previous recipe, so feel free to use the 10.1 Sample Scene again.

3. Create a new shader by duplicating the ScreenGrayscale code; select it from the **Project** tab under the Chapter 9 | Shaders folder and press *Ctrl + D*. Once duplicated, rename the script to ScreenNightVision. Then drag and drop the script into the Chapter 10 | Shaders folder, creating it if needed.

4. Next, go the Chapter 9 | Scripts folder and duplicate the TestRenderImage script. Rename the new file to RenderNightVision and then drag and drop it into the Chapter 10 | Scripts folder, creating it if needed.

Finally, with our screen effect system up and running and our textures gathered, we can begin the process of recreating this night vision effect.

How to do it...

With all of our assets gathered and the screen effect system running smoothly, let's begin to add the code necessary to both the script and shader. We will begin our coding with the RenderNightVision.cs script, so double-click on this file now to open it in your code editor of choice:

1. We will begin by entering the code in our script. Our first step in modifying our script is to rename the class to match our filename, RenderNightVision:

```
[ExecuteInEditMode]
public class RenderNightVision : MonoBehaviour {
```

2. We need to create a few variables that will allow the user of this effect to adjust it in the script's **Inspector**. Enter the following code in the NightVisionEffect.cs script:

```
#region Variables
    public Shader curShader;
    public float contrast = 3.0f;
    public float brightness = 0.1f;
    public Color nightVisionColor = Color.green;
    public Texture2D vignetteTexture;
    public Texture2D scanLineTexture;
    public float scanLineTileAmount = 4.0f;
    public Texture2D nightVisionNoise;
    public float noiseXSpeed = 100.0f;
    public float noiseYSpeed = 100.0f;
    public float distortion = 0.2f;
    public float scale = 0.8f;
    private float randomValue = 0.0f;
    private Material screenMat;
#endregion
```

3. Next, we need to complete our OnRenderImage() function so that we are passing the right data to the shader in order for the shader to process the screen effect properly. Complete the OnRenderImage() function with the following code:

```
void OnRenderImage(RenderTexture sourceTexture, RenderTexture destTexture)
```

```
    {
        if (curShader != null)
        {
            ScreenMat.SetFloat("_Contrast", contrast);
            ScreenMat.SetFloat("_Brightness", brightness);
            ScreenMat.SetColor("_NightVisionColor",
nightVisionColor);
            ScreenMat.SetFloat("_RandomValue", randomValue);
            ScreenMat.SetFloat("_distortion", distortion);
            ScreenMat.SetFloat("_scale", scale);

            if (vignetteTexture)
            {
                ScreenMat.SetTexture("_VignetteTex",
vignetteTexture);
            }

            if (scanLineTexture)
            {
                ScreenMat.SetTexture("_ScanLineTex",
scanLineTexture);
                ScreenMat.SetFloat("_ScanLineTileAmount",
scanLineTileAmount);
            }

            if (nightVisionNoise)
            {
                ScreenMat.SetTexture("_NoiseTex",
nightVisionNoise);
                ScreenMat.SetFloat("_NoiseXSpeed", noiseXSpeed);
                ScreenMat.SetFloat("_NoiseYSpeed", noiseYSpeed);
            }

            Graphics.Blit(sourceTexture, destTexture, ScreenMat);
        }
        else
        {
            Graphics.Blit(sourceTexture, destTexture);
        }
    }
```

4. To complete the `NightVisionEffect.cs` script, we simply need to make sure that we clamp certain variables so that they stay within a range. These ranges are arbitrary and can be changed at a later time. These are just values that worked well:

```
void Update()
{
    contrast = Mathf.Clamp(contrast, 0f, 4f);
    brightness = Mathf.Clamp(brightness, 0f, 2f);
    randomValue = Random.Range(-1f, 1f);
    distortion = Mathf.Clamp(distortion, -1f, 1f);
    scale = Mathf.Clamp(scale, 0f, 3f);
}
```

5. We can now turn our attention over to the shader portion of this screen effect. Open the shader, if you haven't already, and begin by entering the following properties in the `Properties` block:

```
Properties
{
    _MainTex ("Base (RGB)", 2D) = "white" {}
    _VignetteTex ("Vignette Texture", 2D) = "white"{}
    _ScanLineTex ("Scan Line Texture", 2D) = "white"{}
    _NoiseTex ("Noise Texture", 2D) = "white"{}
    _NoiseXSpeed ("Noise X Speed", Float) = 100.0
    _NoiseYSpeed ("Noise Y Speed", Float) = 100.0
    _ScanLineTileAmount ("Scan Line Tile Amount", Float) = 4.0
    _NightVisionColor ("Night Vision Color", Color) = (1,1,1,1)
    _Contrast ("Contrast", Range(0,4)) = 2
    _Brightness ("Brightness", Range(0,2)) = 1
    _RandomValue ("Random Value", Float) = 0
    _distortion ("Distortion", Float) = 0.2
    _scale ("Scale (Zoom)", Float) = 0.8
}
```

6. To make sure that we are passing the data from our `Properties` block to our CGPROGRAM block, we need to make sure to declare them with the same name in the CGPROGRAM block:

```
Pass
{
  CGPROGRAM
  #pragma vertex vert_img
  #pragma fragment frag
  #pragma fragmentoption ARB_precision_hint_fastest
  #include "UnityCG.cginc"
```

```
uniform sampler2D _MainTex;
uniform sampler2D _VignetteTex;
uniform sampler2D _ScanLineTex;
uniform sampler2D _NoiseTex;
fixed4 _NightVisionColor;
fixed _Contrast;
fixed _ScanLineTileAmount;
fixed _Brightness;
fixed _RandomValue;
fixed _NoiseXSpeed;
fixed _NoiseYSpeed;
fixed _distortion;
fixed _scale;
```

7. Our effect is also going to include a lens distortion to further convey the effect that we are looking through a lens and the edges of the image are being distorted by the angle of the lens. Enter the following function just after the variable declarations in the CGPROGRAM block:

```
float2 barrelDistortion(float2 coord)
{
    // lens distortion algorithm
    // See http://www.ssontech.com/content/lensalg.htm

    float2 h = coord.xy - float2(0.5, 0.5);
    float r2 = h.x * h.x + h.y * h.y;
    float f = 1.0 + r2 * (_distortion * sqrt(r2));

    return f * _scale * h + 0.5;
}
```

8. We can now concentrate on the meat of our NightVisionEffect shader. Let's start this by entering the code that is necessary to get the render texture and vignette texture. Enter the following code in the frag() function of our shader:

```
fixed4 frag(v2f_img i) : COLOR
{
    //Get the colors from the RenderTexture and the uv's
    //from the v2f_img struct
    half2 distortedUV = barrelDistortion(i.uv);
    fixed4 renderTex = tex2D(_MainTex, distortedUV);
    fixed4 vignetteTex = tex2D(_VignetteTex, i.uv);
```

9. The next step in our `frag()` function is to process the scan lines and `Noise` textures and apply the proper animated UVs to them:

```
//Process scan lines and noise
half2 scanLinesUV = half2(i.uv.x * _ScanLineTileAmount, i.uv.y
* _ScanLineTileAmount);
fixed4 scanLineTex = tex2D(_ScanLineTex, scanLinesUV);
half2 noiseUV = half2(i.uv.x + (_RandomValue * _SinTime.z *
_NoiseXSpeed),
                i.uv.y + (_Time.x * _NoiseYSpeed));
fixed4 noiseTex = tex2D(_NoiseTex, noiseUV);
```

10. To complete all of our layers in the screen effect, we simply need to process the luminance value of our render texture, and then apply the night vision color to it to achieve that iconic night vision look:

```
// get the luminosity values from the render texture using the
//YIQ values.
        fixed lum = dot (fixed3(0.299, 0.587, 0.114),
renderTex.rgb);
        lum += _Brightness;
        fixed4 finalColor = (lum *2) + _NightVisionColor;
```

11. Lastly, we will combine all the layers together and return the final color of our night vision effect:

```
//Final output
finalColor = pow(finalColor, _Contrast);
finalColor *= vignetteTex;
finalColor *= scanLineTex * noiseTex;
return finalColor;
}
```

12. When you have finished entering the code, return to the Unity editor to let the script and shader compile. If there are no errors, select the `MainCamera` in your scene. Remove the **Render Old Film** component, if it is there already, and add the `RenderNightVision` component. Once there, drag and drop the `ScreenNightVision` shader into the **Cur Shader** property of the component and then assign the **Night Vision Color** property to a green color like the following:

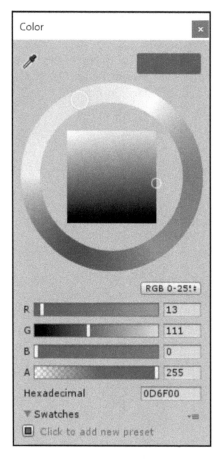

13. Afterward, assign the textures to their proper spot:

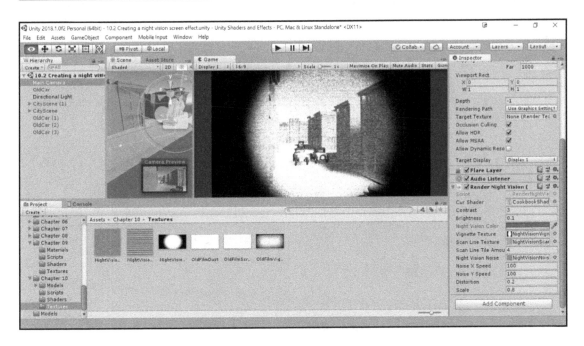

14. Afterward, make sure to play in the editor to see the full, final version of the effect:

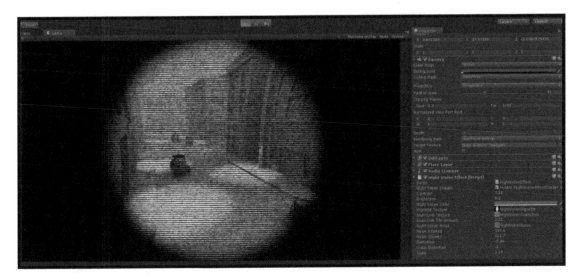

The final result of our night-vision screen effect

How it works...

The night vision effect is actually very similar to the old film screen effect, which shows us just how modular we can make these components. Just by simply swapping the textures that we are using for overlays and changing the speed at which our tiling rates are being calculated, we can achieve very different results using the same code.

The only difference with this effect is the fact that we are including a lens distortion to our screen effect. So let's break this down so that we can get a better understanding of how it works.

The following code snippet illustrates the code used in processing our lens distortion. It is a snippet of code provided to us by the makers of *SynthEyes*, and the code is freely available to use in your own effects:

```
float2 barrelDistortion(float2 coord)
{
    // lens distortion algorithm
    // See http://www.ssontech.com/content/lensalg.htm
    float2 h = coord.xy - float2(0.5, 0.5);
    float r2 = h.x * h.x + h.y * h.y;
    float f = 1.0 + r2 * (_distortion * sqrt(r2));

    return f * _scale * h + 0.5;
}
```

There's more...

It is not uncommon in video games to have the need to highlight certain objects. For instance, a thermal visor should only apply a post-processing effect to people and other sources of heat. Doing this is already possible with the knowledge gathered so far in this book; you can, in fact, change the shader or material of an object by code. However, this is often laborious and has to be replicated on every the object.

A more effective way to use replaced shaders. Each shader has a tag called `RenderType` that has never been used so far. This property can be used to force a camera to apply a shader only to certain objects. You can do this by attaching the following script to the camera:

```
using UnityEngine;

public class ReplacedShader : MonoBehaviour {

    public Shader shader;
    void Start () {
        GetComponent<Camera>().SetReplacementShader(shader, "Heat");
    }
}
```

After entering the play mode, the camera will query all the objects that it has to render. If they don't have a shader decorated with `RenderType` = `"Heat"`, they will not be rendered. Objects with such a tag will be rendered with the shader attached to the script.

Advanced Shading Techniques

11

In this chapter, you will learn the following:

- Using Unity's built-in CgInclude files
- Making your shader world modular with CgInclude
- Implementing a Fur Shader
- Implementing Heatmaps with arrays

Introduction

This chapter covers some advanced shader techniques that you can use for your game. You should remember that many of the most eye-catching effects you see in games are made by testing the limits of what shaders can do. This book provides you with the technical foundations to modify and create shaders, but you are strongly encouraged to play and experiment with them as much as you can. Making a good game is not a quest for photorealism; you should not approach shaders with the intention of replicating reality because this is unlikely to happen. Instead, you should try to use shaders as a tool to make your game truly unique. With the knowledge of this chapter, you will be able to create the materials that you want.

Using Unity's built-in CgInclude files

Our first step in writing our own `CgInclude` files is to understand what Unity is already providing with us for shaders. When writing Surface Shaders, there is a lot happening under the hood, which makes the process of writing Surface Shaders so efficient. We can see this code in the included `CgInclude` files found in the directory that you installed Unity in at `Editor | Data | CGIncludes`. All the files contained within this folder do their part to render our objects with our shaders on the screen. Some of these files take care of shadows and lighting, some take care of helper functions, and some manage platform dependencies. Without them, our shader-writing experience would be much more laborious.

You can find a list of the information that Unity has provided us with at the following link: `http://docs.unity3d.com/Documentation/Components/SL-BuiltinIncludes.html`.

Let's begin the process of understanding these built-in `CgInclude` files, using some of the built-in helper functions from the `UnityCG.cginc` file:

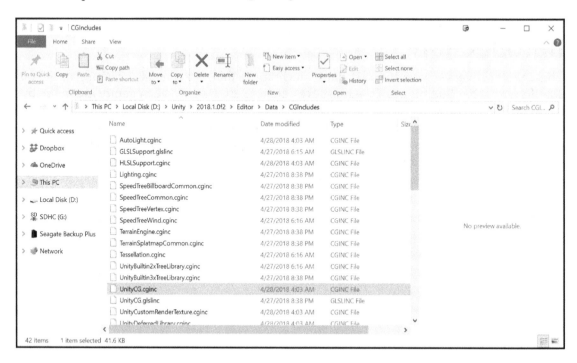

Getting ready

Before we start diving into the meat of writing the shader, we need to get a few items set up in our scene. Let's do the following and then open the shader in your IDE of choice:

1. Create a new scene and fill it with a simple sphere model.
2. Create a new shader (`Desaturate`) and material (`DesaturateMat`).
3. Attach the new shader to the new material and assign the material to the sphere.
4. Create a directional light and position it above your sphere.
5. Finally, open the `UnityCG.cginc` file from Unity's `CgInclude` folder located in Unity's install directory. This will let us analyze some of the helper functions' code so that we can understand what is happening when we use them.
6. You should now have a simple scene set up to work on the shader. Refer to the following screenshot, which is an example:

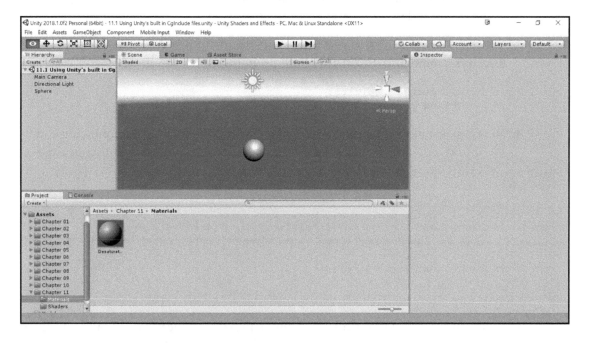

How to do it...

With the scene prepared, we can now begin the process of experimenting with some of the built-in helper functions included with the `UnityCG.cginc` file. Double-click on the shader that was created for this scene in order to open it in your IDE of choice and insert the code given in the following steps:

1. Add the following code to the `Properties` block of the new shader file. We will need a single texture and slide for our example shader:

   ```
   Properties
   {
       _MainTex ("Base (RGB)", 2D) = "white" {}
       _DesatValue ("Desaturate", Range(0,1)) = 0.5
   }
   ```

   We then need to make sure that we create the data connection between our `Properties` and CGPROGRAM blocks.

2. Use the following code, placed after the CGPROGRAM declaration and `#pragma` directives, removing the other default properties:

   ```
   sampler2D _MainTex;
   fixed _DesatValue;
   ```

3. Next, we just have to update our `surf()` function to include the following code. We introduce a new function that we haven't seen yet, which is built into Unity's `UnityCG.cginc` file:

   ```
   void surf (Input IN, inout SurfaceOutputStandard o)
   {
       half4 c = tex2D (_MainTex, IN.uv_MainTex);
       c.rgb = lerp(c.rgb, Luminance(c.rgb), _DesatValue);

       o.Albedo = c.rgb;
       o.Alpha = c.a;
   }
   ```

4. Save your script and return to the Unity editor. From there, you should be able to assign a material to the `DesaturateMat` (I used the `TerrainBlend` texture from the `Chapter 3 | Textures` folder):

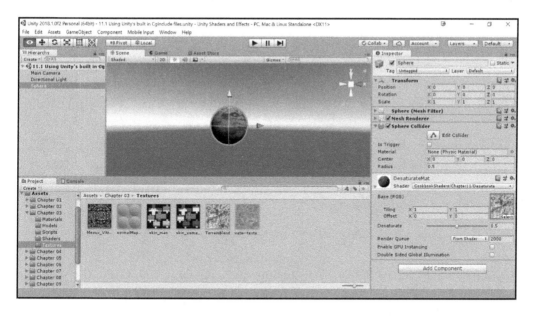

5. With the shader code modified, you should see something similar to the preceding screenshot. We have simply used a helper function, built into Unity's `CgInclude` file, to give us an effect of desaturating the main texture of our shader. Notice that if we change the value to `1`, all of the color leaves, giving us a grayscale effect:

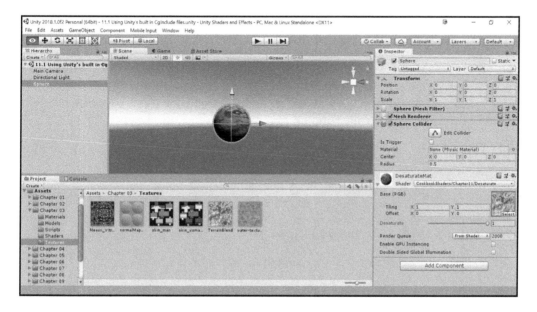

How it works...

Using the built-in helper function named `Luminance()`, we are able to quickly get a desaturation or grayscale effect on our shaders. This is all possible because of the `UnityCG.cginc` file is brought automatically to our shader as we are using a Surface Shader.

If you search through the `UnityCG.cginc` file when opened in a script editor, you will find the implementation of this function at line *473*. The following snippet is taken from the file:

```
// Converts color to luminance (grayscale)
inline half Luminance(half3 rgb)
{
    return dot(rgb, unity_ColorSpaceLuminance.rgb);
}
```

As this function is included in the file and Unity automatically compiles with this file, we can use the function in our code as well, thereby reducing the amount of code that we have to write over and over again.

Notice there is also a `Lighting.cginc` file, which Unity comes with. This file houses all the lighting models that we use when we declare something like `#pragma Surface surf Lambert`. Sifting through this file reveals that all the built-in lighting models are defined here for reuse and modularity.

There's more...

You'll notice that the `Luminance` function we are using will return the dot product between the color passed in and a property called `unity_ColorSpaceLuminance`. To see what that is, you can use **Find** menu in your text editor (*Ctrl + F*) and type it in. After searching for it, you should be able to see the following on line *28*:

```
#ifdef UNITY_COLORSPACE_GAMMA
#define unity_ColorSpaceGrey fixed4(0.5, 0.5, 0.5, 0.5)
#define unity_ColorSpaceDouble fixed4(2.0, 2.0, 2.0, 2.0)
#define unity_ColorSpaceDielectricSpec half4(0.220916301, 0.220916301,
0.220916301, 1.0 - 0.220916301)
#define unity_ColorSpaceLuminance half4(0.22, 0.707, 0.071, 0.0) // Legacy:
alpha is set to 0.0 to specify gamma mode
#else // Linear values
#define unity_ColorSpaceGrey fixed4(0.214041144, 0.214041144, 0.214041144,
0.5)
#define unity_ColorSpaceDouble fixed4(4.59479380, 4.59479380, 4.59479380,
```

```
2.0)
#define unity_ColorSpaceDielectricSpec half4(0.04, 0.04, 0.04, 1.0 - 0.04)
// standard dielectric reflectivity coef at incident angle (= 4%)
#define unity_ColorSpaceLuminance half4(0.0396819152, 0.458021790,
0.00609653955, 1.0) // Legacy: alpha is set to 1.0 to specify linear mode
#endif
```

This means that, depending on the color space being used, the values given will change. By default, Unity uses a Gamma color space as only certain platforms support linear. To check what color space you are using in your project, you can go to **Edit** | **Project Settings** | **Player** | **Other Settings** and look at the **Color Space** property.

For more information on color spaces check out: `http://www.kinematicsoup.com/news/2016/6/15/gamma-and-linear-space-what-they-are-how-they-differ`.

Making your shader world in a modular way with CgInclude

Knowing about the built-in `CgInclude` files is great, but what if we want to build our own `CgInclude` files to store our own lighting models and helper functions? We can, in fact, create our own `CgInclude` files, but we need to learn a little more code syntax before we can start using them efficiently in our shader-writing pipelines. Let's take a look at the process of creating a new `CgInclude` file from scratch.

Getting ready

Let's walk through the process of generating a new item for this recipe:

1. From the **Project** tab, right-click on the `Assets` folder and select **Show in Explorer**. You should see your project folder. Then create a text file by right-clicking and selecting **New | Text Document**:

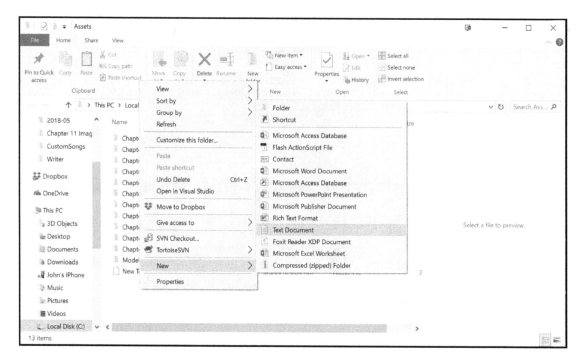

2. Rename the file to `MyCGInclude` and replace the `.txt` file extension with `.cginc`:

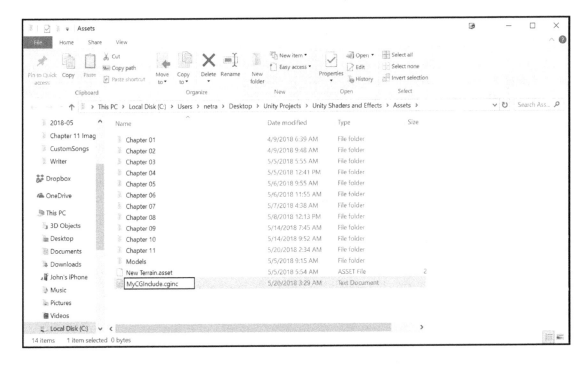

3. Windows will give you a warning message saying that the **File may become unusable**, but it will still work.

4. Import this new `.cginc` file into your Unity project and let it compile. If all goes well, you will see that Unity knew to compile it into a `CgInclude` file.

We are now ready to begin creating our own custom `CgInclude` code. Simply double-click on the `CgInclude` file that you created in order to open it in your IDE of choice.

How to do it...

With our `CgInclude` file open, we can begin to enter the code that will get it working with our Surface Shaders. The following steps will get our `CgInclude` file ready for use within our Surface Shaders and allow us to continually add more code to it as we develop more shaders:

1. We begin our `CgInclude` file with what is called a preprocessor directive. These are statements such as `#pragma` and `#include`. In this case, we want to define a new set of code that will be executed if our shader includes this file in its compiler directives. Enter the following code at the top of your `CgInclude` file:

   ```
   #ifndef MY_CG_INCLUDE
   #define MY_CG_INCLUDE
   ```

2. We always need to make sure that we close `#ifndef` or `#ifdef` with `#endif` to close the definition check, just like an `if` statement needs to be closed with two brackets in C#. Enter the following code just after the `#define` directive:

   ```
   #endif
   ```

3. At this point, we just need to implement the contents of the `CgInclude` file. So, we finish off our `CgInclude` file by entering the following code after the `#define` and before the `#endif`:

   ```
   fixed4 _MyColor;

   inline fixed4 LightingHalfLambert(SurfaceOutput s, fixed3
   lightDir, fixed atten)
   {
       fixed diff = max(0, dot(s.Normal, lightDir));
       diff = (diff + 0.5)*0.5;

       fixed4 c;
       c.rgb = s.Albedo * _LightColor0.rgb * ((diff *
   _MyColor.rgb) * atten);
       c.a = s.Alpha;
       return c;
   }
   #endif
   ```

4. With this completed, you now have your very first `CgInclude` file. With just this little bit of code, we can greatly reduce the amount of code that we have to rewrite, and we can begin to store the lighting models that we use all the time here so that we never lose them. Your `CgInclude` file should look similar to the following code:

```
#ifndef MY_CG_INCLUDE
#define MY_CG_INCLUDE

fixed4 _MyColor;

inline fixed4 LightingHalfLambert(SurfaceOutput s, fixed3
lightDir, fixed atten)
{
    fixed diff = max(0, dot(s.Normal, lightDir));
    diff = (diff + 0.5)*0.5;

    fixed4 c;
    c.rgb = s.Albedo * _LightColor0.rgb * ((diff *
_MyColor.rgb) * atten);
    c.a = s.Alpha;
    return c;
}
#endif
```

There are a couple more steps that we need to complete before we can fully utilize this `CgInclude` file. We simply need to tell the current shader that we are working with to use this file and its code. To complete the process of creating and using `CgInclude` files, let's complete the next set of steps:

1. We have to have our `CgInclude` file in the same directory as our shader, so drag and drop it into the `Chapter 11 | Shaders` folder from the **Project** tab.

If *step 1* is not completed, you will get a compilation error.

2. Now that we are in the folder, select the `Desaturate` shader created in the previous recipe and duplicate it (*Ctrl + D*). Name the duplicate `Colorize`, and double-click on it to open it up.

3. From there, update the shader name:

```
Shader "CookbookShaders/Chapter11/Colorize"
```

4. If you turn your attention to our shader, you will see that we need to tell our CGPROGRAM block to include our new CgInclude file, so that we can access the code it contains. Modify the directives of our CGPROGRAM block to include the following code:

```
CGPROGRAM
#include "MyCGInclude.cginc"
// Physically based Standard lighting model, and enable shadows on
all light types
#pragma surface surf Standard fullforwardshadows
```

5. Our current shader is currently using the built-in Standard lighting model, but we want to use the Half Lambert lighting model that we created in our CgInclude. As we have included the code from our CgInclude file, we can use the Half Lambert lighting model with the following code:

```
CGPROGRAM
#include "MyCGInclude.cginc"
#pragma surface surf HalfLambert
```

6. Finally, we have also declared a custom variable in our CgInclude file to show that we can set up default variables for our shaders to use. To see this in action, enter the following code in the Properties block of your shader:

```
Properties
{
    _MainTex ("Base (RGB)", 2D) = "white" {}
    _DesatValue ("Desaturate", Range(0,1)) = 0.5
    _MyColor ("My Color", Color) = (1,1,1,1)
}
```

7. Lastly, we need to update our surf function header since we use SurfaceOutput in our LightingHalfLambert function:

```
void surf (Input IN, inout SurfaceOutput o)
```

8. Back in Unity, create a new material that will use the newly created Colorize shader (ColorizeMat) and assign it to the sphere we created in the last recipe. Assign the material as normal and modify the **MyColor** value from the **Inspector** to see how it modifies the object. The following screenshot shows the result of using our CgInclude file:

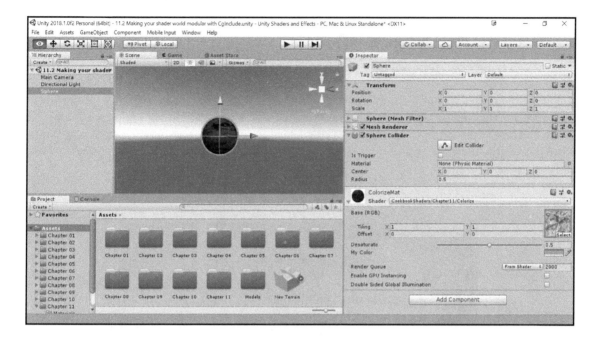

How it works...

When using shaders, we can include other sets of code using the #include preprocessor directive. This tells Unity that we want to let the current shader use the code from within the included file in the shader; this is the reason why these files are called CgInclude files. We are including snippets of Cg code using the #include directive.

Once we have declared the #include directive and Unity is able to find the file in the project, Unity will then look for code snippets that have been defined. This is where we start to use the #ifndef and #endif directives. When we declare the #ifndef directive, we are simply saying "if not defined, define something with a name." In this recipe's case, we said we wanted to #define MY_CG_INCLUDE. So, if Unity doesn't find a definition called MY_CG_INCLUDE, it goes and creates it when the CgInclude file is compiled, thereby giving us access to the code that follows. The #endif method simply says that this is the end of this definition, so stop looking for more code.

You can now see how powerful this is we can now store all of our lighting models and custom variables in one file and greatly reduce the amount of code that we have to write. The real power is when you can begin to give your shaders flexibility by defining multiple states of functions in the CgInclude files.

Implementing a Fur Shader

The look of a material depends on its physical structure. The shaders attempt to simulate them, but, in doing so, they oversimplify the way light behaves. Materials with a complex macroscopic structure are particularly hard to render. This is the case for many fabrics and animal furs. This recipe will show you how it is possible to simulate fur and other materials (such as grass) that are more than just a flat surface. In order to do this, the same material is drawn multiple times over and over, increasing in size every time. This creates the illusion of fur.

The shader presented here is based on the work of Jonathan Czeck and Aras Pranckevičius:

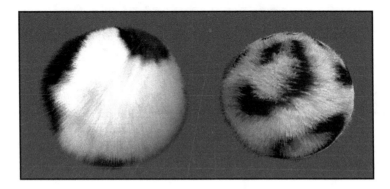

Getting ready

In order for this recipe to work, you will need a texture that shows how you wish to have your fur displayed:

I have provided two examples in `Chapter 11 | Textures` folder with the book's example code (`Faux Fur` and `panda`).

Like all the other shaders before, you will need to create a new **Standard Surface Shader** (`Fur`) and a material (`FurMat`) to host it, and attach it to a sphere for demonstration purposes:

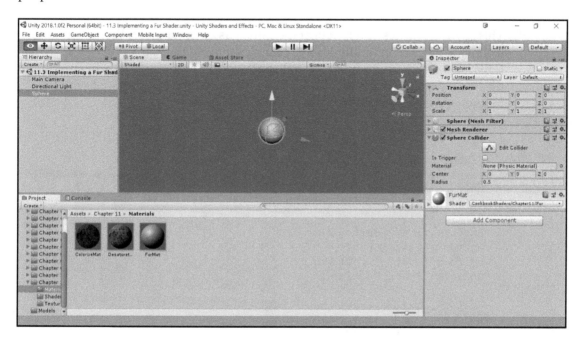

How to do it...

In this recipe, we can start modifying a **Standard Surface Shader**:

1. Double-click on the `Fur` Shader to open it up in your IDE of choice. Once opened, add the following bolded `Properties`:

```
Properties
{
    _Color ("Color", Color) = (1,1,1,1)
    _MainTex ("Albedo (RGB)", 2D) = "white" {}
    _Glossiness ("Smoothness", Range(0,1)) = 0.5
    _Metallic ("Metallic", Range(0,1)) = 0.0

    _FurLength ("Fur Length", Range (.0002, 1)) = .25
```

```
  _Cutoff ("Alpha Cutoff", Range(0,1)) = 0.5 // how "thick"
  _CutoffEnd ("Alpha Cutoff end", Range(0,1)) = 0.5 // how thick
they are at the end
  _EdgeFade ("Edge Fade", Range(0,1)) = 0.4

  _Gravity ("Gravity Direction", Vector) = (0,0,1,0)
  _GravityStrength ("Gravity Strength", Range(0,1)) = 0.25
}
```

2. This shader requires you to repeat the same pass several times. We will use the technique introduced in the *Making your shader world modular with CgIncludes* recipe to group all the code necessary from a single pass in an external file. Let's start creating a new `CgInclude` file called `FurPass.cginc` with the following code:

```
#pragma target 3.0

fixed4 _Color;
sampler2D _MainTex;
half _Glossiness;
half _Metallic;

uniform float _FurLength;
uniform float _Cutoff;
uniform float _CutoffEnd;
uniform float _EdgeFade;

uniform fixed3 _Gravity;
uniform fixed _GravityStrength;

void vert (inout appdata_full v)
{
   fixed3 direction = lerp(v.normal, _Gravity * _GravityStrength +
v.normal * (1-_GravityStrength), FUR_MULTIPLIER);
   v.vertex.xyz += direction * _FurLength * FUR_MULTIPLIER *
v.color.a;
   //v.vertex.xyz += v.normal * _FurLength * FUR_MULTIPLIER *
v.color.a;
}

struct Input {
   float2 uv_MainTex;
   float3 viewDir;
};

void surf (Input IN, inout SurfaceOutputStandard o) {
   fixed4 c = tex2D (_MainTex, IN.uv_MainTex) * _Color;
```

```
    o.Albedo = c.rgb;
    o.Metallic = _Metallic;
    o.Smoothness = _Glossiness;

    //o.Alpha = step(_Cutoff, c.a);
    o.Alpha = step(lerp(_Cutoff,_CutoffEnd,FUR_MULTIPLIER), c.a);

    float alpha = 1 - (FUR_MULTIPLIER * FUR_MULTIPLIER);
    alpha += dot(IN.viewDir, o.Normal) - _EdgeFade;

    o.Alpha *= alpha;
}
```

3. Got back to your original shader and add this extra pass after the ENDCG section:

```
void surf (Input IN, inout SurfaceOutputStandard o) {
    // Albedo comes from a texture tinted by color
    fixed4 c = tex2D (_MainTex, IN.uv_MainTex) * _Color;
    o.Albedo = c.rgb;
    // Metallic and smoothness come from slider variables
    o.Metallic = _Metallic;
    o.Smoothness = _Glossiness;
    o.Alpha = c.a;
}
ENDCG

CGPROGRAM
#pragma surface surf Standard fullforwardshadows alpha:blend
vertex:vert
#define FUR_MULTIPLIER 0.05
#include "FurPass.cginc"
ENDCG
```

4. Go back into Unity and assign the `FauxFur` texture in the **Albedo (RGB)** property. You should notice little dots along the shader:

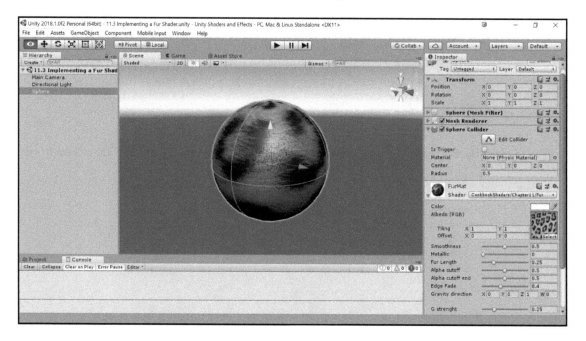

5. Add more passes, progressively increasing `FUR_MULTIPLIER`. You can get decent results with 20 passes, from `0.05` to `0.95`:

```
CGPROGRAM
#pragma surface surf Standard fullforwardshadows alpha:blend
vertex:vert
#define FUR_MULTIPLIER 0.05
#include "FurPass.cginc"
ENDCG

CGPROGRAM
#pragma surface surf Standard fullforwardshadows alpha:blend
vertex:vert
#define FUR_MULTIPLIER 0.1
#include "FurPass.cginc"
ENDCG

CGPROGRAM
#pragma surface surf Standard fullforwardshadows alpha:blend
vertex:vert
#define FUR_MULTIPLIER 0.15
```

```
#include "FurPass.cginc"
ENDCG

// ... 0.2 - 0.85 here

    CGPROGRAM
    #pragma surface surf Standard fullforwardshadows alpha:blend
vertex:vert
    #define FUR_MULTIPLIER 0.90
    #include "FurPass.cginc"
    ENDCG

    CGPROGRAM
    #pragma surface surf Standard fullforwardshadows alpha:blend
vertex:vert
    #define FUR_MULTIPLIER 0.95
    #include "FurPass.cginc"
    ENDCG
  }

  Fallback "Diffuse"
}
```

6. Once the shader has been compiled and attached to a material, you can change its appearance from the **Inspector**.

The Fur Length property determines the space between the fur shells, which will alter the length of the fur. Longer fur might require more passes to look realistic.

Alpha Cutoff and Alpha Cutoff End are used to control the density of the fur and how it gets progressively thinner.

Edge Fade determines the final transparency of the fur and how fuzzy it looks. Softer materials should have a high Edge Fade.

Finally, `Gravity Direction` and `Gravity Strength` curve the fur shells to simulate the effect of gravity:

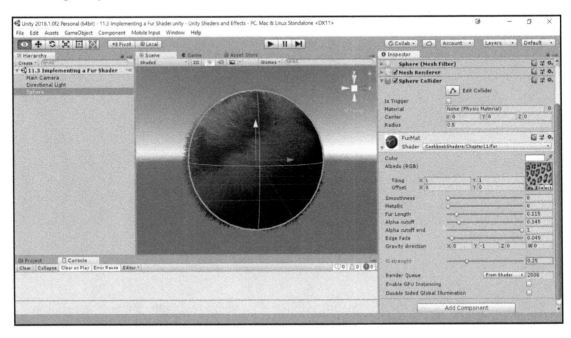

How it works...

The technique presented in this recipe is known as Lengyel's concentric fur-shell technique or simply the shell technique. It works by creating progressively bigger copies of the geometry that needs to be rendered. With the right transparency, it gives the illusion of a continuous thread of hair:

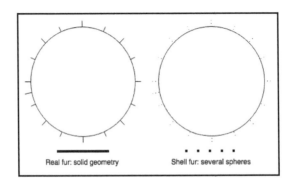

The shell technique is extremely versatile and relatively easy to implement. Realistic fur requires not only extruding the geometry of the model but also altering its vertices. This is possible with tessellation shaders, which are much more advanced and not covered in this book.

Each pass in this Fur Shader is contained in FurPass.cginc. The vertex function creates a slightly bigger version of the model, which is based on the principle of normal extrusion. Additionally, the effect of gravity is taken into account, so that it gets more intense the further we are from the center:

```
void vert (inout appdata_full v)
{
    fixed3 direction = lerp(v.normal, _Gravity * _GravityStrength +
v.normal * (1-_GravityStrength), FUR_MULTIPLIER);
    v.vertex.xyz += direction * _FurLength * FUR_MULTIPLIER * v.color.a;
}
```

In this example, the alpha channel is used to determine the final length of the Fur. This allows for more precise control.

Finally, the surface function reads the control mask from the alpha channel. It uses the cutoff value to determine which pixels to show and which ones to hide. This value changes from the first to the final fur shell to match Alpha Cutoff and Alpha Cutoff End:

```
o.Alpha = step(lerp(_Cutoff,_CutoffEnd,FUR_MULTIPLIER), c.a);

float alpha = 1 - (FUR_MULTIPLIER * FUR_MULTIPLIER);
alpha += dot(IN.viewDir, o.Normal) - _EdgeFade;

o.Alpha *= alpha;
```

The final alpha value of the fur also depends on its angle from the camera, giving it a softer look.

There's more...

The Fur shader has been used to simulate fur. However, it can be used for a variety of other materials. It works very well for materials that are naturally made of multiple layers, such as forest canopies, fuzzy clouds, human hair, and even grass.

Some additional examples of the same shader being used by just tweaking the parameters can be seen in the book's example code:

There are many other improvements that can dramatically increase its realism. You can add a very simple wind animation by changing the direction of the gravity based on the current time. If calibrated correctly, this can give the impression that the fur is moving because of the wind.

Additionally, you can make your fur move when the character is moving. All these little tweaks contribute to the believability of your fur, giving the illusion that it is not just a static material drawn on the surface. Unfortunately, this shader comes at a price: 20 passes are very heavy to compute. The number of passes determines roughly how believable the material is. You should play with fur length and passes in order to get the effect that works best for you. Given the performance impact of this shader, it is advisable to have several materials with different numbers of passes; you can use them at different distances and save a lot of computation.

Implementing Heatmaps with arrays

One characteristic that makes shaders hard to master is the lack of proper documentation. Most developers learn shaders by messing around with the code, without having a deep knowledge of what's going on. The problem is amplified by the fact that Cg/HLSL makes a lot of assumptions, some of which are not properly advertised. Unity3D allows C# scripts to communicate with shaders using methods such as `SetFloat`, `SetInt`, `SetVector`, and so on. Unfortunately, Unity3D doesn't have a `SetArray` method, which leads many developers to believe that Cg/HLSL doesn't support arrays either. This is not true. This post will show you how it's possible to pass arrays to shaders. Just remember that GPUs are highly optimized for parallel computations, and using for loops in a shader will dramatically decrease its performance.

For this recipe, we will implement a heatmap, as shown in the following screenshot:

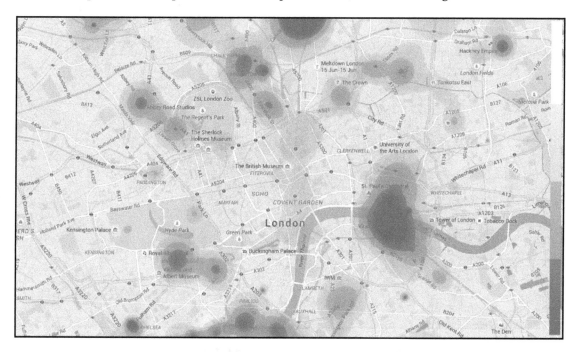

Getting ready

The effect in this recipe creates a heatmap from a set of points. This heatmap can be overlaid on top of another picture, like in the preceding screenshot. The following steps are necessary:

1. Create a quad with the texture that you want to use for the Heatmap (GameObject | 3D Object | Quad). In this example, a map of London has been used. In order to put the texture on the quad, create a new material (Map) using the **Unlit/Texture** shader, and assign the image to the **Base (RGB)** property. Once created, drag and drop that object onto the quad.

2. Create another quad and place it on top of the previous one. Our Heatmap will appear on this quad.

3. Attach a new shader (Heatmap) and material (HeatmapMat) to the second quad:

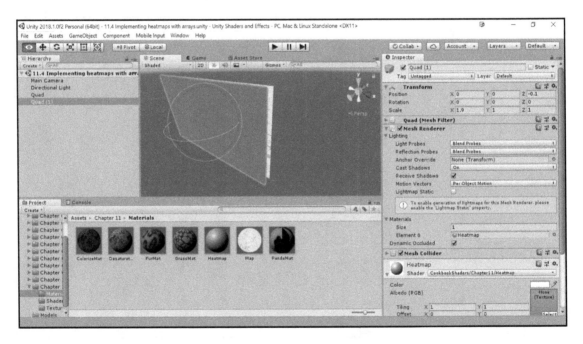

4. For ease of visualization, I also selected the **MainCamera** and changed the **Projection** to Orthographic and the **Size property** to 0.5.

How to do it...

This shader is quite different from the ones created before, yet it is relatively short. For this reason, the entire code is provided in the following steps:

1. Copy this code to the newly created shader:

```
shader " Heatmap" {
    Properties {
        _HeatTex ("Texture", 2D) = "white" {}
    }
    Subshader {
        Tags {"Queue"="Transparent"}
        Blend SrcAlpha OneMinusSrcAlpha // Alpha blend

        Pass {
            CGPROGRAM
            #pragma vertex vert
            #pragma fragment frag

            struct vertInput {
                float4 pos : POSITION;
            };

            struct vertOutput {
                float4 pos : POSITION;
                fixed3 worldPos : TEXCOORD1;
            };

            vertOutput vert(vertInput input) {
                vertOutput o;
                o.pos = mul(UNITY_MATRIX_MVP, input.pos);
                o.worldPos = mul(_Object2World, input.pos).xyz;
                return o;
            }

            uniform int _Points_Length = 0;
            uniform float3 _Points [20];          // (x, y, z) =
    position
            uniform float2 _Properties [20];      // x = radius, y =
    intensity
            sampler2D _HeatTex;

            half4 frag(vertOutput output) : COLOR {
                // Loops over all the points
                half h = 0;
                for (int i = 0; i < _Points_Length; i ++)
```

```
                    {
                            // Calculates the contribution of each point
                            half di = distance(output.worldPos,
        _Points[i].xyz);

                            half ri = _Properties[i].x;
                            half hi = 1 - saturate(di / ri);

                            h += hi * _Properties[i].y;
                    }

                            // Converts (0-1) according to the heat texture
                            h = saturate(h);
                            half4 color = tex2D(_HeatTex, fixed2(h, 0.5));
                            return color;
                    }
                ENDCG
            }
        }
        Fallback "Diffuse"
    }
```

2. Once you have attached this script to your material, you should provide a ramp texture for the heatmap. It's important to configure it so that its **Wrap Mode** is set to **Clamp**:

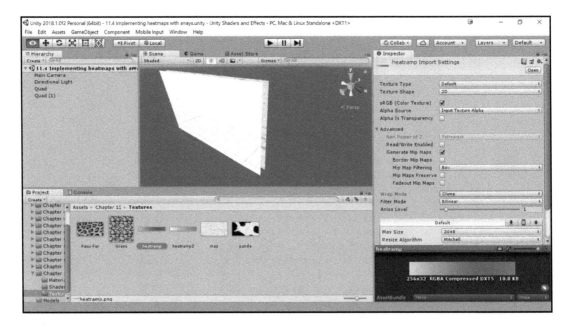

If your heatmap is going to be used as an overlay, then make sure that the ramp texture has an alpha channel and the texture is imported with the **Alpha is Transparency** option.

3. Create a new script called `HeatmapDrawer` using the following code:

```
using UnityEngine;

public class HeatmapDrawer : MonoBehaviour
{

    public Vector4[] positions;
    public float[] radiuses;
    public float[] intensities;
    public Material material;

    void Start()
    {
        material.SetInt("_Points_Length", positions.Length);

        material.SetVectorArray("_Points", positions);

        Vector4[] properties = new Vector4[positions.Length];

        for (int i = 0; i < positions.Length; i++)

        {
            properties[i] = new Vector2(radiuses[i],
intensities[i]);
        }

        material.SetVectorArray("_Properties", properties);
    }
}
```

4. Attach the script to an object in your scene, preferably to the quad. Then, drag the material created for this effect to the `Material` slot of the script. By doing this, the script will be able to access the `Material` and initialize it.

5. Lastly, expand the positions, radiuses, and intensities fields of your script and fill them with the values of your heatmap. Positions indicate the points (in world coordinates) of your heatmaps, radii indicate their size, and intensities indicate how strongly they affect the surrounding area:

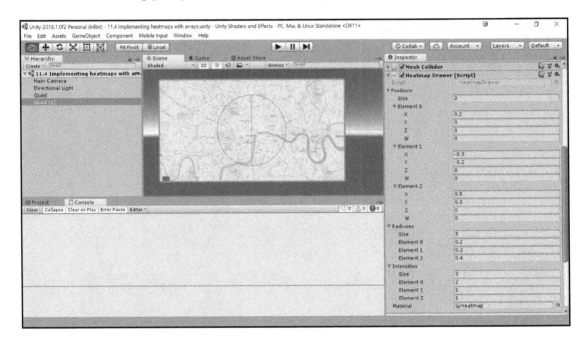

6. If all went well, once you play the game you should notice something similar to the following screenshot:

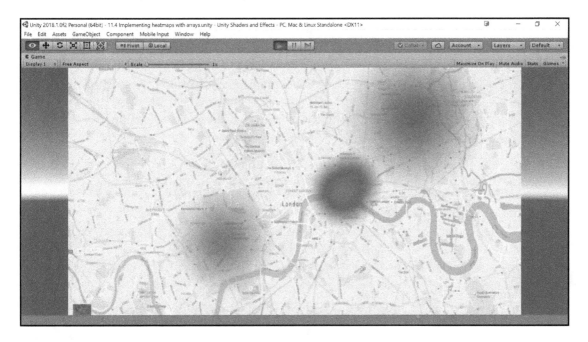

If you do not see this, make sure that the heatmap is placed in front of the map quad and that both objects are in front of the camera.

If you get a warning saying the number of points has changed, go into your shader, modify the script by adding a space, and then save it again.

How it works...

This shader relies on things that have not been introduced before in this book; the first one is arrays. Cg allows arrays that can be created with the following syntax:

```
uniform float3 _Points [20];
```

Cg doesn't support arrays with an unknown size: you must preallocate all the space that you need beforehand. The preceding line of code creates an array of 20 elements.

Unity allows us to set arrays through using a number of methods, including `SetVectorArray`, `SetColorArray`, `SetFloatArray`, and `GetMatrixArray`.

The `SetVectorArray` function only works with the `Vector4` class at present. That will not cause us any issues, though, as you can automatically assign a `Vector3` to a `Vector4`, and Unity will automatically include a zero in for the last element. Also, it is possible to instead use our `Start` code in an `Update` loop to be able to see the values change as we're modifying them, but it would be computationally expensive.

In the fragment function of the shader, there is a similar for loop, which, for each pixel of the material, queries all the points to find their contribution to the heatmap:

```
half h = 0;
for (int i = 0; i < _Points_Length; i ++)
{
    // Calculates the contribution of each point
    half di = distance(output.worldPos, _Points[i].xyz);

    half ri = _Properties[i].x;
    half hi = 1 - saturate(di / ri);

    h += hi * _Properties[i].y;
}
```

The `h` variable stores the heat from all the points, given their radii and intensities. It is then used to look up which color to use from the ramp texture.

The shaders and arrays are a winning combination, especially as very few games are using them at their full potential. However, they introduce a significant bottleneck, as, for each pixel, the shader has to loop through all the points.

12
Shader Graph

In this chapter, you will learn the following recipes:

- Creating a Shader Graph project
- Implementing a simple a Shader Graph
- Exposing properties to the Inspector via Shader Graph
- Implementing a glowing highlight system

Introduction

First released in Unity 2018.1, Shader Graph allows you to create shaders using a visual interface by connecting nodes instead of having to dive into the code. This will allow developers, including artists, to be able to create shaders in a similar manner to material editors in 3D modeling programs such as Autodesk Maya and Blender, or the material editor in the Unreal Engine. At the time of writing, Shader Graph is only supported for certain kinds of projects and doesn't allow the same flexibility as writing the shaders from scratch.

Creating a Shader Graph project

Unlike all of the previous shaders we have written, the Shader Graph tool requires users to have a project that is using the Lightweight Render Pipeline. The Lightweight Render Pipeline is meant for lower-end hardware, and is focused on drawing with a single-pass and decreasing the draw count wherever possible. For this first recipe, you will ensure that your project is set up correctly, by using the settings that Shader Graph needs.

How to do it...

To get started, we first need to create our new project:

1. From the Unity Hub, when creating a new project, set the **Template** to **Lightweight RP (Preview)**:

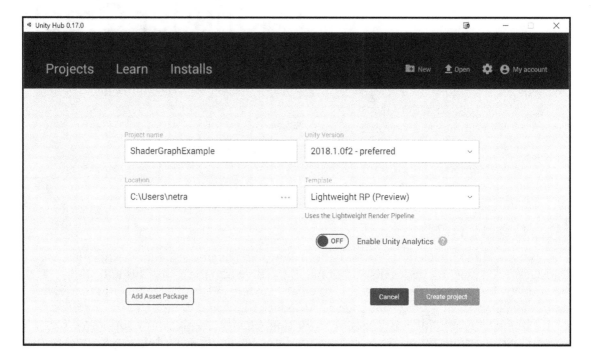

Shader Graph is currently only compatible with the Lightweight Render Pipeline, so this ensures that the graph will work correctly.

Shader Graph is only available with Unity 2018.1 and above. If you are using a prior version, make sure to upgrade before continuing with this chapter.

2. Once selected, press the **Create project** button:

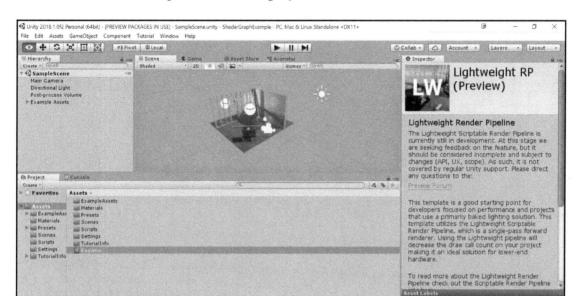

As you can see, this project already includes a number of assets inside it.

3. When the Unity Editor opens, the Shader Graph is not included by default in the Unity editor. To access it, you'll need to make use of the Unity **Package Manager**. From the top menu, go to **Window | Package Manager**. The **Package Manager** will allow you to install or uninstall different aspects of Unity. You'll notice two buttons, one for packages that are in the project (**In Project**) and one for all the packages that are currently available to be downloaded (**All**).

4. From the **Package Manager** window, hit the **All** button, scroll down until you see the **Shader Graph** button, and select it. From there, click on the **Install 1.1.9-preview** button, and wait for it to complete the download and import the content:

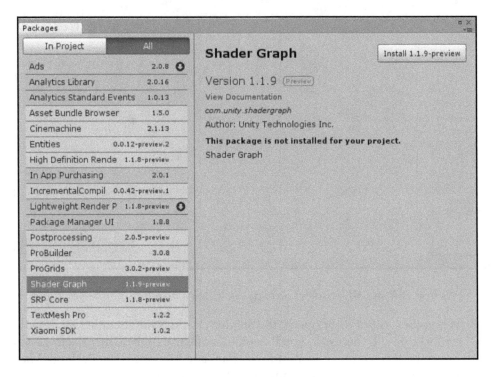

5. Once everything has been downloaded, go to the **Project** tab, select **Create | Shader**, and see if you can find the following new options:
   - **PBR Graph**
   - **Sub Graph**
   - **Unlit Graph**

How it works...

As we mentioned before, Shader Graph is currently only compatible with the Lightweight Render Pipeline. The easiest way to ensure that a project is using that pipeline is by selecting it as the **Template** when creating the project.

Once the project has been created, we make use of the newly added **Package Manager**, which allows you to install or uninstall different aspects of Unity. In this case, you have added the Shader Graph functionality.

If everything's included, Shader Graph has been installed successfully, and you should be able to work on the rest of the recipes for this chapter!

Implementing a simple a Shader Graph

To get acquainted with the interface of the Shader Graph, let's create something similar to what we have seen before by sampling a texture to create a simple shader.

Getting ready

Ensure that you have created a project using the **Lightweight Render Pipeline**, as described in the *Create a Shader Graph project* recipe. Afterward, complete the following steps:

1. Create a new scene, if you haven't done so already, by going to **File | New Scene**
2. Afterward, we need to have something to show our shader, so let's create a new sphere by going to **Game Object | 3D Object| Sphere**:

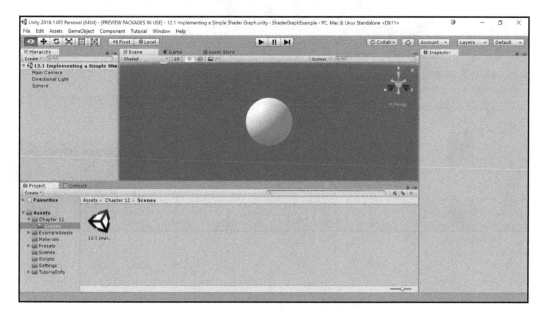

How to do it...

We will start off by creating a simple shader graph.

1. From the **Project** window, create a new shader by going to **Create | Shader | PBR Graph**, and name it `SimpleGraph`.

2. Afterward, create a new material by going to **Create | Material** (I named mine `SimpleGraphMat`). Next, assign the shader to the material by selecting the **Material**, then from the **Inspector** tab, you should select the **Shader** dropdown at the top and select **graphs/SimpleGraph**.

As always, you can also drag and drop the shader on top of the material as well.

3. Next, drag and drop the material onto our spherical object in the scene so we can see our shader being used in action:

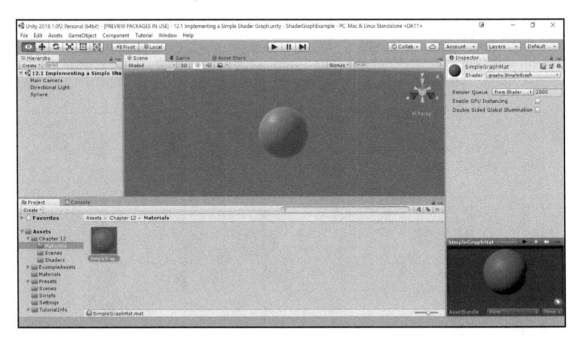

4. Now that the setup is done, we can start creating the graph. If you select the shader, you should notice, the **Inspector** tab that there is a button that says **Open Shader Editor**. Click on the button and the **Shader Graph Editor** will open automatically:

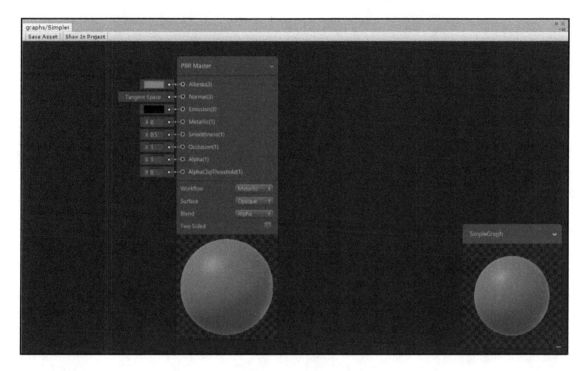

 To move within the Shader Graph Editor, you can use the mouse wheel to zoom in and out, and you can hold the middle mouse button and drag to pan the graph. Alternatively, you can also use *Alt* + left mouse button.

5. To get started, let's add a texture. Right-click to the left of the **PBR Master** and select **Create Node**. From there, you'll see a menu that allows you to either type in the name of a node or select from the menus. To go through the menus, select **Input | Texture| Sample Texture 2D**. Alternatively, you can type in tex, then select the **Sample Texture 2D** option using the arrow keys, and then press *Enter*:

You can also create a new node by moving your mouse over where you want to create one and pressing the Space key.

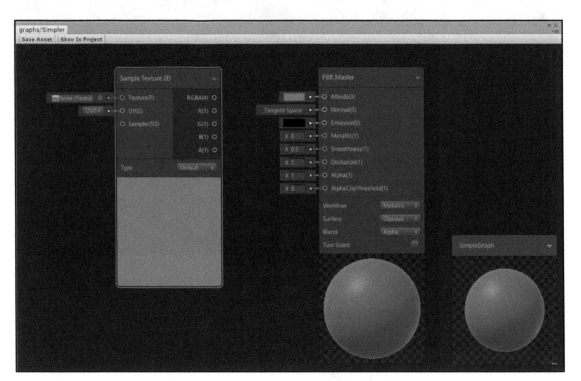

Feel free to click and drag any of the nodes on the Shader Graph to make it easier to see.

6. On the left-hand side of the **Sample Texture 2D** node, click on the circle with the dot in it to assign the texture as something that we can use (I used the **Ground_Albedo** property included with the project):

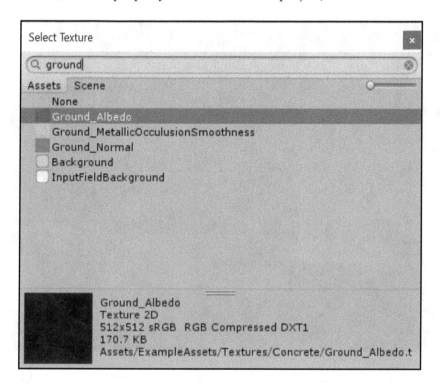

Afterward, you should see the data from the texture given in an image under the node.

7. Click and drag the pink circle on the right-hand side of the **Sample Texture 2D** node to the input **Albedo** node on the **PBR Master** node:

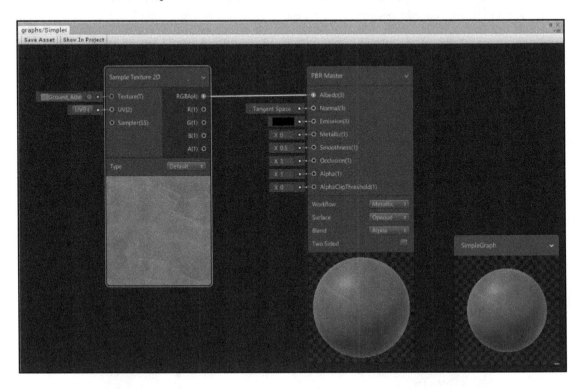

Just like we've learned in previous chapters, we can give a `fixed4` to a `fixed3` and it will just disregard the fourth parameter.

If you are ever interested in what a particular node does or what the properties stand for, feel free to right click on it and select **Open Documentation**. It will open a window that will give you a description of what the node does.

8. Click on the **Save Asset** button on the top menu and then return to the Unity editor:

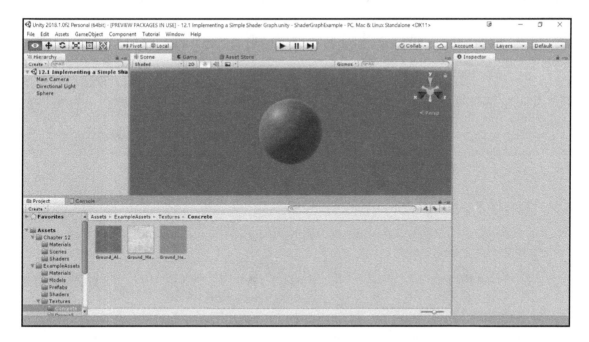

As you can see, the shader has now been updated to contain the information from the Shader Graph editor!

How it works...

From Shader Graph, we are introduced to the first nodes we have encountered. Of note is the **PBR Master** section on the screen. This is where all of the information about the shader will go to. You may notice that the properties are very similar to the regular Standard Shader we've used in the past, and we can modify the properties in a similar manner now, but we can also create additional nodes and connect them together to create unique effects.

The **Sample Texture2D** node allows us to give the **Texture** property as an input and then give the data from it as an **RGBA** output on the right-hand side (things on the right side of a node are outputs while things on the left side are inputs, such as the **Albedo** property on the **PBR Master** node).

Note that the color of the circle from the **Texture** input is red (the T stands for texture), the output of **RGBA** is pink (the 4 stands for `fixed4`), and the input for the **Albedo** input of the **PBR Master** node is yellow (the 3 stands for `fixed3`).

Exposing properties to the Inspector via Shader Graph

It is great to be able to create graphs and set up their properties using the graph editor, but sometimes it is nice to use the same shader with a simple tweak in the same manner that we've used with the previous shaders we've created. To do this, we can make use of the blackboard panel.

Getting ready

Ensure that you have created the SimpleGraph shader in the previous recipe. Afterward, complete the following steps:

1. From the **Project** tab, select the **SimpleGraph** shader and duplicate it by pressing *Ctrl + D*. Once duplicated, name the newly created shader `ExposeProperty`.

2. Next, create a new material (`ExposePropertyMat`) and set the shader it uses to the **graphs/ExposeProperty** selection.

3. Assign the material to the sphere in our scene:

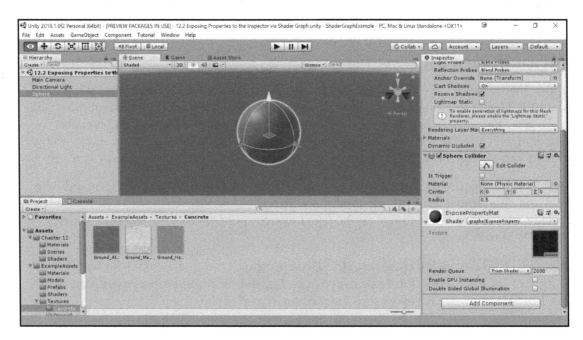

The project should look the same as what we had in the previous recipe since we are using a duplicate of the previous shader.

How to do it...

If you look at our shader from the **Inspector** tab, you may notice the **Texture** property with the **Ground_Albedo** image we assigned in the last recipe. A property like this could be something we want to modify, but, by default, it is grayed out so that we cannot change it without going into the Shader Graph. To adjust this, we can expose the property using the Blackboard aspect of the Shader Graph Editor:

1. Double-click on the **ExposeProperty** shader to open up the Shader Graph:

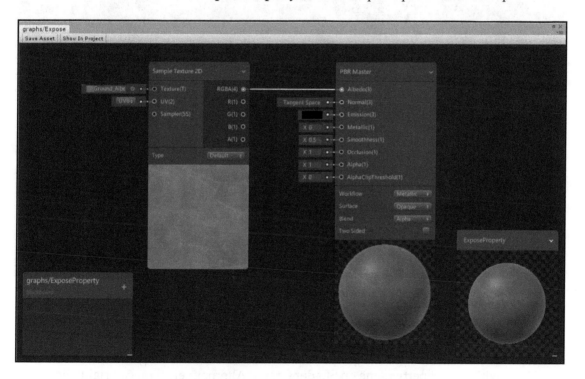

   Notice, on the bottom left, the **graphs/ExposeProperty** blackboard menu. This will contain a list of all the parameters we are able to modify via the Inspector.

As you may already know, Shader Graph is brand new and as such is prone to issues, such as the Blackboard not being visible by default. Unfortunately, at this time, there's no way to turn it on and off through a menu. If you do not see the Blackboard, you might try to save your graph and return. Alternatively, you can reset your layout by going into **Layout | Revert Factory Settings...**

2. From the blackboard panel, click on the + icon and select **Texture**:

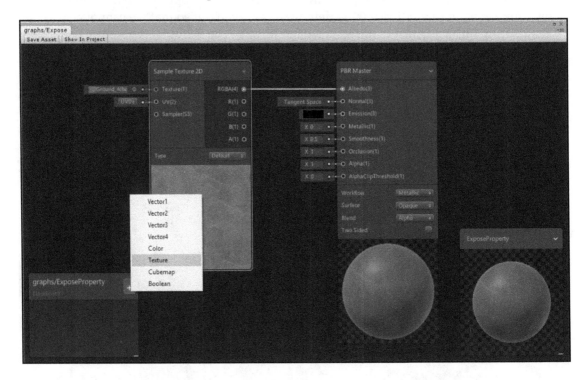

3. From there, you can give the property a name (I used `TextureProperty`). Note that, under **Default**, you can assign a texture in the same way as done previously.

4. From there, to hook the property to our current shader, drag and drop the button with the property name on Shader Graph. Alternatively, you can right-click and select **Create Node**. Once at the menu, you can select **Properties | Property**: **TextureProperty**. Afterward, connect the **TextureProperty** output of the **Property** node to the **Texture** input of the **Sample Texture 2D** node:

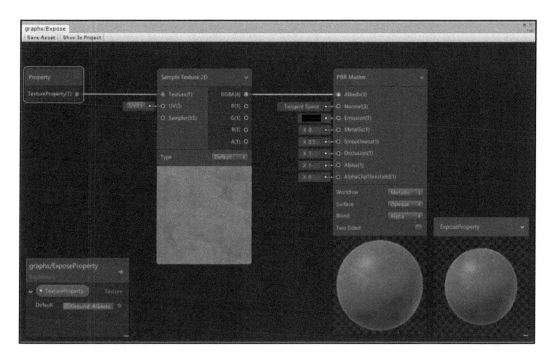

5. Afterward, hit the **Save Asset** button and dive back into the Unity editor:

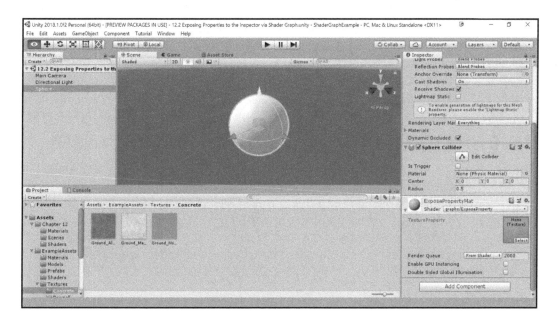

Now, you should be able to assign the **TextureProperty** to whatever you want, through the **Inspector**, and you won't have to dive back into the graph to make those changes!

How it works...

The **Blackboard** menu allows you to create variables that are accessible from the **Inspector**. This works in a similar manner to the `Properties` block in previous chapters. Currently, it supports the following types:

- Vector1
- Vector2
- Vector3
- Vector4
- Color
- Texture
- Cubemap
- Boolean

Properties added to the Blackboard can be reordered by dragging them around, and each property can be renamed by double-clicking on the name.

For more information on the Blackboard, check out the following link: `https://github.com/Unity-Technologies/ShaderGraph/wiki/Blackboard`.

Implementing a glowing highlight system

Now that we have some background information on how to build shaders, let's look at a real-world example of a shader we could potentially use. When playing certain kinds of games, you may notice that, when the player faces an object they can interact with, the object may glow such as in Dontnod Entertainment's *Life is Strange*, The Fullbright Company's *Gone Home*, and even in recent mobile games such as Jam City's *Harry Potter Hogwarts Mystery*. This is something that we can easily do in Shader Graph, which will also allow us to see a non-trivial example of Shader Graph being used.

Getting ready

Ensure that you have created a project using the Lightweight Render Pipeline, as described in the *Creating a Shader Graph project* recipe. Afterward, complete the following steps:

1. Create a new scene, if you haven't done so already, by going to **File | New Scene**
2. Afterward, we need to have something to show our shader, so let's create a new sphere by going to **Game Object | 3D Object | Sphere**

How to do it...

We will start off by creating a simple shader graph:

1. From the **Project** window, create a new shader by going to **Create Shader PBR Graph**, and name it `GlowGraph`.
2. Afterward, create a new material by going to **Create | Material** (I named mine `GlowGraphMat`). Next, assign the shader to the material by selecting the material, and then, from the **Inspector** tab, you should select the **Shader** dropdown at the top and select **graphs/GlowGraph**.
3. Then, drag and drop the material onto our sphere object in the scene, so we can see our shader being used in action.
4. Now that the setup is done, we can start creating the graph. If you select the shader, you should see that, from the **Inspector** tab, there will be a button that says **Open Shader Graph**. Click on the button and the **Shader Graph Editor** will open automatically.
5. Firstly, we will add a new node called a Fresnel (pronounced fer-nel) Effect. To add it, go to the left-hand side of the **PBR Master** node, right-click, and select **Create Node**. From there, type in `Fresnel`, and once it has been selected press the *Enter* key.

> The Fresnel Effect is often used to provide rim-lighting for objects. For more information on it, check out: `https://github.com/Unity-Technologies/ShaderGraph/wiki/Fresnel-Effect-Node`.

6. Once created, connect the **Out** of the **Fresnel Effect** node to the **Emission** property of the **PBR Master** node.

7. To make it easier to tell what each node does, click on the grey color to the left of the **Albedo** property and change it to a different color, such as a bright pink:

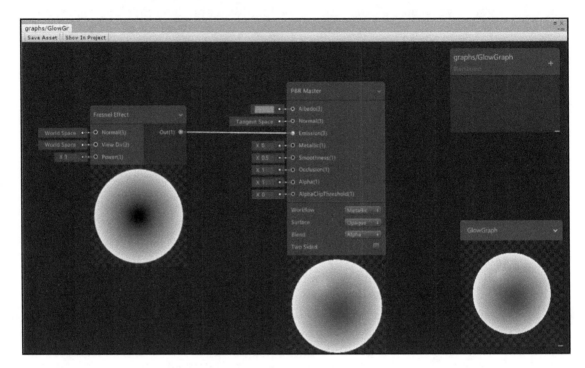

Notice how the Fresnel effect is applied on top of the Albedo color due to it using that value for the **Emission** property.

8. We just want the edges of our object to glow, so change the `Power` property of the **Fresnel Effect** node to 4. Currently, the light around our object is white, but we can make it a different color instead by multiplying it by a color.

9. To do this, go to the Blackboard and create a new color by clicking on the + icon and then selecting **Color**. Once created, give it a name (`HoverColor`) and then set the **Default** color.

10. Once created, drag and drop the property beneath the **Fresnel Effect** node in the same way we learned in the previous recipe:

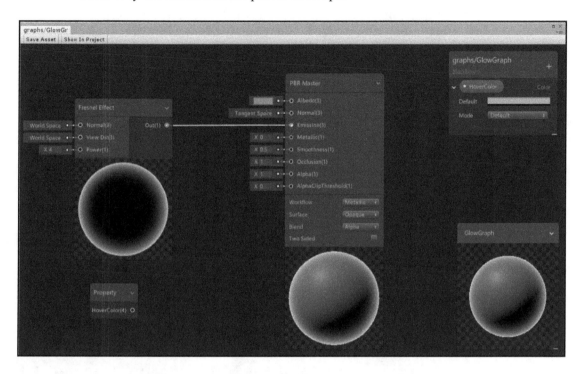

11. Now, we need to multiply these together. Create a new node between them by selecting **Math | Basic | Multiply**. Connect the Out of the **Fresnel Effect** node to the **A** of the **Multiply** node. Then, connect the **HoverColor** property to the **B** of the **Multiply** node. Afterward, connect the **Out** of the **Multiply** node to the **Emission** property:

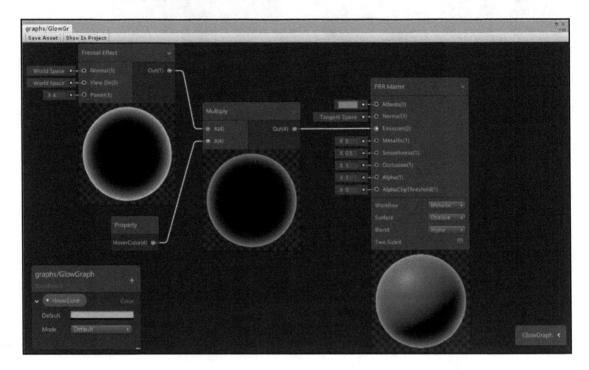

12. Save the graph and dive back into the Unity editor. You should notice that the effect is indeed working as intended.

13. From the **Project** tab, select the `GlowGraph` shader we've created. Notice that the **Inspector** tab includes information on the properties used in the shader:

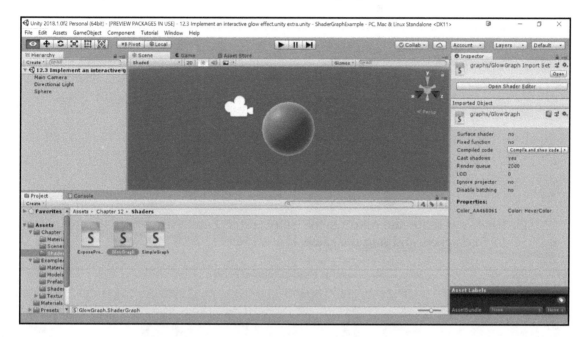

Even though we are using the name **HoverColor** in the shader graph, throughout code it is referred to as `Color_AA468061`. If we wish to refer to this in the code, we will need to use this name latter instead.

14. Create a new C# Script called `HighlightOnHover`. Double-click on it to enter your IDE, and use the following code:

```
using UnityEngine;

public class HighlightOnHover : MonoBehaviour
{

    public Color highlightColor = Color.red;

    private Material material;

    // Use this for initialization
    void Start()
    {
```

```
        material = GetComponent<MeshRenderer>().material;

        // Turn off glow
        OnMouseExit();
    }

    void OnMouseOver()
    {
        material.SetColor("Color_AA468061", highlightColor);
    }

    void OnMouseExit()
    {
        material.SetColor("Color_AA468061", Color.black);
    }

}
```

15. Save your script and return to the Unity editor. From there, attach the component to your sphere and start the game:

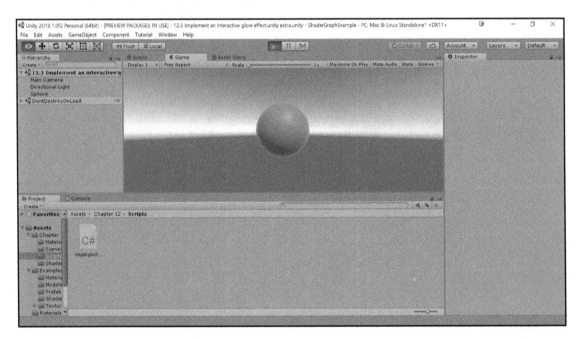

Now, when we highlight the object with the mouse, we will see the hover effect, but, otherwise, it will turn itself off!

How it works...

The **Emission** property is reflective of the light that an object receives. If the **Emission** is white it will be fully lit with that color. If black, it will act as if it doesn't exist. We make use of that by using black by default. However, if we do put our mouse over the object, the `OnMouseOver` function will trigger, causing it to use the color mentioned.

I could write much more on the subject of Shader Graph, but, unfortunately, there isn't enough space in the book. If you would like to explore Shader Graph even more, Andy Touch has put together a lovely group of examples of Shader Graph being used that could be great research material. Check it out at `https://github.com/` `UnityTechnologies/ShaderGraph_ExampleLibrary`.

Other Books You May Enjoy

If you enjoyed this book, you may be interested in these other books by Packt:

Getting Started with Unity 2018 - Third Edition
Dr. Edward Lavieri

ISBN: 9781788830102

- Set up your Unity development environment and navigate its tools
- Import and use custom assets and asset packages to add characters to your game
- Build a 3D game world with a custom terrain, water, sky, mountains, and trees
- Animate game characters, using animation controllers, and scripting
- Apply audio and particle effects to the game
- Create intuitive game menus and interface elements
- Customize your game with sound effects, shadows, lighting effects, and rendering options
- Debug code and provide smooth error handling

Unity Virtual Reality Projects - Second Edition
Jonathan Linowes

ISBN: 9781788478809

- Create 3D scenes with Unity and other 3D tools while learning about world space and scale
- Build and run VR applications for specific headsets, including Oculus, Vive, and Daydream
- Interact with virtual objects using eye gaze, hand controllers, and user input events
- Move around your VR scenes using locomotion and teleportation
- Implement an audio fireball game using physics and particle systems
- Implement an art gallery tour with teleportation and data info
- Design and build a VR storytelling animation with a soundtrack and timelines
- Create social VR experiences with Unity networking

Leave a review - let other readers know what you think

Please share your thoughts on this book with others by leaving a review on the site that you bought it from. If you purchased the book from Amazon, please leave us an honest review on this book's Amazon page. This is vital so that other potential readers can see and use your unbiased opinion to make purchasing decisions, we can understand what our customers think about our products, and our authors can see your feedback on the title that they have worked with Packt to create. It will only take a few minutes of your time, but is valuable to other potential customers, our authors, and Packt. Thank you!

Index

CPSIA information can be obtained
at www.ICGtesting.com
Printed in the USA
FFHW011408021219
56510974-62305FF